ÖDÖN VON HORVÁTH

FOUR PLAYS

BY

ÖDÖN VON HORVÁTH

Kasimir and Karoline
Judgment Day
Faith, Hope and Charity
Figaro Gets a Divorce

INTRODUCTION BY MARTIN ESSLIN

PAJ Publications
[A Division of Performing Arts Journal, Inc.]
New York

Library of Congress Cataloging in Publication Data
Ödön von Horváth: Plays
Library of Congress Catalog Card No.: 86-62158
ISBN: 1-55554-002-3 (cloth)
ISBN: 1-55554-003-1 (paper)

Graphic Design: Gautam Dasgupta
Printed in the United States of America

Publication of this book has been made possible in part by grants received from the National Endowment for the Arts, Washington, D.C., a federal agency, and the New York State Council on the Arts.

General Editors of PAJ Playscripts:
  Bonnie Marranca and Gautam Dasgupta

Contents

Introduction

On June 1, 1938, a sudden thunderstorm descended upon Paris. In the Champs Elysées, opposite the Théâtre Marigny, a group of people sought shelter under the trees. One old tree, hollowed by the years, crashed down and killed a young man standing under it. He had arrived in Paris two days earlier, on his way from Amsterdam to Zurich. In his room, at the Hotel de l'Univers in the Rue Monsieur le Prince, two half-filled glasses of red wine still stood on a table, next to them the manuscript of a novel he had just started to write, *Adieu to Europe*. Thus ended, at the age of thirty-six, the career of one of the most eminent dramatists of the century, Ödön von Horváth. An end, bizarre, ironic and grotesque enough to have figured in one of his own plays.

Horváth had had his first great successes in 1931 and 1932 in Germany with three of his major plays—*Italian Night*, *Tales from the Vienna Woods*, and *Kasimir and Karoline*,—just before Hitler came to power and made production of these left-oriented works impossible in Germany. His death, after five years of trying to get his plays produced in the remaining, shrinking area of the German-speaking world where some freedom still existed, on the eve of a planned move to America—he had come to Paris to discuss a possible film version of one of his novels with Robert Siodmak—caused Horváth's name and reputation to sink into almost total oblivion until well after the war. It was not until the 1960s and 70s that he began slowly to be rediscovered, and today his standing as the most important, next to Brecht, of the dramatists who wrote in German in this century, is unchallenged.

Outside the German-speaking world Horváth is still largely unknown, in spite of highly successful productions of some of his plays at the National Theatre in London and elsewhere. One of the reasons for this lies in the fact that Horváth's principle brilliance is a linguistic one: his plays use language to explore the use of language, and the ravages of its misuse. Hence the extreme difficulty of conveying the full impact of Horváth's work in translation.

Ödön von Horváth was a typical product of the old Austro-Hungarian Empire, that sprawling, multi-lingual country, with its archaic bureaucracy (the workings of which Kafka transmuted into a metaphor for the mysterious workings of the universe), its "despotism mitigated by inefficiency," its love of wine, women, song and an exquisite cuisine, chocolate cake and whipped cream, and its perpetual feeling that its situation was "hopeless but far from desperate."

Ödön (the Hungarian form of Edmund) Josef von Horváth was born on December 9, 1901, the son of an Austro-Hungarian diplomat at Fiume (now Rijeka, in Yugoslavia), then the chief naval base of the Habsburg Empire, where his father was stationed. His father's background was mainly Hungarian, but his ancestry also included Czech, Croat and German ingredients. Following his father's various official positions and transfers, he spent his childhood variously in Budapest, Munich and Vienna. Although the family was Hungarian, they spoke German at home, but he also knew, and had some of his schooling in, Hungarian. He thus acquired the sensitivity for language which often arises from being bilingual in two so strongly contrasting linguistic spheres. (Hungarian is a language with a grammar and vocabulary totally different from any Indo-European idiom.)

After some years of somewhat casual studies at the University of Munich, Horváth decided to devote himself to writing. Accordingly, he took steps, in 1924, to settle at the center of the literary and theatrical life of Germany, Berlin. This was the heyday of the Weimar Republic's brief cultural flowering. The vogue of Expressionism in drama was on the wane, the current slogan was "neue Sachlichkeit" (the "new objectivity"), a return also to more realistic types of drama. At the same time the need to get away from what seemed to the younger generation the grandiloquence, false idealism and artificial language of the German classical and romantic past remained as urgent as ever. Brecht's epic theatre, Piscator's political revues, Zuckmayer's rambunctious rural and proletarian comedies all pursued the same goal—finding a way back to the tradition of the German folk theatre of the seventeenth century: down-to-earth, bawdy and drastic.

Horváth's background—Austro-Bavarian-Hungarian—firmly anchored him in just such a tradition. For in the south of the German-speaking world that seventeenth-century folk theatre had survived and produced some great playwrights: Ferdinand Raimund, Johann Nestroy, Ludwig Anzengruber and Ludwig Thoma, to name but a few. Hence from the very beginning Horváth devoted himself to the revival—and re-functioning—of the genre of the *Volksstück*, the folk play in dialect. Many of his best plays carry that generic designation in their subtitle.

The aristocrat von Horváth, however, observed the speech and mores of the common people with a detachment that was a mixture of pity and contempt. Contempt for the poverty of their means of expression, the stupidity of their lives (the epigraph of *Tales from the Vienna Woods* is: "Nothing can give us the feeling for infinity so clearly as the contemplation of stupidity"); and pity for the tragic situations into which that stupidity and inability to communicate inevitably plunges them.

For Horváth the problem of language and communication was an eminently political one. In this, too, he drew on the Austro-Hungarian tradition, the tradition of "*Sprachkritik*" – the critique of language – which produced such important thinkers as Fritz Mauthner, Ludwig Wittgenstein and Karl Kraus. Among these Horváth's greatest affinities are with Kraus (1874-1936), the great satirist and polemical writer who spent his life castigating the linguistic crimes of the Viennese press in his periodical *Die Fackel* (*The Torch*), which, for forty years, he wrote all by himself and published at irregular intervals, whenever he felt he had something to say.

Kraus's thought is today even more topical than almost a century ago. Kraus was the first to recognize the immense dangers that flowed from the rise of the mass media, of which the first was the mass circulation press catering for a newly literate mass public. Since the introduction of free universal elementary education, no longer, as before, only well-educated people were literate. Suddenly there was a mass of people who could read but had no real education. And what was worse: the newspapers were written by just such half-educated barely literate journalists. This, Kraus argued, was a major cultural disaster; we can only think by using language. If the level of linguistic competence and sophistication declines, the level of thought itself will go down. Thought will be replaced by catch-phrases, slogans producing emotional excitement rather than logical reasoning. Politics will become a welter of hysterical clicheés, rabid nationalistic platitudes, and the result will be chaos and war. Having preached this gospel since the 1890s Kraus found his worst fear confirmed by the First World War with its nationalistic hysteria. His immense drama, *The Last Days of Mankind*, mirrored the horrors of war-time propaganda in all its crass stupidity. In the 1920s, when radio had been added to the arsenal of the mass media, the slogans of the Nazis, the linguistic horrors of Hitler's half-educated oratory, confirmed Kraus's worst fears. Again it seemed inevitable that they would lead to mass hysteria and war.

Horváth's use of language in his "folk plays," whether directly derived from Kraus's ideas or not, closely corresponds to his arguments. What Horváth shows again and again with devastatingly bitter comic effect, is the catastrophic effect of the debasement of language by the mass media, newspapers and cheap romantic novels. Instead of thinking for themselves, instead of acquiring the ability to express their own thoughts or feelings, the half-educated masses were merely parrotting the clichés they had imbibed from these sources. They had lost their own language which is, in the German-speaking world, the local dialect, with its connotation of low social status and incomplete education. To show that they were "educated people," robot-like they mouthed pre-chewed clichés: bloodthirsty nationalistic platitudes in their political discourse, sentimental claptrap about eternal love, and undying loyalty in their sexual relationships.

In one of his few theoretical pronouncements Horváth describes his plays as "dialect plays in which no dialect is spoken": the characters try to speak a stilted and uncertain standard "educated" German, but behind the idiotic catch-phrases pronounced with forced elocution one must always feel that these are people who no longer speak their own authentic language, can no longer feel and think authentically. This inauthentic language Horváth calls "*Bildungs-jargon*" (the jargon of the psuedo-educated). The use of this pre-programmed jargon produces a new type of subtext which Horváth called the "comedy of the subconscious": behind every high-faluting and misunderstood "educated" phrase there lurks the irony of what the speaker actually would have felt and thought in his own dialect-language, the real feelings and thoughts that he could have uttered, if he had not been forced to use those ready-made, emotionally alien clichés he had learned by heart.

Horváth's use of this "*Bildungsjargon*" comprises the falsely romantic clichés of love-making; the moronic generalizations about national characteristics of Germans, Frenchmen, Jews and women; grandiloquent and misapplied quotations from the German classics; proverbs; nationalistic and other political slogans and catch-phrases; advertising jingles; and the whole gamut of the junk-language of the media of his time. The characters in a play like *Tales from the Vienna Woods*, for instance, constantly wallow in the cliché self-image of Vienna as the city of golden-hearted men and sweet loving girls, while, at the same time, behaving to each other in the most heartless and brutal manner and spouting the nationalistic slogans which, a few years later, will plunge the world into war.

Thus, in creating his own latter-day version of it, Horváth deconstructs and subverts the tradition of the "*Volksstück*" which had always been cosy and self-congratulatory. "I am fully aware that I am destroying the old '*Volksstück*,' in its form and in its moral stance, by attempting to find a new form for the folk play," he wrote in 1935.

The production of *Tales from the Vienna Woods* by Max Reinhardt's Deutsches Theater in Berlin on November 2, 1931, was a great success. Peter Lorre played Alfred, Carola Neher (Brecht's great love, the Polly of the *Threepenny Opera* film, later to perish in one of Stalin's Gulags) was Marianne and Hans Moser, one of the greatest of all Viennese folk comedians, the Zauberkönig. Earlier in the same year Horváth's *Italian Night*, a bitter attack against both the Nazis and the effete Social Democrats who did not take them seriously enough, had been performed in Leipzig, and Horváth had been awarded the coveted Kleist Prize (for the most promising new dramatist of the year). In November 1932 *Kasimir and Karoline* also achieved considerable success in Leipzig.

But in January 1933 Hitler came to power. Horváth—a pure, blue-blooded one hundred percent "Aryan" aristocrat—tried for a time to continue to work in Germany, but his next play *Faith, Hope and Charity*, already scheduled for performance at the Deutsches Theater, was banned, and eventually he was officially deprived, as an alien (he had Hungarian nationality), of the right to live and work in Nazi Germany. There were still theatres in the German-speaking parts of Czechoslovakia, of Switzerland and in Austria, but these theatres did not have the lavish means of the big German playhouses. To make a living Horváth continued to write plays, but these now had to be on a more modest scale, with fewer characters and sets. Many of them saw the light of day in tiny avant-garde theatres in Vienna, in the basements of cafés. (They were called "theatres of forty-nine seats" because fire regulations began to apply to premises seating more than fifty spectators.) If anything Horváth had to become even more ingenious in his technique to accommodate himself to these conditions. He had to abandon the epic construction of earlier plays with their multitude of scenes and characters, and return to a more economical use of the stage. *Judgment Day*, completed in 1936, is an example of this later style. It was first performed at the German-language theatre of Moravska-Ostrava in Czechoslovakia in December 1937. In October of the following year Czechoslovakia also succumbed to Hitler.

In the five years of his wanderings after losing the possibility of being performed in Germany, Horváth wrote eight plays and three novels. In *Don Juan Returns from the War* and *Figaro Gets a Divorce* he tried to re-actualize two of the archetypal characters of Mozart's operas. In a number of other satirical comedies he dealt with the plight of émigrés without passports, and in his last play, *Pompeii: The Comedy of an Earthquake*, he depicted a world engaged in petty intrigue, unaware of the impending cataclysm which would bury it forever in dust and lava.

Horváth died before his prophecies came to be fulfilled, only all too accurately. Yet his warnings are as timely and topical today as they were in 1932 and 1938: the dangers of the explosion of mass culture and mass media which Kraus had foreseen from the turn of the century, and Horváth had castigated in the 1930s have, with the rise of television as the ultimate mass medium, become infinitely more menacing and urgent, in the English-speaking world as much—and perhaps more so—than elsewhere. While the same brand of "*Bildungsjargon*" that Horváth depicts hardly exists in the English-speaking countries, simply because being an intellectual—"*gebildet*"—does not carry the same clout as a status symbol here, the systematic attack against logical thought and rational argument, and their replacement by advertising jingles, political catchphrases and the debased human role models of soap opera is infinitely more virulent and all-pervasive here and now than it ever was in Horváth's time.

Horváth's drama is bitter and without reassurance: he disdained catching the audience's goodwill by presenting characters with whom it might identify. There are no heroes, or heroines, in his plays: Marianne in *Tales from the Vienna Woods* is a pitiable victim, but she is shown as the victim of her own stupidity; Karoline is a victim of her need for a man of means. In his preface to *Faith, Hope and Charity* Horváth says:

> In this little Dance of Death, as in all my plays, I have tried not to forget that this hopeless struggle of the individual [against the inhuman bureaucracy of the state] is based on bestial animal instincts and that thus the heroic or cowardly manner of this struggle must be seen as merely the problem of the form of this bestiality, which, as we all know is neither good nor evil. As in all my plays I have not prettified or uglified anything. Anyone who attempts, with watchful eyes, to depict us humans, must come to the conclusion . . . that the expressions of feelings of human beings are "kitschified"; that is: falsified, made cosy, and, in a masochistic vein, lecherous for pity, probably because of a lazy need to be noticed . . .

Horváth's influence, after his rediscovery in the 1960s, has been immense in the German-speaking world: the best of contemporary German and Austrian dramatists—Franz Xaver Kroetz, Martin Sperr, Peter Handke, Wolfgang Bauer, Thomas Bernhard are clearly influenced by him. In a famous article Handke set him up as the counter-influence to that of Brecht—"Horváth is better than Brecht"—more relevant to the present situation than Brecht. There can be no doubt that Horváth's reputation and influence is about to make itself felt outside the German-speaking world as well.

When the tree struck him down in the Champs Elysées in 1938 Horváth was on his way to America. It is an irony of fate that would have amused him that as a writer he will have finally arrived here almost half a century later.

Martin Esslin

Kasimir and Karoline

"And love never faileth."

**translated and adapted by
Violet B. Ketels**

Translation © 1985 copyright by Violet B. Ketels

CHARACTERS:

Kasimir
Karoline
Rauch
Speer
The Barker
The Midget
Schürzinger
Merkl Franz
His girlfriend, Erna
Elli
Maria
The Man with the Bulldog's Head
Juanita
The Fat Lady
The Waitress
The Orderly
The Doctor
Freaks and Octoberfest visitors

This folk play takes place at the Munich Octoberfest grounds in the 1930s.

Note: The characters' grammatical mistakes should suggest their impoverished powers of expression rather than a consistent pattern of illiteracy. More important is their regular resort to clichés and aphorisms never precisely on the mark.

SCENE 1

(*The house lights go down and the orchestra plays the Munich hymn, "As Long as Old Peter Stands." Then the curtain rises.*)

SCENE 2

(*The setting: an amusement park just behind the African Village. To the left an ice cream man with Turkish candy and balloons. To the right a "Hit the Lukas" game. This is the traditional test of strength device. With a mallet, the player strikes a wooden peg that in turn drives another peg up a pole. If the second peg reaches the top of the pole, a bell rings. The player gets a prize each time the bell rings. It is already late afternoon. A zeppelin is flying low over the Octoberfest grounds. In the distance are the sounds of musical flourishes and drum beats.*)

SCENE 3

RAUCH: Bravo Zeppelin! Bravo Eckener! Bravo!
BARKER: Heil!
SPEER: How majestic! Hip, hip, hooray! (*Pause.*)
MIDGET: When you think how far mankind has come—(*He waves his handkerchief. Pause.*)
KAROLINE: Now the zeppelin's almost out of sight—
MIDGET: On the horizon—
KAROLINE: I can hardly see it anymore—
MIDGET: I still see it very plainly—
KAROLINE: Now I see nothing at all. (*She catches sight of Kasimir and smiles.*) Kasimir, sweetheart, soon now we'll all be flying.
KASIMIR: Just leave me alone! (*Kasimir moves to the Lukas game and strikes the mallet. A silent interested crowd gathers to watch him, but the bell doesn't ring until the third swing. Kasimir pays and collects his prize.*)

KAROLINE: Congratulations.

KASIMIR: For what?

KAROLINE: For winning the prize.

KASIMIR: Thanks. (*Silence.*)

KAROLINE: The zeppelin's flying to Oberammergau, but it'll fly back again and do some more circles in the sky.

KASIMIR: What the hell do I care? Twenty big shot businessmen fly around up there and meantime down here millions are starving. That zeppelin's shit, I know that racket, I'm not taken in by it—stupid airship! Don't you see through that? Airship! We're supposed to look at it and get a big thrill, like we're flying up there, too—in the meantime we don't have no decent shoes to put on our feet and we gotta beg for the scraps off their plates to put in our mouths, like dogs.

KAROLINE: When you're so depressed, then I get depressed, too.

KASIMIR: Don't accuse me of being depressing.

KAROLINE: Yes, you are. You're a pessimist.

KASIMIR: You said it. Anybody who's got any brains is a pessimist. (*He walks away from her again and once more tests his strength. This time he rings the bell three times. He pays and collects his prizes. Then he moves back to Karoline.*) It's easy for you to be happy. I told you right off the bat, didn't I, that I wouldn't go to your old Octoberfest today, not under any circumstances. Yesterday I got laid off, tomorrow I'm on the dole, but today I'm supposed to have a good time, just laugh the whole thing off, like you.

KAROLINE: I wasn't laughing.

KASIMIR: Sure you laughed. Why shouldn't you? You still got money coming in and you're living with your parents, who have a pension to live on in their old age. But I don't have my parents no more. I'm on my own in this world, strictly on my own. (*Silence.*)

KAROLINE: Maybe we're just not meant for each other—

KASIMIR: What does that mean?

KAROLINE: Well, you're such a pessimist and I have this tendency to get depress-ed easy—Look what just happened, for instance—with the zeppelin—

KASIMIR: Will you shut the hell up about that zeppelin?

KAROLINE: Will you stop yelling at me all the time? I didn't do nothing to deserve that from you!

KASIMIR: Oh, you can go to hell! (*He exits.*)

SCENE 4

(*Karoline watches him leave; then she slowly crosses to the Ice Cream Man, buys a cone and licks it thoughtfully. Schürzinger is already licking his second cone.*)

KAROLINE: Why are you giving me such a funny look?

SCHÜRZINGER: Sorry! I was thinking about something else.

KAROLINE: Oh. (*Silence.*)

SCHÜRZINGER: I was thinking about the zeppelin. (*Silence.*)

KAROLINE: The zeppelin's flying to Oberammergau.

SCHÜRZINGER: Was the little lady ever in Oberammergau?

KAROLINE: Three times!

SCHÜRZINGER: Well! (*Silence.*)

KAROLINE: But the Oberammergaus aren't no angels either. All people are basically evil.

SCHÜRZINGER: You shouldn't talk like that, Fraulein. People aren't basically good or evil. It's because of the economy today, it follows people have to think about themselves first. They have to survive, after all. See what I mean?

KAROLINE: No.

SCHÜRZINGER: You will, just listen. Let's say, for example, you're in love with a certain guy. And let's say, this certain guy loses his job. Well, then he's bound to lose you as his girlfriend, too. Automatically.

KAROLINE: I disagree.

SCHÜRZINGER: It's true.

KAROLINE: Oh, no! A decent woman stands by her man all the more when he's having a hard time—that's my opinion.

SCHÜRZINGER: Not mine. (*Silence.*)

KAROLINE: Can you read palms?

SCHÜRZINGER: No.

KAROLINE: Well, whatta you do for a living?

SCHÜRZINGER: Take a guess!

KAROLINE: Mechanic?

SCHÜRZINGER: No. Tailor.

KAROLINE: I'd of never guessed that.

SCHÜRZINGER: Why not?

KAROLINE: Because I don't like tailors. They think too much of themselves. (*Silence.*)

SCHÜRZINGER: I'm the exception. I'm busy thinking about the destiny of mankind.

KAROLINE: Do you like ice cream?

SCHÜRZINGER: My only passion, as the saying goes.

KAROLINE: Your only one?

SCHÜRZINGER: Yes.

KAROLINE: That's a shame.

SCHÜRZINGER: Why?

KAROLINE: I think you're really missing something.

SCENE 5

(*Kasimir appears again and beckons to Karoline. She goes to him.*)

KASIMIR: Who's that guy you're talking to over there?

KAROLINE: A friend of mine.

KASIMIR: Since when?

KAROLINE: Oh, for ages. We just happened to run into each other. So, don't you believe me?

KASIMIR: Why shouldn't I? (*Silence.*)

KAROLINE: Whatta you want? (*Silence.*)

KASIMIR: What did you mean, that maybe we're just not meant for each other. (*Karoline remains spitefully silent.*) Is that supposed to mean we don't belong to each other anymore?

KAROLINE: Maybe.

KASIMIR: So, is that supposed to mean we're splitting up—is that what you're thinking?

KAROLINE: Don't ask me right now.

KASIMIR: And why not, if you don't mind?

KAROLINE: Because I'm mad at you right now. And in my present mood, I can't give you a straight answer. (*Silence.*)

KASIMIR: Oh. Huh. So that's the way it is. Just like that. I don't get to say nothing about it. That's really funny.

KAROLINE: What are you talking about?

KASIMIR: That's the way it is.

KAROLINE: The way what is? (*Silence.*)

KASIMIR: Or maybe it isn't just a little funny that on this particular day you get the idea maybe we're just not meant for each other—on the same day I get laid off. (*Silence.*)

KAROLINE: I don't know what you're getting at, Kasimir.

KASIMIR: Just think it over. Just think it over, Fraulein. (*Silence.*)

KAROLINE: (*Suddenly.*) Oh, you ungrateful man! Didn't I always stick up for you? Don't you remember all the trouble I had with my parents? Because I didn't marry the man in the civil service and I wouldn't give you up and I never let them say anything against you?

KASIMIR: Take it easy, Fraulein! Never mind what you didn't do for me, think about what you're doing to me—right now.

KAROLINE: And how about what you're doing to me?

KASIMIR: I'm just getting the record straight, that's all. And now I'm getting out of here—(*He exits.*)

SCENE 6

(*Karoline watches him go; then she turns back to Schürzinger; it is beginning to get dark.*)

SCHÜRZINGER: Who's your friend?
KAROLINE: My fiancé.
SCHÜRZINGER: You're engaged?
KAROLINE: This time he really hurt my feelings. He got laid off yesterday and now he says I want to break up with him because he got laid off.
SCHÜRZINGER: The old story.
KAROLINE: Let's talk about something else. (*Silence.*)
SCHÜRZINGER: He's standing over there, watching us.
KAROLINE: I want to ride the roller coaster.
SCHÜRZINGER: That's an expensive ride.
KAROLINE: But I'm at the Octoberfest and I promised myself a ride. Come on, ride with me.
SCHÜRZINGER: But only once.
KAROLINE: That's up to you. (*The scene fades to black.*)

SCENE 7

(*The orchestra is now playing "The Glowworm Suite."*)

SCENE 8

(*A new setting. Near the roller coaster at the edge of the Octoberfest grounds. The spot is somewhat out of the way and not well-lighted. It is already evening, but in the distance everything is illuminated. Karoline and Schürzinger enter and listen to the roar of the roller coaster and the delighted screams of the riders.*)

SCENE 9

KAROLINE: This is the best roller coaster. The ride's too short on the other one. There's the ticket booth. Oh, something's just ripped on me.
SCHÜRZINGER: What?
KAROLINE: I don't know what. Turn your head, please. (*Silence.*)
SCHÜRZINGER: (*Who has turned away.*) That fiancé of yours is still following us. Now he's talking to another guy and a woman—they're not taking their eyes off us.
KAROLINE: Where?—Oh, that's Merkl Franz and his girlfriend Erna. I know him all right. He used to work with Kasimir. But he got himself into terrible trouble. He's been in jail and all.

SCHÜRZINGER: They nail the little ones and let the big ones go free.

KAROLINE: I guess so. But Merkl Franz beats Erna up. Even though she gives him everything he wants. Beating up a woman – I think that's the lowest you can get.

SCHÜRZINGER: True.

KAROLINE: My Kasimir is hot tempered, too, but he don't ever beat me up.

SCHÜRZINGER: Let's hope he don't make a scene here.

KAROLINE: No, he'd never make a scene in public. He's got too much pride for that, because of his profession.

SCHÜRZINGER: What does he do?

KAROLINE: (*Who has fixed her torn strap.*) He drives automobiles. A chauffeur.

SCHÜRZINGER: Well, they say hot-tempered people are good-natured.

KAROLINE: Are ya scared?

SCHÜRZINGER: What makes you think that? (*Silence.*)

KAROLINE: I want to ride the roller coaster now. (*Karoline and Schürzinger go off and for a few moments there is no one else on stage.*)

SCENE 10

(*Kasimir enters slowly with Merkl Franz and Erna.*)

FRANZ: Parlez-vous français?

KASIMIR: Why?

FRANZ: Too bad.

KASIMIR: Why?

FRANZ: Because you can't say it German. A quotation. That business with the roller coaster and Karoline – (*To Erna.*) If you did something like that to me, I'd kick your teeth in.

ERNA: You'd have every right to.

SCENE 11

(*Karoline shrieks on the roller coaster as it rolls down.*)

KASIMIR: Enjoy yourself, Karoline! Just so you don't hurt yourself. Just so you don't break your neck. That's all I ask.

FRANZ: Don't worry. The two of us are in this together.

KASIMIR: Not me. I'm strictly on my own. (*Silence.*)

FRANZ: Let me give you a bit of advice. First of all, just forget about the guy – it's not his fault he's making time with your girl. It's her you have to have it out with. As soon as she shows up again punch her one in the mouth.

KASIMIR: That's how you look at it.

FRANZ: Naturally.

KASIMIR: Not me.

FRANZ: You're a sucker.

KASIMIR: Apparently. (*Silence.*)

FRANZ: Don't you know what women are? Didn't you ever hear the joke—when the girl was caught fooling around with her own father and brother, what she said—

ERNA: Stop always putting us women down like that! (*Silence.*)

FRANZ: Yeah, what would we do without them?

ERNA: After all, I'm a woman, too!

FRANZ: So don't start getting on my nerves about it! Here! Hold my gloves a while. The man wants to go get himself something over there—to calm his nerves. (*He exits; in the distance a bugle sounds and it is strangely melancholic.*)

SCENE 12

ERNA: Herr Kasimir. Look at the sky. That's the Great Bear.

KASIMIR: Where?

ERNA: There. And there's Orion. With his sword.

KASIMIR: How come you know all that?

ERNA: My boss explained that to me, when I was still working—he was a professor. You know what, whenever I feel blue, then I always think to myself: What's a human being next to a star? And it gives me something to hold onto again.

SCENE 13

(*Schürzinger appears and the bugle stops. Kasimir recognizes him. Schürzinger greets him. Kasimir returns his greeting mechanically.*)

SCHÜRZINGER: Your fiancée is taking another ride.

KASIMIR: (*Staring at him grimly.*) Good for her!

SCENE 14

(*Merkl Franz enters again; he has bought himself two hot dogs and he eats them with relish.*)

SCENE 15

SCHÜRZINGER: I only took one ride with her. But your fiancée wanted one more.

KASIMIR: One more.

SCHÜRZINGER: Right. (*Silence.*)

KASIMIR: Right. Well, so: the gentleman's an old acquaintance of my fiancée's?

SCHÜRZINGER: What?

KASIMIR: What do you mean "what"?

SCHÜRZINGER: Well, there must be some mistake. I just met your fiancée for the first time a little while ago, over there by the ice cream stand—we just happened to get into a conversation.

KASIMIR: Just happened to—

SCHÜRZINGER: That's all it was.

KASIMIR: That's all, huh?

SCHÜRZINGER: Why?

KASIMIR: Because it's very funny. My fiancé just told me she's known you for a long time. For ages, she said.

FRANZ: Uh, oh! (*Silence.*)

SCHÜRZINGER: Sorry.

KASIMIR: So, is it true or isn't it true? I just want to get the record straight. Man to man. (*Silence.*)

SCHÜRZINGER: No. It isn't true.

KASIMIR: Do I have your word on that?

SCHÜRZINGER: You have my word.

KASIMIR: Thank you. (*Silence.*)

FRANZ: You sap, you'll never get anywhere that way, buddy. Punch him in the mouth.

KASIMIR: Don't butt into my business, please. .

FRANZ: Don't be such a pushover! You nosepicker!

KASIMIR: I'm not a nosepicker!

FRANZ: If you keep it up, where do you think you're gonna get end up acting like that? I can just picture it! Crawling on your knees in front of your wife's lover! Kissing the ground she walks on—running her errands, acting grateful if she lets you lick her sweaty foot, you masochist!

KASIMIR: I'm not a masochist! I'm just a human being! (*Silence.*)

FRANZ: That's the thanks you get. Somebody tries to help you and you turn on him. I should just let you stew in your own juices.

ERNA: Let's go, Franz! (*Franz pinches her arm.*) Ow! Ow!

FRANZ: And I don't give a damn how much you scream, either! I'm staying right here as long as I please—in a spot like this a true man don't run out on a friend.

SCENE 16

(*Karoline appears. Silence.*)

SCENE 17

KASIMIR: (*Slowly crosses to Karoline, stopping directly in front of her.*) I asked you before what you meant when you said maybe we're just not meant for each other—and you just said: maybe. That's all you said.

KAROLINE: And you said I'm breaking up with you because you got laid off. That hurt my feelings. A decent woman stands by her man all the more when he's having a hard time.

KASIMIR: Are you a decent woman?

KAROLINE: You'll have to figure that out for yourself.

KASIMIR: And this is what you call standing by me? (*Karoline is silent.*) The least you can do is give me an answer.

KAROLINE: I can't give you an answer. Either you know it or you don't. (*Silence.*)

KASIMIR: Why are you lying?

KAROLINE: I'm not lying.

KASIMIR: Oh, yes, you are. And it doesn't even bother you. (*Silence.*)

KAROLINE: When are you saying I lied?

KASIMIR: Before. When you said you knew that guy over there for a long time. For ages, you said. And all the while you just met him at the Octoberfest. Why did you lie to me? (*Silence.*)

KAROLINE: I was very mad at you.

KASIMIR: That's no excuse.

KAROLINE: For a woman, maybe it is.

KASIMIR: No. (*Silence.*)

KAROLINE: What it was, I just wanted to eat an ice cream—but then we got talking about the zeppelin. You never used to be so suspicious.

KASIMIR: I can't swallow it as easy as that.

KAROLINE: I just wanted to ride the roller coaster. (*Silence.*)

KASIMIR: If you had said to me: Kasimir, I really want to ride the roller coaster because I really enjoy it—then your Kasimir would have said: Go ahead, ride your precious roller coaster.

KAROLINE: Oh, now butter wouldn't melt in your mouth.

KASIMIR: Don't be sarcastic all of a sudden! Who the hell is that guy?

KAROLINE: He's a true gentleman. A tailor. (*Silence.*)

KASIMIR: Are you insinuating a tailor's a better man than a chauffeur who does an honest day's work?

KAROLINE: Don't always twist the facts.

KASIMIR: You're the one who twists the facts. I'm just trying to point out you lied to me and for no reason. So, go on the roller coaster with your "true gentleman." You'll be a lot better off with him than with a poor bastard who got laid off yesterday.

KAROLINE: And so you got laid off, what am I supposed to do—cry about it? You just don't want anybody else to have a good time—you think of nothing but yourself.

KASIMIR: Since when do I think of nothing but myself? You make me laugh. It's not your precious roller coaster, it's the disgraceful way you acted, lying to me!

SCHÜRZINGER: Pardon me—

FRANZ: (*Interrupting.*) You shut up now and get the hell out of here. I'm telling you, get moving!

KASIMIR: Leave him alone, Merkl! They're two of a kind. (*To Karoline.*) You tailor's piece—(*Silence.*)

KAROLINE: What did you say?

FRANZ: He said: "tailor's piece." Or slut, as they say in Berlin.

SCHÜRZINGER: Come on, Fraulein!

KAROLINE: Yes. Now I will come—(*She leaves with Schürzinger.*)

SCENE 18

FRANZ: Have a good trip!

KASIMIR: The two of you!

FRANZ: Women are like shit! (*To Erna.*) Like shit.

ERNA: Don't be so crude. What did I ever do to you?

FRANZ: You're a woman, that's enough. And now Merkl Franz is going to buy himself a glass of beer. To calm his nerves. Come on, Kasimir.

KASIMIR: No. I'm going home and go to bed. (*He exits.*)

SCENE 19

FRANZ: (*Calling after him.*) Good night! (*The scene fades to black.*)

SCENE 20

(*The orchestra plays "The Parade of the Wooden Soldiers."*)

SCENE 21

(*A new setting: near the toboggan. At the end of the chute where the toboganners shoot out on their behinds. When the men are lucky they can see under the dresses of the ladies as they shoot out. Rauch and Speer are looking on. On the left an Ice Cream Man with candy and balloons. On the right a roast chicken stand, which is seldom patronized because the prices are too high. Just now Elli and Maria are spilling out of the chute and the two men can see under their skirts. And the air is full of festival music.*)

SCENE 22

(*Rauch winks at Elli and Maria, who are busily adjusting their bras, which became disarranged as they slid down.*)

ELLI: What an old goat!
MARIA: Yeah.
ELLI: A real pig, that one.
MARIA: I think the other one's a North German.
ELLI: How can you tell?
MARIA: I can tell by his hat. And his shoes. (*Rauch keeps on grinning.*)
ELLI: (*Looks at him flirtatiously, but speaks in a voice he can't hear.*) Hungry for some, shithead? (*Rauch, flattered, greets her. Elli, as before.*) Good evening, Herr Pisspot. (*Rauch's mouth waters.*) You'd really like some, wouldn't you, shithouse? Better think about your death bed, not my bed. (*Gaily laughing, she exits with Maria.*)

SCENE 23

RAUCH: Things are picking up.
SPEER: Two gorgeous little mortal sins, eh?
RAUCH: In spite of the depression and politics—the old Octoberfest brings the old urge right back up. Do I exaggerate?
SPEER: That's a good one! Very good one!
RAUCH: Here the street cleaner rubs shoulders with the mayor, the salesman with the boss, the diplomat with the ordinary worker—that's what I like about democracy! (*He walks with Speer to the chicken stand; the two men wolf down a tender crunchy chicken and guzzle beer.*)

SCENE 24

(*Karoline enters with Schürzinger. She walks a little ahead, then stops suddenly, and so does he, of course.*)

KAROLINE: Why do men have to be so suspicious? Even when you do whatever they want?
SCHÜRZINGER: It's only natural. To really feel like a man, a guy has to have the upper hand at all times. But don't get the wrong idea.
KAROLINE: Why?
SCHÜRZINGER: I mean because I sided with your fiancé back there. He was pretty upset—it's no joke to find yourself suddenly out in the street.
KAROLINE: I guess so. But that's no excuse for what he said, that I'm a slut. You shouldn't mix business with pleasure. You have to keep your private life

separate.

SCHÜRZINGER: In my opinion, these two spheres are fatally intertwined.

KAROLINE: Don't always talk like such a know-it-all! I'm going to buy myself another ice cream. (*She buys herself one from the Ice Cream Man and Schürzinger eats another cone, too.*)

SCENE 25

RAUCH: (*Pointing greedily at Karoline.*) What a nice fanny that little girl has—

SPEER: Very nice.

RAUCH: What's a girl without a fanny, eh?

SPEER: Very true.

SCENE 26

SCHÜRZINGER: I only mean you have to think it over very carefully, a break-up like that, with all its consequences.

KAROLINE: What consequences? I earn my own living.

SCHÜRZINGER: But I mean the psychological aspect. (*Silence.*)

KAROLINE: Well, I don't intend to be insulted. Just because I was stupid enough to give myself, body and soul, to Kasimir—I could've got married twice over by now, to a gentleman in the civil service with a pension coming to him one day. (*Silence.*)

SCHÜRZINGER: I just don't want it to look like I'm to blame for this break-up between you and him—I came between a man and a woman once before. Never again!

KAROLINE: You said if a man loses his job, then he's bound to lose his girlfriend, too—automatically.

SCHÜRZINGER: That's just human nature. Unfortunately.

KAROLINE: What did you say your name is?

SCHÜRZINGER: Eugene.

KAROLINE: Your eyes are so deep.

SCHÜRZINGER: A lot of people have told me that.

KAROLINE: Don't brag about it! (*Silence.*)

SCHÜRZINGER: Do you like the name Eugene?

KAROLINE: It's all right.

SCHÜRZINGER: I'm a lonely man, Fraulein. You see, take my mother, for instance, she's been deaf ever since the inflation, and she's not quite right in the head, either, because she lost everything she had—so I don't have a living soul to talk to.

KAROLINE: Don't you have any brothers and sisters?

SCHÜRZINGER: No, I'm an only child.

KAROLINE: I can't eat anymore ice cream now. (*She exits with Schürzinger.*)

SCENE 27

SPEER: A remarkable generation, the youth of today. In our day we took part in
sports, naturally, but we had remarkably little interest in the so-called
charms of the intellectual life.
RAUCH: The youth of today don't go in for sex much, either.
SPEER: (*Laughing.*) It certainly saves them a lot of trouble.
RAUCH: I've always been lucky myself.
SPEER: Me, too, except once.
RAUCH: Was she pretty at least?
SPEER: In the dark all cats are gray.
RAUCH: (*Raising his glass.*) To your health!

SCENE 28

(*Karoline shoots out of the toboggan slide, followed by Schürzinger. Rauch and Speer
can see under her skirt. Schürzinger glimpses Rauch, winces, and then greets him
politely, repeating his greeting twice.*)

SCENE 29

RAUCH: (*Returning the greeting, surprised; to Speer.*) Who is that? The fellow who
greeted me just then—with the girl who has the nice fanny—

SCENE 30

KAROLINE: (*Fixing her shoulder strap.*) Who's that fellow there?
SCHÜRZINGER: That's him, himself. Commissioner Rauch. My boss. You know
that big company—the four-story building—with the wing in back—
KAROLINE: Oh, yes, yes.
SCHÜRZINGER: He turned it into a corporation in June, only on paper, of
course, for income tax purposes and so forth.

SCENE 31

RAUCH: (*He has said something to Speer and now, somewhat drunk, he approaches
Schürzinger.*) Pardon me, sir. Have we had the pleasure?
SCHÜRZINGER: I'm Schürzinger, Herr Commissioner.
RAUCH: Schürzinger?
SCHÜRZINGER: Children's wear. Coat department. (*Silence.*)
RAUCH: (*To Schürzinger.*) Your fiancée?
KAROLINE: No. (*Silence.*)
RAUCH: (*Shoving a cigar into Schürzinger's mouth.*) Pleased to meet you! (*To Karo-*

line.) May I offer the young lady a kirsch?

KAROLINE: No, thanks. Kirsch doesn't agree with me. I'd prefer a Samos.

RAUCH: A Samos, then! (*He goes to the chicken stand.*) One Samos! (*To Karoline.*) That's my best friend from Erfurt in Thuringen—and I hail from Weiden in Oberpfalz. To your health, Fraulein! And a kirsch for the young man.

SCHÜRZINGER: Excuse me, Herr Commissioner—but I never touch alcohol.

SCENE 32

(*Kasimir appears and looks on.*)

SCENE 33

RAUCH: Well, why in the world, not?

SCHÜRZINGER: Because I'm a teetotaler, Herr Commissioner.

SPEER: On principle?

SCHÜRZINGER: As the saying goes.

RAUCH: Well, we don't recognize principles like that here. We regard them as nonexistent! The young man will certainly drink a kirsch with his superior! Bottoms up, Herr—

SCHÜRZINGER: Schürzinger. (*He empties the glass and makes a face.*)

RAUCH: Schürzinger! I had a teacher once named Schürzinger. What a thick skull! Another Samos here. And kirsch for Herr Teetotaler—whom we've just deflowered, alcoholically speaking. You want one, too, Fraulein?

KAROLINE: Oh, no! I don't drink straight alcohol and I don't care for mixed drinks at all—(*She notices Kasimir.*)

SCENE 34

(*Kasimir beckons her to him. Karoline does not obey. Kasimir beckons more obviously. Karoline empties her glass, puts it down defiantly and ceremoniously and slowly crosses to Kasimir.*)

SCENE 35

RAUCH: Who is that? Don Quixote?

SCHÜRZINGER: That is the young lady's fiancé.

SPEER: What a picture!

SCHÜRZINGER: But she doesn't want to have anything more to do with him.

RAUCH: That's more like it!

SCENE 36

KAROLINE: Now what do you want? (*Silence.*)

KASIMIR: Who are those people over there?

KAROLINE: Just some old friends of mine.

KASIMIR: Don't be spiteful, please.

KAROLINE: I'm not being spiteful. The fat one is the well-known Commissioner Rauch, who's the head of his own company. And the other one is from northern Germany. A chief judge in the district court.

KASIMIR: Nothing but the best. You can't get me upset with that anymore. (*Silence.*)

KAROLINE: What do you want then?

KASIMIR: I wanted to apologize for being suspicious and for being so mean to you. I shouldn't have been! Will you forgive me for that?

KAROLINE: Yes.

KASIMIR: Thank you. Now I feel better again—(*He smiles.*)

KAROLINE: Don't get the wrong idea.

KASIMIR: What idea? (*Silence.*)

KAROLINE: It's just no use, Kasimir. I've thought about it and my mind's made up—(*She turns away to the schnapps booth.*)

KASIMIR: But they're not the right kind of people for you! They'll just use you for their own pleasure.

KAROLINE: So what's new about that? Life is hard and a woman who wants to get someplace in this world has to play up to men of influence, who can help her get there.

KASIMIR: Were you playing up to me?

KAROLINE: Yes. (*Silence.*)

KASIMIR: That isn't true.

KAROLINE: Oh, yes it is. (*Silence.*)

KASIMIR: What do you expect to get out of those guys over there?

KAROLINE: One step higher on the social ladder and all that goes with it.

KASIMIR: Well, you certainly changed, didn't you?

KAROLINE: No, I didn't change—it's just that I used to be dominated by you and I just repeated what you said, that an office worker is no better than a blue collar worker. But deep down inside I always knew better. I just couldn't think straight! I was in a fog because I only listened to you. But that's over now.

KASIMIR: Over?

KAROLINE: You said it. (*Silence.*)

KASIMIR: So. Huh. So that's it. Kasimir got laid off. So, that's that. He doesn't get to say nothing about it. Makes me laugh.

KAROLINE: Do you have anything more to say to me? (*Silence.*)

KASIMIR: I've been hanging around for a long time, making up my mind to apologize to you—but now I'm sorry I did. (*He exits.*)

SCENE 37

(*Karoline watches him go, then turns back to the schnapps booth. Scene fades to black.*)

SCENE 38

(*The orchestra plays "The Last Rose of Summer."*)

SCENE 39

(*A new setting. Inside the freak show tent. It is filled to capacity. Rauch, Speer, Karoline, and Schürzinger are among the audience seated inside.*)

SCENE 40

MASTER OF CEREMONIES: And now for our fifth act, may I present to you, the Man with the Bulldog's Head! (*The Man with the Bulldog's Head enters on stage.*) Johann, the Man with the Bulldog's Head, was sixteen years old the day before yesterday. As you can see, his lower jaw is abnormally well-developed, so that he can touch his nose with his lower lip without any difficulty. (*The Man with the Bulldog's Head does that.*) But Johann cannot open his mouth and so he has to be fed intravenously. Through an exceedingly difficult operation his mouth could be opened, but then he would never be able to close it again. You see here the kind of tricks nature plays on us and the kind of freaks that inhabit our earth.

SCENE 41

MASTER OF CEREMONIES: And now, ladies and gentlemen, we come to our sixth number and the star of our show: Juanita, the Gorilla Girl. (*Juanita appears on stage.*) Juanita was born in a little village near Zwickau. How it happened that she did not come into the world, in respect to her physical anatomy, like other children, is a mystery to medical science. As the ladies and gentlemen can see for themselves, Juanita's entire body is covered with hair, like an animal's, and in the arrangement of her internal organs, she is like an animal, also—

SCENE 42

(*There is a buzzing in the air and it gets louder and louder; from outside general music*) *flourishes, shouts and drumrolls.*)

RAUCH: (*Leaping up.*) The zeppelin! The zeppelin! (*The buzz becomes ear-splitting and the audience rushes outside and now the zeppelin makes several loops over the Octoberfest grounds.*)

SCENE 43

(*Juanita wants to go out, too.*)

MASTER OF CEREMONIES: Hey, get back there! Are you crazy?
JUANITA: But the zeppelin—
MASTER OF CEREMONIES: Nothing doing! You can't go out there! Get back!

SCENE 44

(*The Man with the Bulldog's Head appears with the other side-show freaks: the Fat Lady, the Strong Man, the Bearded Lady, the Camel Man and the Siamese Twins.*)

MASTER OF CEREMONIES: Hey, who called you out here? What the hell are you doing out here?!
THE FAT LADY: But the zeppelin—

SCENE 45

MIDGET: (*Appearing on stage with a dog whip.*) Heinrich! What's going on here?
MASTER OF CEREMONIES: Ringmaster! The freaks are going crazy! They want to see the zeppelin!
MIDGET: (*Sharply.*) And what else do they want?! (*Silence.*) Back to your places! And be quick about it! What do you need to see the zeppelin for? If they see you for free out there, we'll go broke! That's Bolshevism for you!
JUANITA: I'm not going to be insulted! (*She weeps. The Man with the Bulldog's Head makes a sound like a death rattle, sways, and clutches at his heart.*)
THE FAT LADY: Johann! Johann!
MIDGET: Get out of here! Out! Out!
THE FAT LADY: (*Supporting the Man with the Bulldog's Head.*) Poor Johann—he's always had such a weak heart—(*She exits with the other freaks and only Juanita remains.*)

SCENE 46

MIDGET: (*Suddenly tender.*) Please don't cry, my little Juanita—here, have some bonbons—beautiful chocolate creams—

JUANITA: You shouldn't always insult me, Herr Ringmaster—that's very un-christian.

MIDGET: I didn't mean to insult you. Here—(*He gives her the chocolate creams and exits.*)

SCENE 47

(*Juanita listlessly consumes the chocolate creams. Meanwhile Karoline and Schür-zinger come back into the tent and sit down in the last row.*)

SCENE 48

KAROLINE: The zeppelin looks beautiful—even at night, all lit up like that. But we'll never fly in it.

SCHÜRZINGER: That's for sure.

KAROLINE: You're giving me such a funny look.

SCHÜRZINGER: So are you. (*Silence.*)

KAROLINE: I think I'm a little drunk. You never drank alcohol before neither, did you?

SCHÜRZINGER: No, never.

KAROLINE: And are there other things the gentleman hasn't never done?

SCHÜRZINGER: Maybe a few. (*Karoline suddenly gives him a quick kiss. Silence.*) Now I'm completely confused. Is it the alcohol, or—something's happening to me I can't control. If I could just get my hands on some money—

KAROLINE: (*Interrupting him.*) Don't spoil things! (*Silence.*)

SCHÜRZINGER: May I call you by your first name?

KAROLINE: For tonight.

SCHÜRZINGER: And afterwards?

KAROLINE: Maybe. (*Silence.*)

SCENE 49

(*Rauch comes back into the tent, catches sight of Karoline, stops at the entrance and eavesdrops.*)

KAROLINE: Your name is Eugene?

SCHÜRZINGER: Yes.

KAROLINE: And my name is Karoline. Why are you smiling?

SCHÜRZINGER: Because I'm happy.

RAUCH: And my name is Konrad. (*Schürzinger is startled and so is Karoline. Silence. Schürzinger gets to his feet. Rauch grins and threatens playfully with his forefinger.*) Well, well, well, naughty little Karoline, sitting inside here, while the zeppelin's flying around outside.

KAROLINE: Oh, that old zeppelin, I know it by heart already.
RAUCH: (*Staring, annoyed, at Schürzinger.*) Congratulations. (*Schürzinger, unpleasantly affected, bows awkwardly.*) Please continue. Don't let me interrupt such a stimulating conversation.
SCHÜRZINGER: Herr Commissioner! Stimulating isn't the word for it—as the saying goes. (*He smiles politely and sits down again.*)
RAUCH: Isn't it?

SCENE 50

SPEER: (*Who has followed Rauch into the tent.*) A repulsive fellow!
RAUCH: A cynic!
SPEER: Making time in here with Karoline, while we're wasting it out there on the zeppelin.
RAUCH: His time will soon run out.

SCENE 51

(*Now the orchestra softly plays "The Radetsky March" and the audience comes back into the tent because the zeppelin's on its way to Friedrichshafen. When everyone is seated again, the orchestra breaks off in the middle of a measure.*)

SCENE 52

KAROLINE: What did you mean "stimulating isn't the word for it"?
SCHÜRZINGER: That was only a passing remark.
KAROLINE: I just know you're going to walk out on me. You're just as calculating as the rest. Even in love.
SCHÜRZINGER: No, that's a misunderstanding, what you're thinking now.
KAROLINE: I'm not thinking anything at all, I'm just talking.

SCENE 53

MASTER OF CEREMONIES: (*Sounding the gong.*) Ladies and gentlemen! As we were saying when we were interrupted, Juanita's entire body is covered with hair, like an animal's, and her internal organs are arranged like an animal's, too. In spite of that, Juanita has extraordinary intelligence. She speaks perfect English and French, which she taught herself through incredible perseverance and practice. And now Juanita has kindly consented to favor the audience with a sample of her splendid natural singing voice. Allow me to present—(*From a battered old piano come the strains of the "Barcarolle."*)

SCENE 54

(*Juanita sings—and while she sings, Schürzinger puts his arm around Karoline's waist and even the calves of their legs touch.*)

JUANITA: (*Singing the "Barcarolle.*")
  Lovely night, oh night of love
  O smile on our caresses!
  Sweeter than the light of day
  The night of love divine.
  Lustrous moon, too soon I know
  Your glow will fade away.
  To be gone from earth until the close of the day.
  Heaven's azure skies
  Fold the night in a dream, cloak my loved one's eager eyes.
  Take me to Paradise.
  Lovely night, oh night of love
  O smile on our caresses!
  Sweeter than the light of day
  The night of love divine, ah.

SCENE 55

(*During the last stanza the curtain falls. Juanita has finished her song and the Midget crosses the stage in front of the curtain from right to left. He holds a sign which reads: INTERMISSION.*)

SCENE 56

(*Intermission.*)

SCENE 57

(*When the lights go down in the theatre again, the orchestra plays "The Bavarian Parade March" by Scherzer.*)

SCENE 58

(*The scene: near the Wagner brewery. A brass band plays festive airs. Merkl Franz is excited, his Erna is more reserved, while Kasimir crouches nearby in a melancholy mood.*)

SCENE 59

(*All, except Kasimir, sing along with the brass band.*)
So long as our old Peter
On Peter's mountain stands
So long as our green Isar
Through Münchner city flows
So long as down below
Still stands our Hofbrau house
So long the warmth and love of home
Our Münchner will not die!
A cheer, a cheer, for what is dear, our Münchner home!
One, two, three—hurrah!

SCENE 60

FRANZ: Prost, Kasimir! Drink to your future!
KASIMIR: What future is there for me? Minister Commerce, maybe?
FRANZ: Start a new party! And make yourself Minister of Finance!
KASIMIR: They always hit a man when he's down.
FRANZ: He who won't listen to reason can't be helped. (*Silence.*)
KASIMIR: I'm licensed to drive every car and truck on the road.
FRANZ: So be glad you don't have a fiancée anymore, that stuck-up bitch!
KASIMIR: That young lady has an office job.
FRANZ: That's no excuse.
KASIMIR: Generally speaking, all women are inferior beings—present company excepted, of course. They'll sell their souls, and betray, in this particular case, me, for a roller coaster ride.
ERNA: If I was a man, I wouldn't dream of touching a woman. I can't stand the smell of a woman. Especially in winter.

SCENE 61

(*All, except Kasimir, sing again to the music of the brass band.*)
I shoot the stag in the wild wood
In forests dark the doe
The eagle crouched on eyrie rock
Geese swimming down below.
Escape my aim no creature can
When sounds my rifle's start
Yet though I am a man of iron
Still love has touched my heart.
(*Sudden silence.*)

SCENE 62

KASIMIR: "Yet though I am a man of iron / Still love has touched my heart"—
and "it's like a light from heaven that makes a palace of the meanest hut . . ."
And it never dies—as long as you don't get laid off, that is. What's all that
crap, anyway, about perfect love that joins two souls as one? Adam and Eve!
I don't give a shit about all that.—All I've got left in the world is about four
marks in cash, but today I'm going to get drunk on it, and then I'm going to
hang myself.—And tomorrow people will say, "Once upon a time there was
a poor sucker named Kasimir—"

FRANZ: The hell they will! Thousands die every day—and they're forgotten before they're cold. Maybe if you were a dead politician, then they might give
you a fancy funeral, but by tomorrow already you'd still be forgotten—forgotten!

KASIMIR: A man is pretty much alone in this world.

FRANZ: Prost, ass-hole!

SCENE 63

(All, except Kasimir, sing once more to the music of the brass band.)
    Drink, drink, brotherkin, drink
    Leave all your troubles at home
    Forget all your sorrows and pain
    After all, life's just a game.
    Forget all your sorrows and pain
    After all, life's just a game.
(Sudden silence.)

SCENE 64

KASIMIR: (Getting up.) Well. I'm beginning to feel primitive. By rights I should go
right to Karoline's house and rip all her clothes out of her closet and tear
them to shreds, make the feathers fly, show her what's what—now I'm really
getting upset!! (He staggers off.)

SCENE 65

ERNA: Where's he going?

FRANZ: He'll be back, if he doesn't fall flat on his face.

ERNA: I'm worried about him—

FRANZ: Nothing to worry about.

ERNA: But I don't think he has a strong constitution. He's more the sensitive
type.

FRANZ: You're pretty sharp, aren't you? (*Silence.*)

ERNA: Franzl, dear—please leave him alone.

FRANZ: Who?

ERNA: Kasimir.

FRANZ: What do you mean leave him alone?

ERNA: He's not like us. I felt that right away. Don't tempt him, please.

FRANZ: Why not?

ERNA: What we're mixed up in is no damn good.

FRANZ: Since when? (*Silence.*)

ERNA: Get your finger out of my beer!

FRANZ: You're pretty sharp, aren't you?

ERNA: Get your finger out of there—

FRANZ: No. It feels good. Cools my hot blood. (*Erna suddenly pulls his hand out of her beer mug. Franz grins, perplexed.*)

SCENE 66

(*All, except Erna and Franz, start to sing again to the music of the brass band. Rauch, Speer, Karoline and Schürzinger cross the stage with beer mugs in their hands. Of course they join in the singing, too.*)

> Drink, drink, brotherkin, drink
> Leave all your troubles at home
> Forget all your sorrows and pain
> After all, life's just a game.
> Forget all your sorrows and pain
> After all, life's just a game.

(*Sudden silence.*)

SCENE 67

KASIMIR: (*Appears with Elli and Maria, his arms around both their waists.*) Allow me to introduce you. We three charming young people just met in front of the rest rooms. Merkl, can you explain this phenomenon to me: why is it that the women in the world always go to the toilet two by two?

MARIA: Oh, phooey!

FRANZ: No "phooey" here, lady.

KASIMIR: We're all just human beings. Especially today! (*He sits down and lets Elli sit on his lap.*)

ELLI: (*To Franz.*) Is it true he owns a Mercedes?

FRANZ: Of course he owns a Mercedes! And what a car!

MARIA: (*To Elli.*) Go on, don't be taken in by that sharpie! Him and his Mercedes!

KASIMIR: (*To Maria.*) If Kasimir says he's got a Mercedes, then, by God, he's got a Mercedes—remember that, you misfit!

ELLI: (*To Maria.*) Just you shut up, now!

KASIMIR: (*Caressing Elli.*) You're some woman! I'm beginning to like you. You've got such beautiful soft hair and your skin's like velvet.

ELLI: I want a drink.

KASIMIR: Here! Drink!

ELLI: There's not a drop left in it.

KASIMIR: Beer here!

WAITRESS: (*Crossing to him; setting down a mug of beer.*) Pay up, please.

KASIMIR: (*Fumbling in his pockets.*) Pay up, please, pay up—God in heaven, all my money's gone—(*The Waitress takes the beer away. Elli gets up.*)

MARIA: And he's supposed to own a Mercedes? I told you right away at most he had a bicycle. On credit.

KASIMIR: (*To Elli.*) C-mon, let's go—

ELLI: (*Waves.*) Bye, bye, Herr Mercedes—(*She exits with Maria.*)

SCENE 68

KASIMIR: Pay up, please—Oh, poor Kasimir! Without money in your pocket, you're just a no-good bum!

FRANZ: Kasimir the Philosopher!

KASIMIR: If I only knew what party I ought to vote for—(*Pause.*)

FRANZ: Kasimir the Politician.

KASIMIR: Kiss my ass, Merkl. (*Silence.*)

FRANZ: Look at me. (*Kasimir looks at him.*) There's no political party whatsoever I haven't tried, even the splinter parties. But in every one of them, it's the same. Dog eat dog. Every man for himself. In a world like that, you have to act like that, like, for example, a certain Merkl Franz—

KASIMIR: How?

FRANZ: Simple. (*Silence.*) For example, I've been specializing lately—figuring technicalities to get around the law.

KASIMIR: You shouldn't fool around with the law.

FRANZ: You blockhead. (*He waves several ten mark notes under Kasimir's nose. Silence.*)

KASIMIR: No. Individual actions like that are useless.

ERNA: Karoline's sitting over there.

KASIMIR: (*Getting up.*) Where? (*Silence.*)

FRANZ: She's looking at you.

KASIMIR: But she's not coming over. (*Silence.*)

SCENE 69

KASIMIR: (*Making a speech to the distant Karoline.*) Fraulein Karoline! Don't get any idea of coming over here, because we're all through, we're not even friends anymore. It's not your fault, it's just because I got laid off and that's only logical, you crummy bitch! But if I decide to follow in the footsteps of a certain Merkl Franz, then that will be your fault—because now I'm empty inside. You wandered into my life and today you wandered out of it again—and now I'm like a reed in the wind and I can't find nothing to hold onto anymore—(*He sits down.*)

SCENE 70

(*Silence.*)

FRANZ: So?

KASIMIR: I'm burned out.

FRANZ: Kasimir. For the last time, he who won't listen to reason can't be helped.

KASIMIR: I'm not sure yet.

FRANZ: (*Holding out his hand to him.*) It's up to you—

KASIMIR: (*Staring absently ahead.*) I'm still not sure yet.

ERNA: Oh, leave him alone, if he doesn't want to. (*Silence. Franz stares at Erna grimly—suddenly he flings his beer in her face. Erna jumps up.*)

FRANZ: (*Shoving her back into her seat.*) Stay there. Or I'll kick your teeth in.

SCENE 71

(*All, except Kasimir, Erna, and Franz sing.*)
  The roses bloom but once
  And winter flies away
  And we who dwell on earth
  Have only one May
  The birds fly to the south
  And fly again back home
  We who are laid in the earth
  Never return to roam.
(*Scene fades to black.*)

SCENE 72

(*Now the orchestra plays "The Petersburg Sleighride."*)

SCENE 73

(*New setting: in the Hippodrome. Rauch, Speer, Karoline, and Schürzinger enter.*)

SCENE 74

RAUCH: (*To Karoline.*) What do you say to a spirited gallop? We're in the Hippodrome!
KAROLINE: Fine! But no side-saddle—I have a strong grip.
RAUCH: Atta girl!
SPEER: The girl thinks like a horsewoman.
KAROLINE: But if I take one ride, then I'll want two—
RAUCH: Make it three!
KAROLINE: Fine! (*She runs off to the horse track.*)

SCENE 75

SPEER: (*Calling after her.*) Make it four even!
RAUCH: As many as you want! (*He sits down with Speer at a little table on the platform and orders a flask of wine. Schürzinger remains below and keeps his eye on Karoline. Now an old lame horse with a side-saddle, on which a near-sighted ten-year-old is seated, is led past the platform just as the music begins. It always breaks off in the middle of a measure when the horse has gone several trips around the track and the rider has to pay again. The cracking of the whip can be heard. Schürzinger climbs on a chair so he can see better. Of course, Speer and Rauch watch, too.*)

SCENE 76

RAUCH: Bravo! Prima!
SPEER: An Amazon!
RAUCH: An artist! The balcony's shaking! Girls riding on bicycles remind me from behind of swimming ducks.
SPEER: (*Turning back to his wine.*) Rauch, old boy! How long has it been since I had my old nag under me?
RAUCH: Exactly?
SPEER: 1912—Then I could still afford two horses. But today? I'm a poor judge. Those were the days! They were two Arabians. Fillies. Rosalinde and Yvonne.
RAUCH: (*Now he has turned back to his wine, too.*) Did you marry late, too?
SPEER: Never late enough!
RAUCH: (*Raising his glass.*) To your health! (*Silence.*) I had my wife in the hospital at Arosa and who knows where else—My son is sound as a nut.

SPEER: When does he get his doctor's degree?

RAUCH: Next semester. We're getting old. (*Silence.*)

SPEER: I'm a grandfather twice over. At least I'll leave something behind. A little trace.

SCENE 77

(*Karoline appears again and tries to avoid Schürzinger, who is still standing on his chair.*)

SCHÜRZINGER: (*In a low voice.*) Wait! For your own good!

KAROLINE: Oh, yeah.

SCHÜRZINGER: What do you mean, "Oh, yeah!"

KAROLINE: When a man uses that line, he has an ulterior motive.

SCHÜRZINGER: I don't have an ulterior motive. It's just that I'm getting somewhat sober again. Please don't drink anymore alcohol.

KAROLINE: No. I'm going to drink as much as I want today.

SCHÜRZINGER: You can't imagine in your wildest dreams what those two gentlemen over there are saying about you.

KAROLINE: Well, what are they saying about me?

SCHÜRZINGER: They want to get you drunk.

KAROLINE: I can hold my liquor. (*Silence.*)

SCHÜRZINGER: And then he came right out with it, the Commissioner.

KAROLINE: With what?

SCHÜRZINGER: That he wants to go to bed with you. Tonight. (*Silence.*)

KAROLINE: Oh, does he —

SCHÜRZINGER: He said it right in front of me, as if I'm a nothing. He's no fit company for you. That's beneath your dignity. Come on, let's just go.

KAROLINE: Where to? (*Silence.*)

SCHÜRZINGER: We could drink a cup of tea. At my place, maybe. (*Silence.*)

KAROLINE: You're just thinking of yourself, like the rest. Exactly like Kasimir.

SCHÜRZINGER: I don't know what you're talking about.

KAROLINE: That's right, Kasimir.

SCHÜRZINGER: My name is Eugene.

KAROLINE: And mine is Karoline. (*Silence.*)

SCHÜRZINGER: I'm a rather shy person by nature. But back there at the freak show, I was dreaming about sharing the future with you. But I'm just a passing fancy for a certain Fraulein Karoline.

KAROLINE: That's right, Herr Eugene.

SCHÜRZINGER: A man often just wastes his feelings on a —

KAROLINE: People without feelings have it a lot easier in life. (*She leaves him and turns toward the platform. Schürzinger now sits down on the chair.*)

SCENE 78

RAUCH: Congratulations!

SPEER: You are talented. I tell you that as a former Lance Officer.

KAROLINE: I thought the gentleman was a judge—

SPEER: Have you ever met a judge who wasn't an officer? I haven't.

RAUCH: There are a few—

SPEER: Jews!

KAROLINE: No politics, please!

SPEER: That's not politics!

RAUCH: Politics is a dirty word—(*He toasts with Karoline.*) To our next ride!

KAROLINE: I'd like another ride very much. The first three went by so fast.

RAUCH: To three more, then! Uh!

SPEER: (*Lifting his glass.*) Rosalinde and Yvonne! Where are you now? I salute you in spirit. What's a convertible next to a good horse!

KAROLINE: Oh, a convertible's something wonderful!

SPEER: (*Mournfully.*) But it doesn't give you something alive under you—

RAUCH: (*Softly.*) Allow me to inform you that I own a wonderful convertible. I hope you'll take a ride with me. (*Silence.*)

KAROLINE: Where to?

RAUCH: To Altötting.

KAROLINE: To Altötting, sure—(*She runs off again to the horse track, passing Schürzinger, who is now carefully examining a pimple in his pocket mirror.*)

SCENE 79

(*Rauch is really drunk by now. He is waving his arms about, as if he were the conductor of the Hippodrome music. Now a waltz is being played.*)

SPEER: (*Who is even drunker.*) Altötting. Where's Altötting?

RAUCH: (*Singing to the waltz melody.*) In my little room—one, two, three—in my little bed—one, two, three—(*He hums.*)

SPEER: (*Spitefully.*) And your employee over there? (*The music breaks off in the middle of a measure. Rauch hits the table with his hand and glares hatefully at Speer. Now the music starts again, this time a march.*)

RAUCH: (*Grimly singing while h continues to glare at Speer.*)

Yes, we are the gypsies
Wandering the earth
  Winsome are our women
  Earning gold for mirth.
Lying in a cornfield
Arms entwined, I asked
  Whether she did love me

Yes, she said, and laughed.
(*The music breaks off suddenly.*)
SPEER: (*Even more spitefully.*) What about your employee over there?
RAUCH: (*Yelling at him.*) You're just jealous! (*He gets up and staggers over to Schür-zinger.*)

SCENE 80

RAUCH: Herr—
SCHÜRZINGER: (*Who has stood up.*) Schürzinger.
RAUCH: Right. Surprise! (*He again sticks a cigar in Schürzinger's mouth.*) Have another cigar—a successful evening, eh?
SCHÜRZINGER: Very successful, Commissioner.
RAUCH: Speaking of success: Did you ever hear the story about Louis the Fifteenth, King of France?—Listen: one night Louis the Fifteenth went to the Hippodrome with one of his Lieutenants and the Lieutenant's fiancée. And after a little while, the Lieutenant excused himself, because he was very honored that his king showed a little interest in his fiancée—He felt flattered! Flattered! (*Silence.*)
SCHÜRZINGER: Yes, I've heard the story—The Lieutenant soon became a First Lieutenant.
RAUCH: Oh? That's news to me. (*Silence.*)
SCHÜRZINGER: May I excuse myself, Herr Commissioner—(*He exits.*)

SCENE 81

SPEER: (*Approaching Rauch; now totally drunk.*) Herr Commissioner, you must be losing your mind, yelling at me like that—apparently you don't know who you're dealing with! Me! Sperr! Chief Judge of the District Court!
RAUCH: Pleased to meet you!
SPEER: Same here. (*Silence.*)
RAUCH: My dear Werner, in my opinion, you are drunk.
SPEER: Is that your considered opinion, Konrad?
RAUCH: It is. Absolutely. (*Silence.*)
SPEER: The court will adjourn for consultation. The court declares itself to be impartial. No probation. No mitigating circumstances. No probation!
RAUCH: (*Spitefully.*) Don't you have any girls in Erfurt?
SPEER: Hardly any.
RAUCH: (*Grinning.*) Then do you men do it yourself there? (*Speer stares at him grimly. Suddenly he gives him a powerful shove and tries to kick him, but doesn't quite reach him. Silence.*) Should a forty-year friendship be broken for such a reason?
SPEER: In the name of the king—(*He raises his hand as if to swear an oath.*) By the

eyesight of my grandchildren, I swear to you that henceforth we two are divorced—from bed and board! (*He staggers off.*)

SCENE 82

RAUCH: (*Watching him go.*) Sad but true—he's a snake, too. A jealous snake! But Konrad Rauch here, he comes out of sturdy old farming stock and for him such legal technicalities are not worth the paper they're printed on! In spite of his sixty-two years! Ow! (*He suddenly twists in pain and sits down on Schür-zinger's chair.*) Now, what was that?—I hope I'm not going to have a dizzy spell again tonight.—Joseph had a stroke—Watch out, Konrad Rauch! Watch out!

SCENE 83

(*Karoline appears and looks around. Silence.*)

KAROLINE: Where is Herr Schürzinger?
RAUCH: He sends his best regards. (*Silence.*)
KAROLINE: And the Lance Officer left, too?
RAUCH: We are alone. (*Silence.*)
KAROLINE: Are we really driving to Altötting?
RAUCH: Right away. (*He tries to get up, but has to sit down again, obviously in pain.*) How much do you make a month? (*Silence.*)
KAROLINE: Fifty-five marks.
RAUCH: Good!
KAROLINE: And I'm glad I have it, too.
RAUCH: These days.
KAROLINE: It's just that there's no future in it. At best I can only make three times that much. By that time I'll be gray.
RAUCH: The future is all a question of the right connections. (*Now he gets up.*) And Commissioner Konrad Rauch is a connection. On to Altötting! (*A musical fanfare. Darkness.*)

SCENE 84

(*Now the orchestra is playing a little May air.*)

SCENE 85

(*New setting: on the parking lot behind the Octoberfest grounds. In the foreground a bench. Franz appears with Erna and Kasimir.*)

SCENE 86

FRANZ: Now here's the set-up. As far as I know there's only one parking attendant around—and he stands over there most of the time so he gets a better view of the festival grounds. Erna! Pull yourself together now and pay attention!

ERNA: I'm still wet from the beer.

FRANZ: Don't make such a tragedy out of it.

ERNA: Aren't you sorry? (*Silence.*)

FRANZ: No. (*A whistle sounds in the distance. The three of them listen.*) Police?

ERNA: Watch out, Franz!

FRANZ: That's what you're here to do—in case something goes wrong. All kinds of fancy cars parked here today. Bunch of capitalist tax-dodgers—(*He disappears among the limousines.*)

KASIMIR: (*As if to himself.*) Auf Wiedersehen!

SCENE 88

ERNA: Merkl has a strange nature. He can kill a man one minute, and feel sorry for him the next.

KASIMIR: He's not your average person.

ERNA: Because he's so intelligent. He knows how to force a car door open and break a window—without making any noise.

KASIMIR: There's nothing else to do these days.

ERNA: I guess so. (*Silence.*)

KASIMIR: Yesterday if I caught someone breaking into my car, I'd a broke his neck and strangled him—today it's the other way around. That's what life does to you.

ERNA: I can't see well today. The light's blinding me.

KASIMIR: Me, too, a little. (*Silence.*)

ERNA: I often picture a revolution in my mind—and I can see the poor marching under the arch of triumph and the rich in the police wagons, because they tell each other such lies about the poor—You know, I'd be die happy with the flag in my hand for a revolution like that.

KASIMIR: Not me.

ERNA: They shot my brother in a gravel pit—the war was already over at the time—1919.

KASIMIR: So what?

ERNA: My poor brother was a martyr.

KASIMIR: Must have made him even happier to die like a martyr!

ERNA: Don't talk like such a selfish pig! Even Merkl Franz himself shows some respect for my poor dead brother. (*Silence.*)

KASIMIR: Then I'm even more evil than Merkl Franz.

ERNA: And you're very bitter.

KASIMIR: I never said I was any good.

ERNA: Human beings wouldn't never be evil if things wasn't so tough for them. To say that man is basically evil is an outrageous lie!

SCENE 89

FRANZ: (*Appearing from among the limousines with a briefcase.*) What's an outrageous lie?

ERNA: That man is basically evil.

FRANZ: Oh. (*Silence.*)

ERNA: Nobody's all bad.

FRANZ: Don't make me laugh.

KASIMIR: Man's a product of his environment.

FRANZ: Here. A briefcase. – (*He takes a book out of it and reads the title.*) "The Erotic Realm" – and there's an envelope: "Herr Commissioner Konrad Rauch." I think we can return this book to the commissioner – (*To Erna.*) Or are you interested in the erotic realm, perhaps?

ERNA: No.

FRANZ: Hm.

KASIMIR: Neither am I.

FRANZ: Excellent. Excellent. – But you've got to keep walking back and forth – You'll attract attention if you stick to this one spot – (*He disappears again among the limousines.*)

SCENE 90

ERNA: Let's walk back and forth –

KASIMIR: Please forgive me.

ERNA: What for?

KASIMIR: I've been thinking – that was pretty low – that nasty crack I made about your dead brother. (*Silence.*)

ERNA: I knew you didn't mean it, Kasimir. (*She exits with him.*)

SCENE 91

(*Now the orchestra plays the "Military March of 1882" by Schubert and for a time the stage is empty; then Speer enters with Elli and Maria. He is somewhat sobered, but still drunk. The orchestra breaks off in the middle of a measure.*)

SCENE 92

MARIA: No, there are only private cars here. The taxis are all over there, in front of the First Aid Station. (*Elli suddenly draws back.*)

SPEER: Now what's the matter with her, that poisonous blonde—

MARIA: I don't know what it is. She often does that—suddenly goes on strike—(*She calls.*) Elli! (*Elli doesn't answer.*) Elli! Come on, now! (*Elli doesn't stir.*)

SPEER: In the name of the law!

MARIA: I'll get her—(*She goes to Elli.*)

SCENE 93

MARIA: (*To Elli.*) Don't be so cutesy!

ELLI: No. I'm not getting mixed up in it. (*Speer eavesdrops, but hears nothing.*)

MARIA: That's great—first you're all for it, you just can't wait to get some guy in your clutches, then you chicken out! Don't be such a coward! We're getting ten marks for this. You five and me five. Think about all the bills you owe. (*Silence.*)

ELLI: But that old pig's a total pervert!

MARIA: Go on, it's just dirty talk.

SPEER: (*Senilely.*) Elli! Elli! Ellile—Ellile—

MARIA: Come on, loosen up—(*She leads Elli to Speer and they exit.*)

SCENE 94

(*Now the stage is empty again for a time and the orchestra continues the "Military March of 1822" by Schubert. Rauch enters with Karoline. They stop in front of an old convertible and he looks for his key. The orchestra breaks off again in the middle of a measure.*)

SCENE 95

KAROLINE: Is that an Austrian-Daimler?

RAUCH: Right on the nose. Bravo!

KAROLINE: My former fiancé drove an Austrian-Daimler. He was a chauffeur. A strange guy. For instance, three months ago, the two of us took a little drive out in the country and he got into a terrible argument with some man who was driving a horse and wagon, all because the man was beating his horse. Imagine, just because of a horse. And he's only a chauffeur himself. You gotta give him credit for that.

RAUCH: (*Who has finally found his car keys and opens the car door.*) Allow me, my dear lady—

SCENE 96

(*Kasimir passes by with Erna. He notices Karoline. She recognizes him and they stare*) *at each other.)*

SCENE 97

KAROLINE: *(She leaves Rauch and steps right up to Karoline.)* Goodbye, Kasimir.
KASIMIR: Goodbye.
KAROLINE: Yes. And lots of luck.
KASIMIR: Prost. *(Silence.)*
KAROLINE: I'm going to Altötting.
KASIMIR: Have a good time. *(Silence.)* That's a beautiful convertible you got there. Just like the one I used to drive. The day before yesterday.
RAUCH: Allow me, my dear lady! *(Karoline slowly turns away from Kasimir and gets into the car with Rauch. Soon the convertible is out of sight.)*

SCENE 98

KASIMIR: *(Watching the departing convertible; imitating Rauch.)* Allow me, my dear lady—*(Scene fades to black.)*

SCENE 99

(And again the orchestra is playing the "Military March of 1822" by Schubert, this time to the end.)

SCENE 100

(A new setting: in front of the First Aid Station on the Octoberfest grounds. An Orderly is busily treating Rauch, who is sitting on a bench in front of the First Aid Station and ceremoniously taking two pills with water. Karoline is nearby, too. And the air is still full of popular music.)

SCENE 101

KAROLINE: *(Carefully watching Rauch.)* Are you feeling any better? *(Rauch doesn't answer, but stretches out on his back on the bench.)*
ORDERLY: He's not feeling any better yet, Fraulein. *(Silence.)*
KAROLINE: All we wanted was just to drive to Altötting, but then the Commissioner suddenly got sick.—Saliva was running out of his mouth and if I hadn't jammed on the brakes at the last minute, we'd be in the next world by this time.
ORDERLY: Then he has you to thank for his life.
KAROLINE: Probably.
ORDERLY: Stands to reason. In that you had presence of mind.

KAROLINE: Yes, I'm familiar with driving because my former fiancé was a chauffeur.

SCENE 102

(*Now the orchestra is playing softly the waltz "Are You Laughing, Lady Luck?" and out of the First Aid Station come Octoberfest visitors, dazed and limping, with bandaged heads and limbs. Even the Midget and the Master of Ceremonies are among them. They're all dragging themselves home, and the orchestra breaks off in the middle of the waltz again, as usual in the middle of a measure.*)

SCENE 103

KAROLINE: (*Softly.*) Herr Orderly. What happened? Some terrible catastrophe?
ORDERLY: Why?
KAROLINE: Did the roller coaster jump the track?
ORDERLY: Far from it. Just a common ordinary brawl.
KAROLINE: For what reason?
ORDERLY: For no reason.
KAROLINE: For no reason? Then people are just like wild beasts.
ORDERLY: They'll never be anything else.
KAROLINE: Nevertheless—(*Silence.*)
ORDERLY: Supposedly some old Casanova was trying to get in a taxi with two girls and he was attacked by a bunch of teenagers. Supposedly one of the teenagers took off his shoe and held it under the old Casanova's nose to make him smell it—but the old guy wouldn't do it. So another teenager punched him in the face. The result was in no time flat a hundred people were in the fight. Nobody knew what it was about anymore, but they just kept hitting each other anyhow. People are so jumpy these days, they won't put up with anything anymore.

SCENE 104

DOCTOR: (*Appearing at the door.*) Stretchers here yet?
ORDERLY: Not yet, Doctor.
DOCTOR: Well, we've got six concussions, a broken jaw, four broken arms, one of them with complications, and the rest bruises. A real zoo! Germans fighting against Germans! (*He exits.*)

SCENE 105

KAROLINE: Broken jaw—oh, that must hurt.
ORDERLY: It ain't half as bad nowadays with all the new medical discoveries.

KAROLINE: You could be scarred for life. What if you got an ear cut off or something. Especially a woman.

ORDERLY: It wasn't a woman who got socked in the jaw, but the old Casanova I was telling you about.

KAROLINE: Well, that's good.

ORDERLY: He's some kind of important judge. From northern Germany. A guy named Speer.

RAUCH: (*Has been listening and now yells.*) What?! (*He gets up.*) Speer? Casanova? Judge? (*He clutches at his heart. Silence.*)

KAROLINE: You mustn't get excited, Herr Commissioner —

RAUCH: What are you still hanging around for, Fraulein? Goodbye. My respects. Bye, bye. (*Silence.*) Broken jaw. My poor old comrade — Those bitches. Wouldn't touch 'em with a ten foot pole. Filthy rotten pack. Ought to be exterminated — All of them!

KAROLINE: I didn't do nothing to deserve that from you, Herr Commissioner —

RAUCH: Deserve? Still harping on that? (*Silence.*)

KAROLINE: I saved your life.

RAUCH: My life? (*Silence.*) You'd like to think so, wouldn't you? (*Silence.*) Goodbye. (*To Orderly.*) Where did you put the judge? Inside there?

ORDERLY: Yes, sir, Herr Commissioner.

SCENE 106

(*Rauch goes slowly toward the First Aid Station — as Elli and Maria appear in the doorway. Maria with her arm in a sling and Elli with a heavily bandaged eye. Maria recognizes Rauch and stares at him. Rauch in turn recognizes her and stops for a moment.*)

SCENE 107

MARIA: (*Grinning.*) Ah, Mr. Pisspot himself! Look at him, Elli, just look —

ELLI: (*Raising her head and trying to look at him.*) Ow, my eye! (*Silence. Rauch straightens his tie and walks past Elli and Maria into the First Aid Station.*)

KAROLINE: (*Suddenly screaming.*) Auf Weidersehen, Mr. Pisspot! (*Scene fades to black.*)

SCENE 108

(*Now the orchestra plays the waltz "Are You Laughing, Lady Luck?"*)

SCENE 109

(*A new setting: the parking lot again, but a different part of it this time, where the ex-*

hibition flags are hardly visible. Kasimir and Erna are still walking back and forth. Suddenly Kasimir stops. And so does Erna.)

SCENE 110

KASIMIR: Where do you think Merkl got to?

ERNA: He'll turn up somewhere or other. (*Silence.*)

KASIMIR: And I don't give a damn where Karoline got to, either.

ERNA: No, she's not the right woman for you. I got a sharp eye for things like that.

KASIMIR: A woman like her is like a car that don't work right—it always needs repair. The gas is the blood and the ignition's like the heart—and if the spark's too weak, the engine won't start and if it's got too much oil in it, then it smokes and stinks—

ERNA: What an imagination you have! Very few men have that. For example, Merkl don't—Anyway, you were right when you said Merkl treats me badly. —No! I'm never gonna put up with that stuff again—(*She suppresses a scream suddenly.*) Jesus, Mary and Joseph! Merkl! Franz! Jesus, Mary—(*She claps her hand to her mouth and whimpers.*)

KASIMIR: What's the matter?

ERNA: Over there.—They've got him. My Franz! See the two policemen—Forgive me, Franz!—No, I'll never complain again, I'll never complain—(*Silence.*)

KASIMIR: It's all that slut's fault. That bitch! Karoline!

ERNA: He's not even resisting—just going along with them. (*She sits down on the bench.*) I'll never see him again.

KASIMIR: Come on, they're not going to kill him on the spot.

ERNA: They might as well. He's been arrested so many times—they'll give him five years this time, just like nothing—and then he'll never get out again. He had tuberculosis the last time he was in jail—He'll never come out alive. (*Silence.*)

KASIMIR: Have you been in jail, too?

ERNA: Yes. (*Kasimir sits down beside Erna. Silence.*) How old do you think I am?

KASIMIR: Twenty-five.

ERNA: Twenty.

KASIMIR: These days we're all older than our age. (*Silence.*) There comes Merkl now.

ERNA: (*Shrinking back.*) Where? (*Silence.*)

SCENE 111

(*Merkl Franz goes by, handcuffed to a detective. He throws one last glance at Erna.*)

SCENE 112

ERNA: (*Silence.*) Poor Franz. The poor man—

KASIMIR: That's life.

ERNA: Gone before you know it. (*Silence.*)

KASIMIR: I always said breaking the law doesn't make sense—I think I'll always remember the sight of poor Merkl Franz, as a warning.

ERNA: Better to go on the dole.

KASIMIR: Better go hungry.

ERNA: Yes. (*Silence.*) I told poor Franz to let you alone. I knew right away you were different—that's why he threw the beer in my face.

KASIMIR: Is that why?

ERNA: Yes. Because of you.

KASIMIR: I didn't realize that. It was all because of me that you—What did I do to deserve that?

ERNA: I don't know. (*Silence.*)

KASIMIR: Is that the Great Bear over there?

ERNA: And there is Orion.

KASIMIR: With his sword.

ERNA: (*Laughing softly.*) How did you remember that—(*Silence.*)

KASIMIR: (*Still staring at the sky.*) The world's far from perfect.

ERNA: We can do something to make it a little more perfect.

KASIMIR: Are you in good health? I mean, you didn't catch tuberculosis from the poor man, did you?

ERNA: No. As far as I know, I'm in perfect health.

KASIMIR: I think we have a lot in common.

ERNA: Me, too, it's like we'd known each other a long time. (*Silence.*)

KASIMIR: What was your dead brother's name?

ERNA: Ludwig. Ludwig Rittmeier. (*Silence.*)

KASIMIR: I was a driver once for a man named Rittmeier—He had a wool factory. Wholesale. (*He puts his arm around her.*)

ERNA: (*Putting her head on his chest.*) Here comes Karoline.

SCENE 113

KAROLINE: (*Entering and looking searchingly around. Glimpsing Kasimir and Erna, she approaches slowly and stops right in front of them.*) Good evening, Kasimir. (*Silence.*) Don't look so suspicious.

KASIMIR: Easy for you to say. (*Silence.*)

KAROLINE: You were right.

KASIMIR: About what?

KAROLINE: All I wanted was an ice cream—but then the zeppelin flew by and I rode the roller coaster. And then you said I automatically broke off with you because you lost your job. Automatically, you said.

KASIMIR: That's right, Fraulein.

KAROLINE: I fooled myself into thinking I could make a rosy future for myself—and for a little while I was willing to do anything to get it. But I had to lower myself so far down just to get one step higher. For example, I saved the Commissioner's life, but he didn't want to hear anything about it.

KASIMIR: That's life, Fraulein. (*Silence.*)

KAROLINE: You said the Commissioner just wanted to use me for his own pleasure and that I should listen to you—you were right.

KASIMIR: I don't give a damn about any of that now! I'm way past it, Fraulein! What's dead is dead and there ain't no ghosts, especially not between the sexes! (*Silence. Karoline suddenly gives him a kiss.*) Brrh! Get off! Go to hell! (*He spits.*) Brrh!

ERNA: I don't understand how someone who calls herself a woman can have such little sensitivity.

KAROLINE: (*To Kasimir.*) Is she the new Karoline?

KASIMIR: That's none of your damned business, Fraulein!

KAROLINE: And betraying Merkl Franz, is that what you mean by sensitivity?

ERNA: Merkl Franz is dead, Fraulein. (*Silence.*)

KAROLINE: Dead? (*She laughs—but suddenly falls silent.*) Do you expect me to believe that, you jailbird?

KASIMIR: Shut up and get moving.

ERNA: (*To Kasimir.*) Leave her alone. She doesn't know what she's doing. (*Silence.*)

SCENE 114

KAROLINE: (*To herself.*) You start out in life with such beautiful dreams—but then your wings get broken and life goes by as if you'd never lived—

SCENE 115

SCHÜRZINGER: (*Appears in a cheerful mood—with a balloon on a string tied to his buttonhole; he spies Karoline.*) Now there's a sight for sore eyes. Destiny has brought us together again, Karoline. Tomorrow Second Lieutenant Eugene Schürzinger will become First Lieutenant Eugene Schürzinger in the army of his Majesty, Ludwig the Fifteenth—and I owe it all to you.

KAROLINE: There must be some mistake.

SCHÜRZINGER: I'm joking! (*Silence.*)

KAROLINE: Eugene. I hurt your feelings and that was wrong. You always get punished in the end—

SCHÜRZINGER: You need a man, Karoline—

KAROLINE: Always the same shit.

SCHÜRZINGER: Ssh! Things are getting better and better.
KAROLINE: Who says so?
SCHÜRZINGER: Come. (*Silence.*) Come on, things are getting better—
KAROLINE: (*Repeating after him, tonelessly.*) Things are getting better—
SCHÜRZINGER: Everything's getting better and better—
KAROLINE: Everything's getting better and better—(*Schürzinger embraces her and gives her a long kiss. Karoline doesn't resist.*)
SCHÜRZINGER: You really need a man.
KAROLINE: (*Smiling.*) Everything's getting better—
SCHÜRZINGER: Come on—(*He exits with her.*)

SCENE 116

KASIMIR: Dreams are illusions.
ERNA: As long as we don't hang ourselves, we won't starve. (*Silence.*)
KASIMIR: Erna, sweetheart—
ERNA: What?
KASIMIR: Nothing. (*Silence.*)
ERNA: (*Sings softly and Kasimir joins in.*)
   The roses bloom but once
   And winter flies away
   And we who dwell on this earth
   Have but just one May
   The birds fly to the south
   And fly again back home
   We who are laid in the earth
   Never return to roam.

END

Judgment Day

a play in seven scenes

translated by Martin and Renata Esslin

CHARACTERS:

Thomas Hudetz, Stationmaster
Mrs. Hudetz
Alfons, her brother, a chemist
Landlord of "The Wild Boar"
Anna, his daughter
Ferdinand, her fiancé, a butcher from out of town
Leni, waitress at "The Wild Boar"
Mrs. Leimgruber
A Forestry Worker
Traveling Salesman
A Policeman
Kohut, a railway fireman
Public Prosecutor
A Police Inspector
A Detective
A Railway Worker (Maintenance Man)
Pokorny, engine driver, dead
A Guest
A Child

The action takes place:

Scene 1: A small railway station
Scene 2: On the track where two trains have collided
Scene 3: At "The Wild Boar"
Scene 4: At the viaduct
Scene 5: At "The Wild Boar"
Scene 6: At the chemists'
Scene 7: On the track where the two trains had collided

The time is the thirties. Four months pass between Scenes 2 and 3. Interval after Scene 5.

SCENE 1

(*In front of the station building. From left to right a door leading to the first floor, a booking office, and a second door with frosted glass and a notice "Station Master." Next to it some signal apparatus, signal bells, etc. There are timetables and railway advertisements on the walls. Two benches. From right upstage to downstage a barrier, giving access to the platform, but the track is not visible. Arriving, departing and passing trains can be heard. Express and fast trains do not stop here as the place to which the station belongs is only slightly more than a large village. It is a small station but on a main line.*

There are two travelers waiting on the benches: Mrs. Leimgruber, the wife of the baker, and a Forestry Worker with an empty rucksack and a tree saw. The signal bell rings, then all is quiet. A third traveler enters left, carrying a suitcase and a briefcase. He is a Traveling Salesman from the city. He stops and looks at the station clock. It is nine o'clock in the evening on a warm spring night. The Traveling Salesman goes to the booking office and knocks. There is no movement. He knocks again, energetically.)

FORESTRY WORKER: You can knock as much as you like. He's only going to open up just before the train arrives.

TRAVELING SALESMAN: (*Looking at the clock.*) Is the train late then?

MRS. LEIMGRUBER: (*Laughs loudly. To Forestry Worker.*) Listen to him!

FORESTRY WORKER: (*Grins.*) This gentleman must have come from the moon. (*To the Salesman.*) Of course it's late, three-quarters of an hour.

TRAVELING SALESMAN: Three-quarters of an hour? Damn inefficiency! (*He lights a cigarette, furiously.*)

MRS. LEIMGRUBER: What do you expect, they're in a bad way—

FORESTRY WORKER: (*Interrupts.*) That's because they're cutting and cutting services. They'll go on rationalizing until there are no trains at all.

TRAVELING SALESMAN: (*Blowing cigarette smoke.*) Rationalization—don't give me that again.

FORESTRY WORKER: They're firing everybody, a waste of good manpower.

MRS. LEIMGRUBER: (*Suddenly becoming talkative, to the Traveling Salesman.*) Look at this station—what do you think of their big staff? One man, one single man is all we have.

TRAVELING SALESMAN: (*Puzzled.*) Why only one?

MRS. LEIMGRUBER: It's lucky our station master is really efficient, an educated, polite, hard-working fellow. A rare kind of a really reliable man! He's not afraid to work, he carries the luggage, nails down the packing cases, works the switches, sells tickets, sends signals and mans the telephone—all by himself! *And* he's badly paid.

FORESTRY WORKER: Who is?

MRS. LEIMGRUBER: The station master, of course.

FORESTRY WORKER: You call that badly paid? I think the pay is first-rate . . . think of the free accommodation they have up there! (*He points to the first floor.*) He's even got a sitting room up there and in the morning, when he gets up, he hears the birds singing and looks right out over the countryside— (*He grins. The signal bell rings and the station master, Thomas Hudetz, quickly comes out of his door, operates the signal and a fast train rushes past. He salutes formally and goes off.*)

MRS. LEIMGRUBER: That was the express, it doesn't stop here.

TRAVELING SALESMAN: I don't blame it. What's the population of this dump?

FORESTRY WORKER: Two thousand three hundred and sixty-four. (*Silence.*)

MRS. LEIMGRUBER: (*Eyeing the Traveling Salesman.*) Didn't you like it here?

TRAVELING SALESMAN: I am a traveling salesman, Madame, and I have traveled far and wide across the world, but nowhere have I come across such total lack of interest as here. I've never seen anything like it! You're quite unique in that respect!

MRS. LEIMGRUBER: What are you selling then?

TRAVELING SALESMAN: Cosmetics.

FORESTRY WORKER: Eh?

TRAVELING SALESMAN: Beauty products.

FORESTRY WORKER: Beauty? (*Grinning.*) We're quite beautiful enough here.

TRAVELING SALESMAN: As long as you like your own looks! (*Turns to Mrs. Leimgruber.*) I had just one customer who took pity on me—(*He smiles.*)

MRS. LEIMGRUBER: (*With curiosity.*) And who was that?

TRAVELING SALESMAN: The waitress at "The Wild Boar."

FORESTRY WORKER: (*Surprised.*) Leni? I don't believe it!

TRAVELING SALESMAN: Why not?

FORESTRY WORKER: She would know better, she wouldn't fall for such crap.

TRAVELING SALESMAN: (*Angrily.*) How can you talk like that. Considering we live in an age of . . .

MRS. LEIMGRUBER: (*Interrupting him, to the Forestry Worker.*) Surely the gentleman knows who he has sold something to.

TRAVELING SALESMAN: (*Annoyed.*) Small and slim she was—almost a child.

MRS. LEIMGRUBER: (*To the Forestry Worker.*) He means Anna!

FORESTRY WORKER: Ah, well!

MRS. LEIMGRUBER: (*Talkative, to the Traveling Salesman.*) That's not the waitress, that's Anna, the landlord's daughter! She's engaged to the butcher, but he's from out-of-town and only comes to see her once a week.

TRAVELING SALESMAN: So what.

FORESTRY WORKER: That girl, she wasn't born yesterday.

MRS. LEIMGRUBER: (*Surprised.*) Who?

FORESTRY WORKER: Anna, of course. (*Sarcastically.*) Almost a child, as the gentleman says!

MRS. LEIMGRUBER: How can you say that! Anna is innocence personified in person.

FORESTRY WORKER: She may be innocent but she's not wet behind the ears.

MRS. LEIMGRUBER: (*To Traveling Salesman.*) You see, that's how people get a bad name.

TRAVELING SALESMAN: (*More to himself.*) The rise of the masses. The decline of the West—(*The station master's wife, Mrs. Hudetz, enters through door on left with her brother Alfons, the pharmacist.*)

MRS. LEIMGRUBER: (*Greets her.*) Good evening, Mrs. Hudetz.

MRS. HUDETZ: Good evening, Mrs. Leimgruber. (*She talks quietly to Alfons.*)

MRS. LEIMGRUBER: (*Tries to listen but is unable to hear, turns to the Traveling Salesman, who is sitting beside her and points discreetly to Mrs. Hudetz, whispering.*) That's the wife of the station master.

TRAVELING SALESMAN: (*Uninterested.*) Very interesting.

MRS. LEIMGRUBER: And that man is her brother.

TRAVELING SALESMAN: (*Without looking up.*) Oh, yes.

MRS. LEIMGRUBER: (*Vindictive.*) Brother and sister—one's as good as the other—(*The signal bell rings again and Hudetz comes quickly out of his door, operates the signal and the train rushes past. He salutes again and is about to go off when, with surprise, he notices his wife and Alfons. The two men look at each other, then Alfons greets him, Hudetz replies and exits through his door.*)

MRS. HUDETZ: (*Quietly to Alfons.*) He hasn't spoken to me for days.

ALFONS: Don't let it worry you.

MRS. HUDETZ: You'll see, he'll drive me mad.

ALFONS: You're on edge because you're always fighting.

MRS. HUDETZ: But I keep hearing voices—

ALFONS: (*Interrupts her.*) There has never been a case of mental illness in our family. It's just nerves, overexcitement, nothing else. Any doctor will tell you that. Your marriage is finished and there is only one solution.

MRS. HUDETZ: (*Interrupting him.*) No. I wouldn't think of it. He and another woman—I told him before we got married: think it over, I said, I am thirteen years older than you. And he said, there is nothing to think over.

ALFONS: (*Interrupts.*) And that was a lie.

MRS. HUDETZ: No, not then. (*Silence.*)

ALFONS: It's never been right between you two.

MRS. HUDETZ: But I'm not going to get a divorce, do you hear, I'd rather —

ALFONS: Quiet. (*He glances suspiciously at Mrs. Leimgruber and then talks softly to Mrs. Hudetz.*)

MRS. LEIMGRUBER: (*Softly to the Traveling Salesman, who is looking at his notebooks, working out figures and is hardly listening.*) She's a nasty pill, that hateful creature, always tormenting our poor station master, such a nice, kind man — it's a real shame.

TRAVELING SALESMAN: Is it?

MRS. LEIMGRUBER: Always nagging the poor man with her blind jealousy, he hardly dares show his face at the bar nowadays. She sneaks after him and if he as much as looks at the waitress, there is hell to pay at home —

TRAVELING SALESMAN: Really.

MRS. LEIMGRUBER: After the Christmas Dance she screamed and yelled up there so you could hear it in the village, that hysterical bitch — he wasn't even touching her and she kept screaming: "He's going to kill me, he's going to kill me!" My goodness me, she wants to have her bottom spanked so she can't sit down for a week.

TRAVELING SALESMAN: (*Suddenly listening.*) What bottom?

MRS. LEIMGRUBER: (*Offended.*) Now you haven't been listening at all and there I am telling you all these intimate details.

TRAVELING SALESMAN: Sorry. (*Silence.*)

ALFONS: (*Quietly to Mrs. Hudetz.*) What about going away for a bit — see that poster? You can get to the seaside on a cheap ticket.

MRS. HUDETZ: And how do I pay for it?

ALFONS: I can lend you something, I've saved a bit.

MRS. HUDETZ: (*Smiling.*) Alfons, you really are a dear, if only people knew how kind you are.

ALFONS: I'm no saint. But those people . . .

MRS. HUDETZ: I can't bear them.

ALFONS: You're so right.

MRS. HUDETZ: They can all go to hell for all I care.

ALFONS: (*Smiling.*) Come, come.

MRS. HUDETZ: (*Smiling sweetly.*) The lot of them. Goodbye, my dear.

ALFONS: Think it over — you can go to the seaside if you want to.

MRS. HUDETZ: (*Suddenly serious and hard.*) No, I'm staying. Goodbye, Alfons. (*She exits through door left. The Traveling Salesman now notices Alfons and stares at him.*)

ALFONS: (*Stares after Mrs. Hudetz and murmurs.*) Goodbye. (*Exits left lost in thought.*)

TRAVELING SALESMAN: (*Watches him go and turns to Mrs. Leimgruber.*) Wasn't that the pharmacist?

MRS. LEIMGRUBER: That's right.

TRAVELING SALESMAN: A most unpleasant man, the way he treated me today!

MRS. LEIMGRUBER: What way?

TRAVELING SALESMAN: (*Shrugging his shoulders.*) It's hard to say—(*Silence.*)

MRS. LEIMGRUBER: He's isn't popular.

TRAVELING SALESMAN: I can see why.

MRS. LEIMGRUBER: He and his sister. Nobody wants anything to do with them. They always look at you so proud and hurt that they make you feel guilty, as if we had done something to them—but is it our fault that he lost all his money and that she got the station master to marry her when she's thirteen years older than he is?

TRAVELING SALESMAN: (*Interrupting.*) Thirteen years?

MRS. LEIMGRUBER: Such an upright, sensitive young man he was. The slut!

TRAVELING SALESMAN: Ah well, women—first they bring you up and then they let you down. (*Ferdinand, the butcher from out of town, enters with his fiancée Anna, the landlord's daughter. They enter quickly from left. Both are out of breath from running.*)

FERDINAND: (*Hurriedly to the Forestry Worker who has been sitting there for some time now eating a large slice of bread and not taking any interest in what is going on around him.*) Has the train gone?

FORESTRY WORKER: No.

ANNA: (*To Ferdinand.*) You see, I told you, it's always late.

FERDINAND: You can't rely on it.

ANNA: (*Placing her hand on her heart.*) My goodness, I've been running.

FERDINAND: (*Worried.*) Does it hurt, your darling little heart?

ANNA: No, it's just beating rather fast—(*Ferdinand puts his hand on her heart and listens.*) Can you hear it?

FERDINAND: Yes.

MRS. LEIMGRUBER: (*Softly to Traveling Salesman.*) That's Anna.

TRAVELING SALESMAN: Who's Anna?

MRS. LEIMGRUBER: The one you thought was almost a child.

TRAVELING SALESMAN: (*Recognizes Anna.*) Oh, the landlord's daughter. My only customer—(*He greets her murmuring.*) Here comes my beauty queen—(*Anna thanks him shyly.*)

FERDINAND: (*To Anna, suspiciously.*) Who's that?

ANNA: I won't tell.

FERDINAND: Why not?

ANNA: Because you're going to be angry again.

FERDINAND: I'm never angry.

ANNA: Oh, aren't you! (*Ferdinand stares at the Traveling Salesman.*)

TRAVELING SALESMAN: (*Becoming uncomfortable, softly to Mrs. Leimgruber.*) Who is that fellow staring at me?

MRS. LEIMGRUBER: That's Anna's fiancé from out of town. He's a butcher.

TRAVELING SALESMAN: (*Becoming more and more uncomfortable.*) Oh, a butcher.

MRS. LEIMGRUBER: A hulk of a man, but a gentle giant. (*Hudetz opens the booking office.*)

TRAVELING SALESMAN: (*Sighs with relief.*) At last! (*He goes to the booking office and buys a ticket.*)

FERDINAND: (*To Anna.*) Tell me at once or I'll break his neck.

ANNA: (*Smiling.*) All right, all right. It's the sales rep I bought the face cream from this morning.

FERDINAND: (*Reassured.*) Oh well. But you don't need no cream or powder or nothing—

ANNA: (*Interrupts him.*) Here you go again—(*Silence.*)

FERDINAND: (*Subdued.*) Annie, I only mean that your tender rosy little cheeks don't need nothing artificial—

ANNA: Do you remember that last film we saw? I thought that woman was so beautiful.

FERDINAND: I didn't.

ANNA: Don't say that. You're making a fool of yourself. (*Silence.*)

FERDINAND: (*Sadly.*) Oh, Annie. (*Putting his arm around her shoulder and looking up at the stars.*) You know, when I see our little stars, I want to be with you all the time.

ANNA: (*Also looks up.*) You'll see me again soon.

FERDINAND: (*Sadly.*) In a week. And tomorrow is another weekday and I have to get out of bed at four in the morning—

ANNA: What are you slaughtering?

FERDINAND: Only two calves—(*The signal bell rings. Hudetz comes quickly out of his door and opens the barrier. The Forestry Worker, Mrs. Leimgruber and the Traveling Salesman go to the platform. Hudetz punches the tickets.*)

TRAVELING SALESMAN: (*To Hudetz.*) Is this usual? Three quarters of an hour late? (*Hudetz shrugs his shoulders and smiles.*) Some inefficiency—

MRS. LEIMGRUBER: (*To Traveling Salesman.*) But that's not the station master's fault. (*Hudetz smiles at Mrs. Leimgruber and politely raises his hand to his cap. The slow train arrives and stops.*)

FERDINAND: (*To Anna.*) Don't forget me now! (*He embraces her and hurries on to the platform. Anna goes slowly up to the barrier. Hudetz gives the departure signal. The train leaves and the signal bell rings. Anna waves after the departing train. Hudetz closes the barrier.*)

ANNA: (*Watching him.*) Has no one got off?

HUDETZ: No. (*He operates the signal and is about to exit through his door.*)

ANNA: Just a moment. Why don't we see you any more? My father was wondering whether you had become a regular somewhere else.

HUDETZ: I never have time now, Miss. I'm always on duty.

ANNA: That's all right then. I was afraid you weren't coming because of me.

HUDETZ: (*With genuine surprise.*) Why because of you?

ANNA: I thought because of your wife.

HUDETZ: What's my wife got to do with you?

ANNA: She doesn't like me.

HUDETZ: Go on, you're imagining things. (*He stops suddenly and looks up to the second floor. Silence.*)

ANNA: (*Sarcastically.*) Who's up there?

HUDETZ: Nobody.

ANNA: Are you afraid that your wife will see you with a young girl? Aren't you allowed to speak to me?

HUDETZ: You seem to know all about it.

ANNA: If you talk to me now you're going to have it out tomorrow, is that it?

HUDETZ: Who says so?

ANNA: Everybody. (*Silence.*)

HUDETZ: (*Stares at her.*) I wish you would all leave my wife alone, do you understand? All of you, and you most of all. You are much too young to talk about such things—

ANNA: (*Mocking.*) Do you think so?

HUDETZ: You've got a lot to learn before you can begin to understand—

ANNA: (*As before.*) Come on, teach me something, Mr. Teacher—

HUDETZ: You'll learn by yourself that you mustn't hurt other people and then you won't be sorry.

ANNA: You're talking like the priest now. (*She laughs.*)

HUDETZ: Just you laugh, the time will come—(*He is about to go.*)

ANNA: Everybody is laughing about you, Mr. Hudetz. What is he up to, they ask, that handsome fellow, never out of his station, day and night—

HUDETZ: (*Grimly.*) People seem to be very concerned about me.

ANNA: Yes, they say, the station master isn't a man at all. (*Silence.*)

HUDETZ: Who says that?

ANNA: Oh, everybody. I'm the only one who speaks up for you sometimes. (*She smiles maliciously, suddenly she kisses him and points to the second floor.*) Now she's seen that I've kissed you. (*She laughs.*) Now you're going to get it, aren't you? (*She laughs.*) She's going to give it to you, isn't she? (*She makes the gesture of spanking someone.*)

HUDETZ: (*Stares at her.*) If you don't clear out at once I don't know what I'll do.

ANNA: Are you going to kill me?

HUDETZ: Stop it! Get out! (*He seizes her arm.*)

ANNA: Ouch! Leave me alone you brute! (*She pulls herself free and rubs her arm.*) Can't you take a joke?

HUDETZ: (*Roughly.*) No! (*A fast train passes by.*) Good God! (*He violently pulls the lever, the signal bell rings, he clutches at his heart.*)

ANNA: (*Afraid.*) What's happened?

HUDETZ: (*Staring in front of him, in a whisper.*) The 9:05 Express and I've forgotten the signal!—(*Turns on her.*) There's your joke for you. And I . . . I've always done my duty!

ANNA: Come on. Nothing's going to happen—

HUDETZ: Shut up. (*He exits through door.*)

SCENE 2

(*The 9:05 Express which had not been given a signal has run into a freight train not far from the small station.*

The scene of the accident. A tangle of train wreckage is lying on the line in the background. The injured and the dead have been taken away. Army engineers are busy clearing the wreckage. In right foreground is a small black table with a lamp on it. The Public Prosecutor and his staff have been at the station for some time. He is now inspecting the signal—it is at red. Sightseers have arrived from all around, among them the Landlord of "The Wild Boar," his daughter Anna and Leni, the waitress. In left foreground a Policeman is keeping back the sightseers. Dawn is breaking, it looks like a gray day. People shiver.)

POLICEMAN: Get back! Get back everybody. Haven't you seen enough of this mess?

LANDLORD: Well, you don't get to see that kind of thing every day, do you—

LENI: (*To Policeman.*) Was the train derailed?

POLICEMAN: No, it crashed. The fast train crashed into a freight train—five and a half hours ago.

LENI: It's dreadful! It's as if a volcano had exploded—(*For some unexplained reason she presses closer to the Landlord.*) I'll have nightmares about it.

LANDLORD: (*Pulling her closer.*) It is the hand of God, for good or ill. (*The Fireman of the crashed train enters, wearing a bandage round his head.*)

LENI: (*To the Landlord.*) Look, he's injured!

FIREMAN: (*To Leni, talkative.*) Oh yes, it was nearly see you later. I wasn't thinking about anything, and suddenly there was this hellish noise and a jerk, I was flying through the air, like a plane, and then all went black before my eyes. When I woke I was lying in the meadow in the hay, not a bone broken. But my head is spinning like a wheel.

LANDLORD: A very special angel must have watched over you.

FIREMAN: It's possible. You know, I was standing on the footplate—

LENI: (*Interrupting him.*) Are you the engine driver then?

FIREMAN: No, I'm not Pokorny, poor chap. My name is Kohut.

POLICEMAN: He was only the fireman.

LANDLORD: Was he?

FIREMAN: A fireman is important too, you know. The fireman is sometimes more important than the driver.

LENI: (*To Fireman.*) Were there really more than a hundred dead?

FIREMAN: I heard seventeen.

POLICEMAN: (*To Fireman.*) They told me eighteen.

LANDLORD: That's enough, isn't it.

FIREMAN: He went past a signal, they said, or rather, the signal was never given, or rather it was given afterwards, in other words too late. The Prosecutor has been here for more than three hours, he's just looking at the signal . . . for the hundreth time.

LANDLORD: And whose fault was it?

POLICEMAN: That'll come out, I dare say.

FIREMAN: I would say the station master's.

LANDLORD: Our Hudetz?

FIREMAN: I don't know how you spell his name. But I do know that poor old Pokorny, bless his soul, was a first-class engine driver. He had eyes like a hawk.

LANDLORD: I can't believe that it was Hudetz's fault! That's out of the question.

FIREMAN: It'll all come out in the wash. If your friend Hudetz didn't set the signal in time—he won't get away with less than three years.

POLICEMAN: And he'll lose his job.

FIREMAN: Plus his pension.

POLICEMAN: Naturally.

FIREMAN: He'll need a witness to swear that he set the signal in time.

POLICEMAN: Yes, that would get him off. But the fact is he was alone, not a soul around.

FIREMAN: A real tragedy.

ANNA: (*Softly, to the Landlord.*) Father, I want to tell you something—

LANDLORD: What?

ANNA: It's very important. The station master was not alone when it happened—

LANDLORD: What? What do you know about it?

ANNA: The station master has got a witness—

LANDLORD: Well, come on then, out with it!

ANNA: Me. I was at the station when it happened.

LANDLORD: You? At the station?

ANNA: Shh. You know I went to the station to see off Ferdinand and then I had a few words with the station master—just a few words—

LANDLORD: And—what?

ANNA: (*Speaks very softly.*) And—(*Her words are inaudible.*)

LENI: Are there still some dead among the wreckage?

FIREMAN: What do you think, miss?

LENI: And no more injured?

FIREMAN: What do you think? If there was they would be screaming their heads off. You'd be covering up your ears.

POLICEMAN: You're right there. (*Laughs. The Public Prosecutor enters with his Inspector, tired and shivering. He is followed, at a distance, by Hudetz accompanied by a Policeman.*)

POLICEMAN: Stand back, everybody, stand back. (*He pushes the Landlord, Anna, Leni and the other bystanders over to the left. Only the Fireman remains.*)

PROSECUTOR: (*Quietly to Inspector, so that Hudetz cannot hear what is being said.*) The signal is unfortunately in order. It is set on half. But it can't be proved whether it was set like that before or after the event.

INSPECTOR: Those who could have told us are unfortunately no longer able to testify.

PROSECUTOR: Damn. I have a hunch that this fellow Hudetz is not innocent. He seems calm enough – (*He smiles.*)

INSPECTOR: (*Smiling.*) A bit too calm for my liking.

PROSECUTOR: (*Sighing.*) Let's try again, for the tenth time – (*He sits at the small black table and looks at his papers.*)

A DETECTIVE: (*Enters quickly from the right and greets the Prosecutor.*) I've just been to the station, sir, and have interviewed Mrs. Hudetz. I can't help feeling that the woman has something to tell us –

PROSECUTOR: "Can't help feeling" – I don't like to hear that kind of thing. Be more precise, please.

DETECTIVE: I'm sorry, but I sometimes rely on my intuition and I'll be damned if Mrs. Hudetz isn't keeping something to herself.

PROSECUTOR: What makes you think that?

DETECTIVE: Something seems to be worrying her. She looks as if she has been crying.

PROSECUTOR: Bring her here!

DETECTIVE: Right away. (*Goes off right.*)

PROSECUTOR: (*Calls.*) Mr. Kohut! Mr. Joseph Kohut!

FIREMAN: (*Comes forward.*) Present.

PROSECUTOR: (*In a low voice so that Hudetz cannot hear.*) So you still maintain that you did not see the signal? Speak quietly.

FIREMAN: I didn't see anything, sir. I was standing with my back to the engine and was shovelling coal when there was a jerk –

PROSECUTOR: (*Impatiently.*) Yes, you've already told us about the jerk.

FIREMAN: There's nothing else to tell you except the jerk. I can only swear to you that poor old Pokorny never went past a signal in his life. Not even in thickest fog!

PROSECUTOR: That's right. His record is first class.

FIREMAN: He was a first-class chap, a kind fellow, sir. Now he's left three orphans behind – (*Looking up.*) Poor old Pokorny. Now you're standing before the Lord's judgment seat.

PROSECUTOR: Let's keep to the point.

FIREMAN: Well, when that jerk occurred Pokorny was talking about a wages claim –

PROSECUTOR: (*Interrupts him.*) That's got nothing to do with it. Thank you, Mr.

Kohut.

FIREMAN: (*As if touching his cap.*) Not at all, not at all. (*Exits.*)

PROSECUTOR: (*Calls.*) Mr. Thomas Hudetz! (*Hudetz steps forward.*) I take it you continue to assert that you set the signal on half in time?

HUDETZ: (*Outwardly composed but inwardly unsure.*) But sir, I can't imagine that I wouldn't—I have always done my duty without fail—

PROSECUTOR: (*Interrupts him.*) You've already told us that a hundred times.

HUDETZ: That's all I can say. (*Silence.*)

PROSECUTOR: (*Staring at him, quietly but insistent.*) I can't help feeling—

HUDETZ: I've got nothing to hide. (*Silence.*)

PROSECUTOR: (*Pointing at him.*) Mr. Hudetz, a collision is no joke—

HUDETZ: (*Suddenly frightened.*) But sir—

PROSECUTOR: (*Shouts at him.*) Don't you imagine that the truth is not going to come out. Even if by a lucky chance for you the train driver and the guard are dead, there is still one person who, by a miracle, is still alive. Joseph Kohut, the fireman. And this man has already told us some most interesting facts, facts that will not please you at all, I can tell you that.

HUDETZ: (*Unsure.*) I can only tell you that I have never missed a signal yet. (*He smiles. Silence.*)

PROSECUTOR: (*Suddenly kindly.*) Ask yourself, Thomas Hudetz. Think of those eighteen poor souls, all those injured who are now suffering in the hospital. Do you want to carry that burden around with you all your life? You are a decent man, Mr. Hudetz. Relieve your conscience—(*Silence.*)

HUDETZ: It wasn't my fault.

PROSECUTOR: (*Sarcastically.*) Whose fault was it then?

HUDETZ: Not mine.

PROSECUTOR: (*As before.*) A mysterious Mr. X perhaps?

HUDETZ: Perhaps—(*The Policeman, the Landlord, and Anna enter left.*)

INSPECTOR: (*To Policeman.*) What is it? (*Prosecutor listens.*)

POLICEMAN: The Landlord of "The Wild Boar" tells me that his daughter wants to make an important statement.

PROSECUTOR: (*Interrupts.*) Well? Why only now?

LANDLORD: My daughter is almost a child, sir, and she didn't have the courage at first. So first she confided in me and I told her, you must report this at once because it might be a matter of life and death for our dear Mr. Hudetz—

PROSECUTOR: Let's wait and see.

LANDLORD: I told her, there's a human being at stake, I said. You wouldn't have a quiet moment for the rest of your life, nor would I, if our station master had to suffer. She saw it with her own eyes, sir, that he set the signal at half soon enough!

PROSECUTOR: Soon enough? (*Looks at Anna.*) Come here, my dear. Now don't be frightened, we're not going to bite you—(*Anna steps forward.*) I only want to draw your attention to the fact that everything you tell me here you will have to repeat in Court–under oath. Do you know what that means?

ANNA: Yes. (*Hudetz looks at Anna, horrified.*)

PROSECUTOR: (*Leaning back.*) Now tell us what you know.

ANNA: He set the signal in time–

PROSECUTOR: (*Interrupts her.*) One thing after another, please, one thing after another. Now come on, one thing after another! (*Silence.*)

ANNA: (*As if reciting a school exercise.*) I accompanied my fiancé to the last train last night, and it was very late, and then, after the train had left, I waved, and then I spoke a few words with the station master, and I asked him why he doesn't come to our pub any more, he doesn't go anywhere any more–

PROSECUTOR: What concern is that of yours?

ANNA: I am the landlord's daughter and our business concerns me. (*She smiles.*)

LANDLORD: (*To the Prosecutor.*) Excuse my interrupting, but the station master doesn't go anywhere now because his wife won't let him.

PROSECUTOR: (*Eagerly.*) His wife?

LANDLORD: Do you know, sir, what a wicked wife is?

PROSECUTOR: (*Sighs.*) Yes, I do know.

HUDETZ: My wife is not wicked.

LANDLORD: Come off it, Hudetz. (*To the Prosecutor.*) He is always taking her side, it makes me wild. (*To Hudetz.*) She nags you day and night.

HUDETZ: She doesn't!

LANDLORD: Of course, she does. Everybody knows it!

HUDETZ: You don't know anything, nothing! There's always a reason for everything and you have no idea. I'm not behaving properly towards her–

LANDLORD: He hardly dares leave the house, sir. He always thinks it's his fault because she keeps telling him, day and night, year after year. And why? Because their relationship has gone wrong. And no wonder, as she's so much older.

HUDETZ: (*Shouts at the Landlord.*) That's got nothing to do with it.

LANDLORD: (*To Hudetz.*) Don't shout at me.

PROSECUTOR: Silence. Mr. Hudetz, it certainly says a lot for your truthfulness that you are speaking up for your wife and the authorities take note of that. But there would be no purpose in persuading yourself–

HUDETZ: (*Interrupts him.*) But I am not persuading myself.

PROSECUTOR: Let's leave this business with your wife now. You are going to see the psychiatrist anyway–

LANDLORD: She's driven him mad, mad!

PROSECUTOR: Silence! (*To Anna.*) Continue, please.

ANNA: I've nearly finished. I heard the signal bell, and then the station master set the signal, and then the Express went past–

PROSECUTOR: Only then?

ANNA: Yes–(*Mrs. Hudetz enters from the right with the Detective. They stop and* listen unnoticed by the others.)

PROSECUTOR: (*Emphatically.*) Let's have that again: first the bell—

ANNA: Then the signal.

PROSECUTOR: And only then the train?

ANNA: Yes. And then—(*She stops.*)

PROSECUTOR: Yes?

ANNA: And then I heard thunder in the distance, a terrible crash and thunder and screaming—terrible screams. I can still hear them—(*She covers her ears.*)

PROSECUTOR: Mr. Hudetz. Why did you not tell us that you had a witness? (*Hudetz does not know what to reply. Mrs. Hudetz looks at him with malice. To Hudetz.*) Well? (*Hudetz shrugs his shoulders.*) Funny.

ANNA: But sir, he didn't know that I had seen everything—

MRS. HUDETZ: (*Harshly.*) Seen everything? (*All look at her in surprise.*)

DETECTIVE: (*To Prosecutor.*) Mrs. Hudetz.

PROSECUTOR: Oh. (*Mrs. Hudetz looks at Anna with hatred.*)

DETECTIVE: (*Quietly to Prosecutor.*) I can't get anything out of her. She says, she didn't see anything. She was already asleep—(*Continues inaudibly.*)

MRS. HUDETZ: (*To Anna.*) You just wanted to annoy me, didn't you.

LANDLORD: (*To Mrs. Hudetz.*) What do you want with my daughter?

MRS. HUDETZ: (*To Hudetz, pointing to Anna.*) Is that your defense witness? Congratulations, congratulations. (*She grins.*)

LANDLORD: Be quiet, Mrs. Hudetz.

MRS. HUDETZ: I wasn't speaking to you.

LANDLORD: Don't you get on your high horse with me!

MRS. HUDETZ: You don't have to tell me what to do. Better tell your daughter not to go running around after strange men at night.

LANDLORD: What are you saying? My daughter running around with men? Mrs. Hudetz, don't go too far!

PROSECUTOR: Mrs. Josephine Hudetz, please step forward. (*Mrs. Hudetz steps forward.*) I understand you have nothing to tell us?

MRS. HUDETZ: (*Glancing maliciously at Hudetz and Anna, after a pause.*) Nothing.

PROSECUTOR: Heard nothing, seen nothing. Thank you. We don't require you any more. You may go—(*He turns the pages of his papers.*)

MRS. HUDETZ: (*Screaming suddenly.*) I'm not going! I'm not going! I'm not going to let you treat me like that. You think you can do what you like with me, with me and my poor brother. No, I'm not going to keep quiet. I'm going to talk, I'm going to say what I want.

LANDLORD: Shut up!

MRS. HUDETZ: You're not going to tell me to shut up. You tell your dear little daughter to shut up, so that she isn't going to perjure herself. Yes, I'm saying it straight out, I am! Last night I was standing at the window on the second floor and I saw everything, and I heard everything. Everything, everything, everything! I saw it quite clearly how this little slut kissed my husband—I saw it!

LANDLORD: A kiss? Never!

ANNA: (*Screaming.*) She's lying, she's lying, she's lying!

MRS. HUDETZ: I'm telling the truth and I'll swear to it! She kissed him just to annoy me. But there is a God of vengeance and that's why he missed the signal—I can swear to it, swear to it, swear to it—

ANNA: (*Screams, beside herself.*) You perjure yourself then. You perjure yourself! You are a wicked person. Just because you are too old for your husband, you're trying to ruin him. You're ready to kill him, just because he won't touch you any more. You're notorious, you are. I didn't kiss him, God help me! I am happily engaged to be married and you want to ruin my life too— (*She cries bitterly and presses her head against her father's chest. He tries to comfort her.*)

PROSECUTOR: (*To Mrs. Hudetz.*) Are you aware, Mrs. Hudetz, that your statement heavily incriminates your husband?

LANDLORD: (*Indignantly to Mrs. Hudetz.*) You should be ashamed of yourself, just when he has been taking your side.

ANNA: (*Sobbing to Mrs. Hudetz.*) He's always taking your side. Always!

MRS. HUDETZ: My side? (*She smiles sarcastically.*) Thomas, you've been taking my side?

HUDETZ: Yes.

LANDLORD: (*To Hudetz.*) And has she deserved it?

HUDETZ: No.

LANDLORD: There you are then.

HUDETZ: Sir, everything my wife has said was lies. Neither did this young lady kiss me, nor did I miss the signal. I'm afraid my wife is not quite normal.

MRS. HUDETZ: Not quite normal? You'd like that, wouldn't you?

HUDETZ: (*To Prosecutor.*) She often hears voices when she is by herself. She's told me herself. And her brother.

MRS. HUDETZ: You won't get rid of me like that. Not me, you won't.

HUDETZ: Now I will—if a wife incriminates her own husband in such a way—

MRS. HUDETZ: (*Interrupts him.*) "Husband," I keep hearing "husband." (*Laughs hysterically.*) Do you think you are one? You aren't a man!

HUDETZ: (*Shouting at her.*) That will do! That's enough!

PROSECUTOR: (*Rises.*) That will do! It's not our concern here whether you are a man or not. What concerns us here is a railway accident, if you don't mind. And it's one testimony against another. Much as I regret it, Mr. Hudetz, on the grounds of the incriminating statement by your wife, I shall have to take you into custody.

LANDLORD: Into custody?

PROSECUTOR: (*Gathering up his papers.*) The truth will come out in the course of the proceedings, it will come out—If it's a question of perjury (*Glancing at Mrs. Hudetz.*)

MRS. HUDETZ: (*Unerring calm.*) You can look at me as long as you like, sir. I'm very fond of the truth.

SCENE 3

(*Four months have passed. The scene is in the bar of "The Wild Boar" Inn. At the back is the bar counter and two windows, on the left an entrance door and on the right a door to the dining room. On the wall is a picture of a wild boar. Leni, the waitress, is standing on top of a pair of steps fixing a sign with "Welcome" above the dining room door. The whole room is decorated with paper lanterns and greenery. There is only one customer, a truck driver, who is devouring his meal. It is autumn but sunny outside.*)

CUSTOMER: (*Suddenly.*) Where is my beer?

LENI: (*Without moving from the steps.*) Coming. (*Silence.*)

CUSTOMER: (*Choking with anger.*) Are you going to bring me that beer or not?

LENI: (*As before.*) In a moment!

CUSTOMER: (*Beating the table with his fist.*) What d'you think you're doing. I'm on my break now and I haven't had my beer yet. I'm damn thirsty. What the hell are you decorating up there? Where's the landlord for Christ's sake?

LANDLORD: (*Entering from left.*) Here I am. My apologies—(*To Leni.*) Go and get him a beer at once, d'you hear? What kind of service is that?

LENI: (*Subdued.*) But the sign—

LANDLORD: (*Interrupts her.*) The customer comes first.

CUSTOMER: I should say so. (*Leni comes down, offended, and draws a pint at the counter.*)

LANDLORD: My apologies. Everything is upside down here today because we've got a special celebration on—

CUSTOMER: (*Pointing to sign.*) Who are you expecting? The Emperor of China?

LANDLORD: (*Smiling.*) No, just one of our most respected citizens. Do you remember the big rail disaster four months ago?

CUSTOMER: No idea. I'm a driver.

LANDLORD: Well, our station master was wrongly suspected at the time, a terrible injustice—he has been in prison for four months, but yesterday afternoon he was cleared—and acquitted.

CUSTOMER: You don't say. I wonder that anyone is ever acquitted.

LANDLORD: It is encouraging to see that the truth will out and justice wins the day.

CUSTOMER: Where's that beer?

LENI: (*Bringing it.*) Here you are.

CUSTOMER: And my bill—(*He drinks the pint in one go.*)

LENI: One menu, one beer and four rolls—two twenty.

CUSTOMER: More than enough. (*Throws the money on the table.*)

LENI: Thank you.

LANDLORD: Thank you! I hope we'll have the pleasure again!

CUSTOMER: Not very likely. (*Exits left.*)

LANDLORD: (*Watching him go, sadly.*) There are some sad people in this world—(*He turns to Leni who is up on the steps again and tries to peer under her skirt.*) People who are not interested in anything—who are not interested whether someone is sent to prison, or found guilty or not—all they can think of is their beer.

LENI: Well, everyone thinks of something different.

LANDLORD: You're right there.

LENI: (*Has at last fixed the welcome sign.*) There. That will stay up there for ever. (*She steps down.*) What do you think Mrs. Hudetz is going to do now?

LANDLORD: I shouldn't think she'd want to show her face anywhere—she'd be lynched, like the niggers in America.

LENI: Well, she asked for it.

LANDLORD: She saw Anna kiss him, she saw it! And she saw how he missed the signal and everything! You could see the lies written all over her face, not even the Public Prosecutor believed one word of what she said, even though she swore an oath. She should be glad to get away without being convicted for perjury. I'm telling you, Mrs. Hudetz is finished. She's finished and done with. Now he'll get a divorce—and that puts an end to that. Amen! (*Silence.*)

LENI: Do you think he's going to marry again?

LANDLORD: Maybe he hasn't had enough of it yet. Do you fancy him, our friend Mr. Hudetz?

LENI: (*Smiling.*) There's something about him.

LANDLORD: (*Interested.*) How do you know?

LENI: I just know. (*Silence.*)

LANDLORD: (*Joking.*) Maybe he'll lead you up the aisle. (*Laughs.*)

LENI: (*Looks at him sadly.*) I'm no glamor girl—(*Silence.*)

LANDLORD: (*Regretting that he has hurt her, comes closer and puts his arm around her waist, singing softly to cheer her up. Leni remains serious throughout.*)
Leni, Leni, give me your answer, do
I'm half crazy all for the love of you.
It won't be a stylish marriage,
'cos I can't afford a carriage.
But you'll look sweet
Upon the seat
Of a bicycle made for two.
(*Ferdinand enters quickly from the left. Landlord lets go of Leni and says, pleasantly surprised.*) Hallo, hallo, whom have we here—my daughter's intended! Hallo there, Ferdinand!

FERDINAND: Hallo, Father. Surprised to see me? I thought I'd come on my motor bike, on the spur of the moment.

LANDLORD: Got much work then?

FERDINAND: Today of all days. It wasn't easy to get off because of the cattle auction—

LANDLORD: (*Surprised.*) Cattle auction today?

FERDINAND: Why not?

LANDLORD: On a Wednesday?

FERDINAND: (*Uninterested.*) They've changed the date—(*With enthusiasm.*) You should have seen those oxen, they were like elephants—but I didn't waste time on them. There isn't a single ox more important to me than Anna. Where is she?

LENI: She's changing.

LANDLORD: (*To Leni.*) Go and call her. (*Leni quickly exits right.*) Let me tell you something, Ferdinand. I'm glad you are going to marry my Anna, you'll look after my business well. Eighty-six years it's been in the family—just remember that when I'm gone. (*Anna enters right wearing a white dress.*)

FERDINAND: Anna! (*He embraces and kisses her.*)

ANNA: I'm so glad—

FERDINAND: You've become a celebrity since I saw you last week. The leading witness in a sensational court case. Look what they are saying about you— (*He takes a paper from his pocket and shows her the headlines.*) "Beautiful publican's daughter"—in big letters.

LANDLORD: She has much to be proud of.

FERDINAND: And so have I.

ANNA: (*Smiling strangely.*) That sort of fame soon fades away.

LANDLORD: How well she speaks. How exquisitely she expresses herself, my daughter.

FERDINAND: Good Lord, I feel as if my bride was a filmstar! Let me look at you, star witness, let me see if you've changed—(*He looks her up and down.*)

ANNA: (*Again smiling strangely.*) Hardly. (*A band is heard in the distance, coming closer. They listen.*)

FERDINAND: Music?

LANDLORD: They're coming, they're coming—(*Looking excited at his watch.*) Yes, that's right. He'll be here in a minute—our dear Mr. Hudetz. They're meeting him at the station, the whole village! (*Anna looks pale and puts her hand to her heart.*)

FERDINAND: What is it Anna? Your heart again?

ANNA: (*Very softly.*) Yes.

LANDLORD: (*To Ferdinand.*) This whole trial has been too much excitement.

FERDINAND: (*Stroking Anna's hand gently.*) But now it's all over, isn't it, Anna?

ANNA: (*Smiling vaguely.*) Yes, it's all over—

LANDLORD: (*Hands her a glass.*) Have a drink, that's the best medicine!

FERDINAND: I'll have one too—(*He helps himself to a glass, to Anna.*) To you, Anna!

ANNA: (*Softly.*) To you Ferdinand! (*They drink up and the music approaches. People are calling "hurrah" nearby.*)

LENI: (*Comes running in excitedly from the right. She too has changed her dress.*) He's coming, he's coming, he's coming! (*She runs to the window and calls out.*) Hurray! (*The Landlord and Ferdinand join her. The sun begins to set and dusk falls quickly.*)

ANNA: (*Stares straight ahead. Then she quickly pours herself another glass, muttering.*) Hurrah. (*She empties the glass quickly. The party enter through the door on the left. Half the village is there: Mrs. Leimgruber, the Forestry Worker and the Policeman in his best uniform. Hudetz enters, a frozen smile on his face, acknowledging his welcome. He has become paler during his time in prison.*)

ALL: Hurrah, hurrah, hurrah!

LANDLORD: (*Begins to make a speech.*) Thomas Hudetz! Dear old friend! Our respected station master! All of us who are assembled here today have always been convinced of your absolute innocence—and it is a personal joy and honor to me that fate should have selected my own child to be the witness to prove your innocence.

SOME CALL: Hurrah, Anna, hurrah!

LANDLORD: Yes, there is an Almighty up there in Heaven, who watches over us, so that truth will out and justice prevail! Let us welcome you, you who were not guilty but had to suffer imprisonment all the same and bear this great suffering. Long live Thomas Hudetz, our favorite station master—the man who never forgets his duty. May he live long! (*He goes up to Hudetz and shakes both his hands.*)

ALL: Hurrah, hurrah, hurrah! (*The band sounds.*)

A CHILD: (*Carrying a posy enters and curtsies before Hudetz. She recites.*)
  Let us now praise the famous man
  Whose life with glorious deeds began.
  Organs and bells to him belong
  Whose praises must be sung in song.
  Thank God that sing and praise I can
  The deeds of this most famous man!
(*She curtsies again and hands the flowers to Hudetz. All applaud.*)

HUDETZ: (*Strokes the child's cheek but suddenly sees Anna. He stops, looks at her and walks slowly over to her taking her hand.*) Good evening, Anna.

ANNA: Good evening, Mr. Hudetz.

HUDETZ: How are you?

ANNA: Very well, thank you. (*She smiles. All look at Anna and Hudetz waiting for their next words.*)

HUDETZ: (*Becoming embarrassed, suddenly turns away and pointing to Anna calls.*) My guardian angel! Long may she live! Hurrah, hurrah! (*He hands her the flowers.*)

ALL: (*Enthusiastically.*) Hurrah, hurrah, hurrah! (*The lights are now turned down *in the big room and the band plays a waltz.*)

LANDLORD: (*Climbing onto a chair.*) Ladies and gentlemen! May I ask you to move into the dining room. I think we can all do with a little food and drink and it's getting dark in here! (*Laughter and shouts of bravo.*)

FERDINAND: (*Offers his arm to Anna.*) May I have the pleasure—(*All, except Leni, go off right in a happy mood. Leni goes to the bar and begins to draw several mugs of beer. She hums the waltz tune which we hear from the dining room. Alfons enters left. Leni sees him and stares at him horrified.*)

ALFONS: Good evening, Leni. Why do you look so surprised?

LENI: How dare you come here? Tonight of all nights?

ALFONS: (*Smiles.*) And why not?

LENI: When your sister, Mrs. Hudetz—

ALFONS: (*Interrupts her.*) I have no sister.

LENI: No one is going to believe that. They'll throw you out, you'll see. (*Alfons sits. Leni is worried.*) Why don't you leave. You're going to get beaten up. They're drinking in there and you'll get hurt.

ALFONS: (*Smiles.*) Let them—

LENI: (*Annoyed.*) Oh well, if you won't take my advice, I can't help you. (*She exits quickly to the right carrying beer mugs. Someone is singing "We'll gather lilacs in the spring again." Alfons listens, stands up and goes slowly towards the dining room. He stops and hesitates. The song is finished and people are yelling and shouting bravo. Alfons is taken aback by the noise, puts on his hat and exits left. Silence.*)

ANNA: (*Enters quickly with Hudetz from the right; they speak in subdued voices while she looks anxiously around.*) No one will see us here.

HUDETZ: What do you want?

ANNA: I've got to tell you something.

HUDETZ: Why not in there?

ANNA: Because everybody is watching us—I must speak to you alone. There's something I've got to tell you.

HUDETZ: What do you want to tell me?

ANNA: (*Smiles.*) Oh, so much! (*Silence.*)

HUDETZ: It will be better for both of us if we don't meet.

ANNA: No, no, we won't—I can't stand it much longer—(*She smiles.*)

HUDETZ: Quietly! (*He looks around. Silence.*) Now we must go back. What would your fiancé say if he saw us here? He would think there was something between us and that would be the last straw.

ANNA: Please have pity on me. You must listen to me tomorrow—

HUDETZ: You talk as if your life depended on it.

ANNA: Perhaps—(*She smiles. Silence.*)

HUDETZ: All right then, tomorrow. But where?

ANNA: At the viaduct.

HUDETZ: On top or underneath?

ANNA: Underneath.

HUDETZ: At what time?

ANNA: At night. At nine o'clock.

HUDETZ: At nine o'clock? At night?

ANNA: (*Smiling.*) So that no one can see us. At least no living person.

HUDETZ: (*Shrugging his shoulders.*) All right then.

ANNA: (*Holds out her hand.*) All right.

HUDETZ: (*Takes it.*) All right.

ANNA: (*Smiles.*) Good. (*Exits quickly to right. Another waltz is being played. Alfons enters quickly from the left, sees Hudetz and clutches at his heart.*)

HUDETZ: (*Looks at him and says softly.*) Is that you Alfons?

ALFONS: Yes. (*Pause.*)

HUDETZ: (*Smiling.*) Good evening, brother-in-law—

ALFONS: Good evening, Thomas. You mustn't say brother-in-law like that—a woman who behaves as my sister has done no longer exists as far as I am concerned.

HUDETZ: Let's forget about it. It's over and done with.

ALFONS: Not for me, it isn't. (*Hudetz looks at him. Pause.*) I was here earlier tonight but I was told I would get beaten up. (*He smiles and then becomes serious again.*) But I am not afraid now. I have thought it all out. There is only one way open to me and that is to say publicly that I have broken with my sister. It's all finished between her and me. I can't go on like that. No one greets me or speaks to me. I've always been boycotted by people but now they want to ruin me altogether. Thomas, we have never had any arguments. Please help me—(*The Landlord, Mrs. Leimgruber, Ferdinand, Anna and the Forestry Worker come out of the dining room.*)

LANDLORD: (*Turns on the light and sees Hudetz.*) There you are, we're looking for you—(*He stops and sees Alfons.*) Hey—what do I see. How dare you come in here? What nerve! Get out!

MRS. LEIMGRUBER: Get out! Get out!

ALFONS: No, I want to tell you something—

LANDLORD: (*Interrupts him roughly.*) You don't want to tell us anything—get out or else—

FORESTRY WORKER: (*Approaching Alfons.*) You perjured quack, you—(*Tries to push him.*)

HUDETZ: Stop! He has just told me that he has broken with his sister—

FERDINAND: Liar!

HUDETZ: (*Sharply.*) He's not lying!

LANDLORD: (*Surprised to Hudetz.*) Now why should you of all people say that—

HUDETZ: Do me a favor, will you, and leave him in peace. (*Exits right.*)

SCENE 4

(A gorge. The pillars of the viaduct stretch up towards the sky. It is a quiet night. The moon is up, it is autumn and everything is peaceful and at rest. The Policeman is on his round.)

POLICEMAN: *(Stops suddenly and listens in the darkness.)* Anybody there? Hey, who's there?

HUDETZ: *(Steps forward.)* Good evening, officer.

POLICEMAN: *(Reassured.)* Ah, the station master. What are you doing here by the viaduct?

HUDETZ: Just going for a walk.

POLICEMAN: In the middle of the night?

HUDETZ: The night doesn't worry me—*(He smiles.)*

POLICEMAN: Well, be careful. There are all sorts of people about in the night. I've just had an official message, gypsies, I think.

HUDETZ: I'm not afraid.

POLICEMAN: *(Smiling.)* Ah well, people with a clear conscience need not be afraid. They can sleep peacefully in their beds at night. How much convalescent leave have they given you?

HUDETZ: A week.

POLICEMAN: Is that all? You'll have to take it easy then and not go to too many parties like the one last night. It did go on, didn't it. Till six in the morning!

HUDETZ: It was great fun.

POLICEMAN: Quite a few got sozzled, didn't they. It got almost dangerous. Till when did you sleep this morning?

HUDETZ: I didn't sleep at all. I don't sleep well nowadays.

POLICEMAN: I know just what that's like. I suffer from the same thing. There you are lying in the dark and you start thinking of all kinds of things—all the things you could have done better.

HUDETZ: That and other things too.

POLICEMAN: Well, so long then, Mr. Hudetz. And have a good rest. *(Exits.)*

HUDETZ: Goodbye, officer. *(He watches him go and lights a cigarette. A signal bell is heard up on the viaduct, similar to the signal bell at the station. He listens and looks up. Anna enters, sees him and is startled.)* What's wrong?

ANNA: *(Smiling.)* You were suddenly in front of me—*(A church clock strikes in the distance.)*

HUDETZ: *(Counting the strokes quietly.)*—Nine—I have been here since a quarter to—*(He grins.)* You shouldn't keep ladies waiting. *(Silence.)*

ANNA: *(Looking around anxiously.)* I came out secretly. I don't want anyone to know that we are meeting here.

HUDETZ: I couldn't agree more.

ANNA: People would talk, wouldn't they, and there is no reason, is there?

HUDETZ: I shouldn't have thought so. (*The train passes over the viaduct.*)

ANNA: (*Looks up.*) The local?

HUDETZ: (*Looks up too.*) No, that's the express.

ANNA: I thought it was going rather slowly —

HUDETZ: That's deceptive.

ANNA: Even so — (*Silence.*)

HUDETZ: What have you got to tell me?

ANNA: Oh much, oh so much.

HUDETZ: Well, come on then. First, second and third. (*Silence.*)

ANNA: Don't you have a feeling for this kind of thing? (*Hudetz stares at her.*) What would you say if I told everyone that I had told a lie, that I had committed perjury, that you didn't —

HUDETZ: (*Angrily.*) Be quiet! (*He looks around. Silence.*)

ANNA: (*Softly but with eager expectation.*) What would you do?

HUDETZ: I — hm, I don't know what I would do.

ANNA: That's not true.

HUDETZ: You ought to know.

ANNA: Oh, I get to hear things. (*Silence.*)

HUDETZ: I wouldn't kill you.

ANNA: (*Smiles.*) What a pity. (*Hudetz looks surprised. Silence. Anna simply.*) I don't want to go on living.

HUDETZ: It was your duty to swear that oath the way you did.

ANNA: (*Harshly.*) You're wrong if you think that it was all my fault. Oh no, I'm not going to stand for that, I'm not.

HUDETZ: Whose fault was it then other than yours?

ANNA: Oh no, it wasn't just me.

HUDETZ: (*Sarcastic, like the Public Prosecutor.*) Maybe it was the mysterious Mr. X?

ANNA: Maybe it was. (*Another signal bell sounds on top of the viaduct. Hudetz looks up. Anna afraid.*) What was that?

HUDETZ: A signal.

ANNA: (*Stopping her ears, softly.*) I keep hearing screams — when I am on my own the dead come for me. They are angry and they are going to get me — (*Silence.*)

HUDETZ: Now listen to me. I have been on my own for four months, in solitary confinement, all on my own, and I have had plenty of opportunity to talk it all over with myself, all day long. We discussed it a lot, Anna, and the result was that my inner voice said to me: "You have always been a conscientious railwayman. You have never missed a signal, you are not guilty, Thomas" —

ANNA: (*Interrupting him.*) Not guilty?

HUDETZ: Absolutely not.

ANNA: (*Harshly.*) Don't you make it too easy for yourself.

HUDETZ: (*Screams at her.*) I'm not making anything easy for myself. My only fault was that I didn't chase you off right away. I was too polite with you. I should have whacked you one, do you understand? (*Silence.*)

ANNA: (*Smiles.*) You should have whacked me one?

HUDETZ: Yes. (*Silence.*)

ANNA: Pity you didn't—

HUDETZ: Yes, I'm sorry too.

ANNA: Why don't you whack me one now. Perhaps that will make it better.

HUDETZ: (*Screams again.*) Don't make stupid jokes now, will you.

ANNA: It's not a joke. When I gave you that kiss, that was a joke—

HUDETZ: (*Interrupts her.*) Let's not talk about that!

ANNA: (*Smiles.*) That's all I've got to talk about.

HUDETZ: Shut up then, or there'll be trouble. (*Silence.*)

ANNA: How do you mean?

HUDETZ: What?

ANNA: There'll be trouble. What is going to happen? (*Silence.*)

HUDETZ: (*Looking at her.*) I have been pronounced innocent, Anna, completely innocent!

ANNA: Then you'll have to do something worse to get a conviction—(*She smiles. Silence.*)

HUDETZ: (*Angrily.*) Don't look at me like that!

ANNA: (*Smiles.*) Are you afraid of me?

HUDETZ: (*Staring at her.*) You are quite pale.

ANNA: That's the moonlight—

HUDETZ: As if there wasn't a drop of blood left, not a drop—

ANNA: Oh, I think I've still got enough. (*She laughs.*)

HUDETZ: (*Harshly.*) Stop it! (*Silence.*) I'm going.

ANNA: Where?

HUDETZ: To sleep.

ANNA: Can you sleep?

HUDETZ: Yes. (*He starts to go.*)

ANNA: Wait! My life is suddenly completely changed. I thought nothing of it at first, but now it's different. And when night falls I don't remember the stars. Our house has shrunk and as for Ferdinand, I see him with different eyes. All have become strangers, my father, Leni, all of them—but not you. When you came in yesterday, I knew what you would look like, your nose, your eyes, your chin, your ears—I remembered it all, although we'd never noticed each other. But now I know you well. Do you feel the same about me?

HUDETZ: (*Does not look at her. After a short pause.*) Yes.

ANNA: (*Smiles.*) Good. (*Silence.*) When I am dead one day, I shall belong to you. We shall meet again and again—

HUDETZ: (*Moves slowly towards her and lifts her chin. He looks into her eyes as if he was calling.*) Anna, Anna—

ANNA: (*Very softly.*) Do you recognize me?

HUDETZ: Yes. (*He kisses and embraces her.*)

SCENE 5

(*Three days later at "The Wild Boar." The "Welcome" sign and decorations have gone. It is raining outside. Leni is reading the paper at a table. Hudetz enters left.*)

LENI: Good evening, sir.

HUDETZ: A glass of red wine, please. (*He sits.*)

LENI: (*Surprised.*) Since when are you drinking red wine?

HUDETZ: Since today.

LENI: That's odd. (*She pours. Silence.*)

HUDETZ: What's the news?

LENI: (*Bringing him the wine.*) Nothing yet. We're completely in the dark.

HUDETZ: Hm. (*Drinks.*)

LENI: It'll be three days tonight that she disappeared, our Anna—just disappeared, as if the earth had swallowed her up. I was the last to see her—she said she was going to bed because she was tired from the night before. But in the morning her bed was untouched, quite untouched—

HUDETZ: Hm.

LENI: Her father is offering a reward for any information about her—they were discussing the amount for a long time yesterday, he and Ferdinand. I only hope she hasn't been kidnapped by white slave traders or people like that—

HUDETZ: That's old wives tales.

LENI: D'you know, sir, I don't want to say it out loud, but I think she is no longer alive—(*She stops and looks at his cheek with interest.*) What's that?

HUDETZ: Where?

LENI: Who's been scratching you?

HUDETZ: No one. I hurt myself on a rusty nail—(*He smiles.*)

LENI: (*Flirtatiously.*) Well, well, well. I can think what I like. (*She wipes some glasses.*) By the way, do you know who's been back here since last night? Your wife.

HUDETZ: (*Puzzled.*) Who?

LENI: Your wife, your ex—divorced—

HUDETZ: (*Interrupts.*) Oh, her!

LENI: She is staying with her brother at the drug store even though the pharmacist said publicly that he had no sister and you even took his side. What do you say to that?

HUDETZ: (*Grimly.*) I don't think I'll say anything about anything any more.

LENI: And do you know what people are saying? They seem to think it is absolutely all right and nobody is criticizing her. Since poor Anna has gone the pharmacist is God Almighty again, suddenly everyone speaks of him with the greatest respect. Just goes to show how fickle people are! (*The church clock strikes.*)

HUDETZ: I don't care about people! (*He counts.*) Six.

LENI: Six already. How time flies—

HUDETZ: Yes. (*He drinks. Deliberately disinterested, quite by the way.*) Why do you think Miss Anna is no longer alive?

LENI: (*Looks about her carefully and comes closer. Softly.*) I swear to you she's done away with herself—(*Hudetz stares at her. Leni watches him.*) Can't you understand that, sir?

HUDETZ: (*Confused.*) What do you mean?

LENI: (*As above.*) Haven't you heard?

HUDETZ: What? What's it got to do with me? Tell me.

LENI: Don't get angry with me—

HUDETZ: I'm not angry, come on!

LENI: (*Looking about her carefully and even more quietly than before.*) Since poor Anna has gone people don't believe her any more. They even say that the station master won't be all that upset if Miss Anna can't talk any more—(*Hudetz stares at her.*) They say that Anna wanted to be dead because she could no longer find peace, that her conscience—

HUDETZ: Her conscience?

LENI: People are saying that Anna swore a false oath, committed perjury, because—(*She pauses.*)

HUDETZ: (*Warily.*) Because what?

LENI: Because you, sir, they say, did not switch the signal in time—(*Silence. Hudetz laughs and then becomes serious again. Silence.*) What are you going to do?

HUDETZ: Of course I operated the signal in time. I've always done my duty—(*He drinks. Policeman enters from left. He looks serious.*)

LENI: Good evening, officer.

POLICEMAN: Is the landlord in?

LENI: Yes.

POLICEMAN: I must see him at once.

LENI: (*Horrified.*) Why, what's happened?

POLICEMAN: We found Anna. She's dead.

LENI: Heaven preserve us! (*Makes the sign of the cross.*) So she did away with herself.

POLICEMAN: No, she didn't. She was murdered.

LENI: Murdered—

POLICEMAN: We are following a definite trail. She was found at the viaduct, underneath, and we had reports that there had been some dangerous people about, gypsies—(*To Hudetz.*) I think I told you, didn't I—

HUDETZ: Yes, you did.

POLICEMAN: It was in the same night when we met near the viaduct, underneath—

HUDETZ: That's right.

POLICEMAN: Tell me, didn't you notice anything suspicious that night?

HUDETZ: No.

POLICEMAN: Hm. (*Looking at Hudetz.*) The mills of the Lord grind wondrous slow—

HUDETZ: I didn't see any gypsies.

POLICEMAN: She wasn't murdered by gypsies. See you soon, station master.

HUDETZ: So long. (*Policeman exits right. Silence.*)

LENI: (*Stares at him.*) You were at the viaduct that night?

HUDETZ: Yes (*He rises.*)

LENI: Going already?

HUDETZ: The bill, please.

LENI: (*Suddenly screams at him.*) What were you doing at the viaduct?

HUDETZ: What was I doing? (*He smiles.*) I got engaged to Miss Anna—(*Exits quickly to left.*)

SCENE 6

(*Three days later at the pharmacist's. A desk in background, a small table and two chairs in foreground. The entrance door on the right and part of the window display as seen from the inside. On the left a door leading to the private quarters. Late afternoon, shortly before closing time.*)

MRS. LEIMGRUBER: What a pity you didn't come to the dear child's funeral. It was absolutely splendid. People came from all over, even more than were at the train disaster, even some journalists came, and they took photos of the grave from all angles, for the *Illustrated Daily News*. And you should have seen the flowers—what a show! You've really missed something. Mind you, I can understand perfectly that you didn't want to be present at poor Annie's last journey, when your former brother-in-law—I quite understand—I quite understand! It's a matter of tact, plain tact! What are you doing there? That parcel is much too big, better make it two.

ALFONS: As you wish—

MRS. LEIMGRUBER: I would be grateful. You know, her father, poor man, although stricken by grief, was very calm, but her fiancé, Ferdinand, he broke down completely, that big hulk in ruins, tears streaming down his face, it was a pitiful sight. You wouldn't believe there was so much tender feeling in such a rough fellow like a butcher and vice versa. I always say, it's the rough fellow that often has the heart of a little child. Poor Annie! Now you are lying there in the ground, all by yourself. No one tucks you in when it rains. Look, these are the photographs they took when she was laid out—to remember the funeral by—I'll give you one, I've got a whole lot—(*She puts one on the desk.*)

ALFONS: (*Without looking.*) Thank you, Mrs. Leimgruber. (*Silence.*)

MRS. LEIMGRUBER: And how is your dear sister? How is her health?

ALFONS: (*Smiling.*) She's bearing up.

MRS. LEIMGRUBER: Of course, of course! She's had a lot to put up with. But if I were in her shoes I would be happy that he didn't kill me—that could have happened too. I kept thinking during the funeral today that it must be a great satisfaction to her that they are after that man, that "nice" station master, Mr. Hudetz, that murderer—I hope they get him soon. You know, I'm really glad that the ice between us has been broken at last. Everybody speaks most highly of you and your unfortunate sister, as if they were sorry—

ALFONS: Sorry—no one has ever regretted being sorry. But I want to make one thing plain: I don't feel any satisfaction at all. As far as I am concerned it would have been better if the whole terrible business had never happened.

MRS. LEIMGRUBER: Come, come! That's going too far! Just watch that you don't become too generous in the end, or people will turn against you again.

ALFONS: I'm telling you what I really feel.

MRS. LEIMGRUBER: The truth is different.

ALFONS: People spat on my sister because she spoke the truth.

MRS. LEIMGRUBER: But that's what I'm saying, it was a mistake, a dreadful mistake. But in this business with Thomas Hudetz there can be no mistake. This man Hudetz persuaded poor little Annie to perjure herself. It was his criminal influence, nothing else. But when she broke down under the heavy burden of guilt and wanted to confess, he just killed her. And it wasn't her who kissed him at the station that time, it was him, and not just a kiss, he wanted to rape her in his office, and that's why she fell onto the signal lever—

ALFONS: (*Interrupts her angrily.*) How do you know all that? Were you there?

MRS. LEIMGRUBER: Do you mind!

ALFONS: I can't stand this talk! I'm telling you, as long as it hasn't been proved beyond the shadow of a doubt that he is the murderer, as long as he doesn't confess of his own free will, I won't believe in his guilt.

MRS. LEIMGRUBER: It seems to me you don't believe in anything. Not in God or anything.

ALFONS: I don't need you to tell me about God. Hudetz is not the worst by a long stretch, remember that Mrs. Leimgruber!

MRS. LEIMGRUBER: (*Offended.*) So we are being compared with murderers now.

ALFONS: Just remember how he took my side when you all wanted to beat me up.

MRS. LEIMGRUBER: (*Spitefully.*) Perhaps it would have been better if he hadn't taken your side. My goodness me, one really can't be friends with you—it simply doesn't work! (*She takes her two parcels and quickly exits to right.*)

ALFONS: (*Alone. He smiles and covers his eyes with his hands. The church clock strikes seven. He looks at his watch.*) That's it for another day. (*He exits slowly through the shop door and we hear the sound of the iron shutter being pulled down in front of the shop window. Mrs. Hudetz enters through the side door, carrying a tray with supper. She lays the table. Alfons re-enters through the shop door and locks it from inside. He sits at the small table and begins to eat.*)

MRS. HUDETZ: (*Also sitting and eating, suddenly.*) Have you been talking to a customer again about him?

ALFONS: Yes.

MRS. HUDETZ: I can hear you in the kitchen. Not everything, but you were taking his side again?

ALFONS: Yes. (*Silence.*)

MRS. HUDETZ: Couldn't we eat in the room? It smells so much of soap and things in here.

ALFONS: Then we'd have to heat that room.

MRS. HUDETZ: (*Smiling, a little piqued.*) I never knew you were a miser—

ALFONS: If I weren't a miser you wouldn't be going to the seaside. (*Silence.*)

MRS. HUDETZ: Let's eat in the kitchen from tomorrow.

ALFONS: I've never eaten in the kitchen, but if you like—(*Silence.*)

MRS. HUDETZ: Food all right?

ALFONS: Yes. (*Silence.*)

MRS. HUDETZ: What would you like tomorrow?

ALFONS: Whatever you are making.

MRS. HUDETZ: (*Stops eating and puts her knife and fork down next to her plate.*) Sometimes I ask myself what crimes it is we are paying for—

ALFONS: Our own.

MRS. HUDETZ: But I haven't—

ALFONS: Yes, you have.

MRS. HUDETZ: I'm not aware of any crimes.

ALFONS: That doesn't mean anything. You've just forgotten.

MRS. HUDETZ: (*Sharply.*) Do you think so?

ALFONS: I believe it absolutely.

MRS. HUDETZ: The truth is different.

ALFONS: You talk like Mrs. Leimgruber.

MRS. HUDETZ: (*Offended.*) So we are being compared to people like that now.

ALFONS: (*Smiles.*) Mrs. Leimgruber, Mrs. Leimgruber!

MRS. HUDETZ: (*Looks at him coldly, then shrugs her shoulders.*) I am innocent.

ALFONS: Innocent? (*He laughs.*)

MRS. HUDETZ: (*Angrily.*) Don't laugh. Tell me of one crime, just a single crime!

ALFONS: (*Rises and walks up and down.*) I remember you telling me: Thomas doesn't want me anymore. But I won't let him look at another woman, not a single one! You had no right to say that, that was a crime.

MRS. HUDETZ: (*Sarcastically.*) For that crime I'll accept responsibility.

ALFONS: Then don't complain when you are being punished. Don't accuse people of persecuting you. You were thirteen years older, you ought to have known and felt it—but you wanted to blackmail him to love you, yes, blackmail!

MRS. HUDETZ: Go on, have it your way! What do you know about women! None of them wants you—

ALFONS: (*Stares at her.*) Did you or did you not say: "I hate him, yes I hate him and I could kill him when he lies next to me in the night." (*Harshly.*) Did you say that? Yes or no?

MRS. HUDETZ: (*Frighteningly calm.*) Yes, I did. But I didn't kill him. (*She smiles.*)

ALFONS: Perhaps. (*Silence.*)

MRS. HUDETZ: You're talking as if I had missed the signal, as if eighteen people had been killed by me.

ALFONS: (*Interrupts her.*) It all ties in together.

MRS. HUDETZ: (*Screaming.*) Perhaps I also killed that girl, Anna—(*There is a knock at the door. They are startled and listen. Mrs. Hudetz looks worried.*) Who could that be? (*There is another knock.*)

ALFONS: (*Goes toward the door.*) Let's see—

MRS. HUDETZ: Be careful, Alfons!

ALFONS: (*Opens the door and starts back. Softly.*) It's you. (*Hudetz enters in his crumpled uniform without his cap.*)

MRS. HUDETZ: (*Cries in a muffled voice.*) Thomas! (*Alfons quickly closes the door. Hudetz does not look at them, walks slowly to the table, looks at what is left of the food, takes a bread roll and eats lethargically. They look at him.*)

HUDETZ: (*Stops eating, looks at them and smiles.*) How are you?

MRS. HUDETZ: Thomas, are you out of your mind?

HUDETZ: (*Harshly.*) Quiet, don't shout! (*He looks around suspiciously.*)

ALFONS: Are they after you?

HUDETZ: (*Grins.*) Of course. (*Silence.*)

ALFONS: What do you want?

HUDETZ: I've been hiding in the woods until today and now I'm here—(*He grins.*) Don't be afraid. No one has seen me. (*Becoming serious, matter of fact.*) I need some clothes. I most go away and I can't do that in this uniform. (*Silence.*) Will you give me a suit or not?

MRS. HUDETZ: (*Angrily.*) Why do you want to involve us? That would be aiding and abetting. Leave my brother out of this. You've caused me enough unhappiness. Leave us in peace.

HUDETZ: (*Grinning.*) Are you at peace? (*Silence.*)

ALFONS: We're looking for peace. And trying to show good will.

HUDETZ: You, perhaps—

ALFONS: (*Annoyed.*) Don't talk in that tone of voice. Take a look at yourself! (*Silence.*)

HUDETZ:; (*Grinning.*) Where shall I look? Into myself? What would I find there?

ALFONS: Look and see. (*Hudetz listens and stops grinning. Silence.*)

HUDETZ: Everything is surrounded by the police and the military. But I can get through. I am not going to serve a sentence. It wasn't my fault.

ALFONS: You don't think so?

HUDETZ: I am innocent.

MRS. HUDETZ: (*Laughing hysterically.*) Just like Mrs. Leimgruber, Mrs. Leimgruber.

HUDETZ: Don't laugh!

MRS. HUDETZ: But it really is too funny—(*She sits at the small table, bends over it and cries.*)

HUDETZ: (*To Alfons.*) What's the matter with her? (*Silence.*)

ALFONS: Thomas, I didn't want to believe it—

HUDETZ: What?— Oh, I see.— Well, I can't help you. You'll have to believe it. I got "engaged" to Anna.

MRS. HUDETZ: (*Aghast.*) Engaged?

HUDETZ: (*Nods.*) Yes. At the viaduct. Hm—(*He smiles.*) I grabbed her and shook her, but she was no longer there—I called her but she didn't make a sound. Then I went home and lay down. Suddenly I was able to sleep again, after four months, just like I used to when I had done my duty as a good civil servant—(*He smiles.*) Ah well. (*He thinks and holds his head.*) Oh yes, I wanted to ask you something: I know that I killed her but I don't know how. (*He looks at Alfons and Mrs. Hudetz.*) How did I do it? (*They look at him aghast.*) Didn't you read it in the papers?

ALFONS: No, we didn't want to read anything about it.

HUDETZ: If only I knew—

ALFONS: What then?

HUDETZ: Well then—then I'd know myself, a little better—(*Silence.*)

HUDETZ: (*To Mrs. Hudetz.*) You know that I've always spoken up for you?

MRS. HUDETZ: Yes. But you always thought of another woman when you were with me—

HUDETZ: (*Smiles at her.*) Yes, of my fiancée—

MRS. HUDETZ: Let's not talk about it, Thomas. I am so tired.

HUDETZ: So am I. But I've got to get far away—

ALFONS: (*To Mrs. Hudetz.*) Get him my gray suit. Go on.

MRS. HUDETZ: You're going to get yourself into trouble!

ALFONS: Go on! (*Mrs. Hudetz exits through the side door. Silence.*)

HUDETZ: Someone once said to me: You were acquitted, sir, and you will have to commit a major crime in order to be punished. (*He holds his hand in front of his eyes.*) Who said that—who?

ALFONS: Wasn't it Anna?

HUDETZ: (*Startled, looks at Alfons with surprise.*) Yes. How do you know?

ALFONS: I wasn't there. (*He smiles. Silence.*)

HUDETZ: (*Looks at Alfons.*) You weren't there? Neither was I—(*He smiles and sees the dead girl's photo on the desk.*) What's that? (*Reads.*) "In pious memory of

Anna Lechner, virgin, our innkeeper's daughter, now in Heaven." (*To Alfons.*) Was it a good funeral?

ALFONS: Yes, it was.

HUDETZ: (*Smiling to himself, happily, looks at the photograph. He becomes serious and reads it as if he was just reading it out to someone.*)

Wayfarer,
Stand still.
Look at my wounds
For good or ill.
The hours pass
The wounds remain
Take care, beware
The verdict I shall say
About you on Judgment Day—

MRS. HUDETZ: (*Enters with the gray suit and puts in on a chair. To Hudetz who is deep in thought.*) Go on now, Thomas—

HUDETZ: (*As if to himself.*) Yes—(*He goes towards the door.*)

MRS. HUDETZ: The suit?

HUDETZ: (*Looks at the suit and then at both of them. He smiles.*) No, thank you. (*Exits through shop door.*)

SCENE 7

(*On the railway line, at the place where the 9:05 Express had crashed with a freight train. The night is dark and the signal is green, go ahead. Policeman enters right. The Landlord and Ferdinand follow him armed with their hunting rifles. They go left.*)

LANDLORD: (*Stops suddenly and listens in the dark.*) There's somebody there.— Who's there? (*Silence.*)

POLICEMAN: Nothing. Sometimes you can hear the dark.

LANDLORD: (*Grimly.*) He'll get away, you know—

POLICEMAN: He can't, believe me. The entire neighborhood is on alert, everything is surrounded.

FERDINAND: (*Suddenly sobs sentimentally.*) Oh, Annie, my poor dear Annie— where are you now?

POLICEMAN: In paradise.

FERDINAND: What good is that to me—(*Takes a bottle and drinks*).

LANDLORD: (*Quietly.*) Don't drink so much.

FERDINAND: But I'm going to get pissed because I didn't protect her, you know. Oh, Annie, Annie, I'm such a wicked person, such a bad apple.

LANDLORD: Be a man.

FERDINAND: (*Crossly to Landlord.*) I won't be a man. You are only her father but I am her fiancé and she was the love of my life. If you don't mind. (*He drinks*

again. Alfons enters right. He sees them and stops. They see him and stare at him.)
ALFONS: Good evening. (*Silence.*)
LANDLORD: (*The first to recover his speech.*) How dare you show yourself—
ALFONS: (*Interrupts.*) Well—(*To Policeman.*) I'm looking for you, officer.
POLICEMAN: Where is your brother-in-law?
ALFONS: (*Smiling uncertainly.*) Oh, you know about it—
POLICEMAN: (*Puzzled.*) About what?
LANDLORD: Look how he smiles. (*He stares spitefully at Alfons.*)
ALFONS: My brother-in-law, Thomas Hudetz, suddenly appeared at my place tonight—
FERDINAND: (*Interrupts him.*) Suddenly appeared?
ALFONS: Unexpectedly.
LANDLORD: (*Sarcastically.*) Unexpectedly?
ALFONS: Yes. (*To Policeman.*) He came to ask me for a suit—
POLICEMAN: (*Interrupts him harshly.*) And what did you do? Did you give it to him?
ALFONS: (*After a short pause.*) He changed his mind—(*He smiles.*) He decided not to take it. And I was trying to make up my mind, constable, whether I should report the fact that he came to me for help, but I think it is better to report it—in his own interest, too.
FERDINAND: His interest is not our concern, remember that!
LANDLORD: Where is he then, your dear brother-in-law? Where has he got to now, our beloved station master?
ALFONS: I followed him as soon as he had gone—but then I lost him. He was going towards the viaduct.
LANDLORD: The viaduct?
ALFONS: Yes. God help him. (*Silence.*) Now do you understand why he didn't want the suit?
POLICEMAN: Why not?
ALFONS: A viaduct is usually very high—(*He smiles strangely. Silence.*)
POLICEMAN: Do you think he's going to jump?
FERDINAND: Jump?
ALFONS: I'm afraid he's going to be his own judge.
LANDLORD: His own judge? No way. I won't allow that. That would make it too simple. What does he think? Kill my child, my only child, and then simply kill himself? That would be too easy!
FERDINAND: He's got to be put in prison and then hanged. Hanged by the neck, by the neck.
POLICEMAN: A proper court procedure—
LANDLORD: (*Interrupts him.*) I'm going to get him. Let's go to the viaduct! (*Exits quickly to left.*)
FERDINAND: I'm going to get him too. Come on, constable. (*To Alfons.*) You, go to bed, you. (*Quickly exits left.*)

ALFONS: No, I'm going to get him too. He mustn't escape his punishment on this earth.

POLICEMAN: Good! (*Exits to left with Alfons.*)

POKORNY: (*The late engine driver comes out of the dark smoking a cigarette. He watches Alfons and grins.*) Idiot! You and your punishment on this earth—

(*The signal bell rings and the signal changes to red. A Maintenance Man walks along the track carrying a lamp around his chest. His face is not visible.*)

POKORNY: (*Quietly.*) Good evening, Kreitmeyer.

MAN: (*Stops, he has a soft voice.*) I'm happy to see you, Mr. Pokorny.

POKORNY: Where is he?

MAN: At the viaduct.

POKORNY: Has he jumped yet?

MAN: No. He seems to be afraid—

POKORNY: Afraid? Perhaps I should have another word with him—

MAN: (*Afraid.*) Don't do that!

POKORNY: But I will! And if it costs me a thousand years—it's worth it! After all, you were one of the victims too! You were on that train! Just remember how we woke up and the night went on for ever!

MAN: That's true.

POKORNY: So there you are. I hope they won't catch him before he does it.—

MAN: (*Interrupts him.*) Quiet! (*He listens.*)

POKORNY: (*Listens too.*) I hear him coming—

MAN: Here he is. (*Silence.*)

POKORNY: He's thinking that a viaduct is quite high but not high enough to finish the job—

MAN: He's wondering whether it's better to throw himself in front of the train—

POKORNY: The surest way—(*Hudetz enters slowly from left. The Maintenance Man directs his light towards him. He is taken aback and stops.*)

MAN: Good evening, station master! (*Hudetz stares at him, terrified.*) I'm just checking that the track is all right—(*Hudetz sees Pokorny and wants to turn back quickly.*)

POKORNY: Stop! (*Hudetz stops.*)

MAN: Mr. Pokorny only wants a word with you, station master—

POKORNY: (*Bows slightly.*) I am the engine driver Pokorny.

MAN: Don't go, we're not going to give you away.

HUDETZ: (*Afraid.*) Who's that?

POKORNY: I was the driver of the 9:05 Express, the train that crashed here. Why are you staring at me like that? Do you think that you can't speak to the dead? You can, but only if the dead want to—(*He laughs.*)

MAN: (*Smiling.*) That makes you think, doesn't it?

HUDETZ: (*Shouts to the Man.*) Turn that lamp round so that I can see your face!

MAN: (*Quietly.*) I haven't got a face. (*The wind howls sounding like distant trumpets. Hudetz listens.*)

POKORNY: (*Cheerfully, but not without malice, to the Man.*) Look how frightened he is—mind you he has every reason, because it's his fault that I am no more.

HUDETZ: (*Interrupting him.*) No, not my fault.

POKORNY: (*Coming slower.*) So you want to escape justice here on earth—quite right too! What sort of a life can you expect? A life sentence at best. (*Silence.*)

HUDETZ: You are saying my own thoughts out loud—but my thoughts go even further than that.

POKORNY: (*Puzzled.*) Further than that?

HUDETZ: Yes. You see, I am really innocent—and if I am to be judged I would like to go before the highest court straight away. If there is a God, He will understand me—

POKORNY: (*Grins.*) I'm sure of that. (*Sound of wind as before. Hudetz listens uncomfortably. Anna enters slowly from the right and stops.*)

HUDETZ: (*Sees her, horrified.*) Anna! (*Silence.*)

ANNA: (*Looking at Hudetz with big eyes.*) There was a signal you—

POKORNY: (*Interrupts her.*) It was your fault, miss, yours and no one else's.

MAN: Is that true?

ANNA: (*Reciting, like something she has learnt by heart.*) He forgot about the signal because I kissed him, but I wouldn't have kissed him if he hadn't had a wife whom he had never loved—

POKORNY: (*Interrupts her.*) What has that to do with it?

ANNA: (*Looking at Hudetz.*) I can't lie any more.

HUDETZ: (*Angrily.*) As if I had invented lying. (*Silence.*)

ANNA: (*With her eyes fixed on Hudetz.*) Do you remember when I asked you at the viaduct: Do you recognize me?

HUDETZ: (*Softly.*) Yes.

ANNA: You did recognize me.

HUDETZ: (*Unsure.*) I don't know.

ANNA: But I know. Because you embraced me in the same way as then.

HUDETZ: When?

ANNA: As that time when we went away together. Heaven was like a strict angel, we heard the words and were afraid to understand them—oh, so afraid—times were hard, do you remember? By the sweat of our brow—

HUDETZ: (*Interrupts her.*) It was your fault! Who was it who said to me: Take all! Take all!

ANNA: I did.

HUDETZ: And what did I do?

ANNA: (*Smiles.*) You've killed me so often and will kill me so many more times that it doesn't hurt any more.

HUDETZ: Are you enjoying it then? (*Anna shudders and stares at him. The signal bell rings and the signal changes to green.*)

MAN: The train will be here soon.

POKORNY: It's usually late.

MAN: That's right, because it has to wait for the connection—

HUDETZ: Where are we? Oh, peaceful, very peaceful! You know, like a quiet country inn at dusk—and outside there is snow, and all you hear is the clock—for ever and ever—and you sit there reading your paper and drinking your beer, and you never get a bill—

HUDETZ: (*Smiles.*) Really?

POKORNY: And we often play cards and everybody wins—or everybody loses, according to what he prefers. In a way you are pleased not to be alive. (*The 9:05 Express approaches. Everybody listens. Pokorny quietly to Hudetz so that Anna cannot hear.*) There's your train—(*Hudetz turns slowly towards the line.*)

ANNA: (*Suddenly screams at him, horrified.*) No! What are you doing?

POKORNY: (*To Anna.*) Don't interfere!

HUDETZ: (*To Anna.*) I'm meeting my friend Pokorny.

POKORNY: We'll play cards.

ANNA: Cards?

HUDETZ: Yes, there's snow outside but inside there's a fire and it's warm—

ANNA: (*To Hudetz.*) There's no fire and it's not warm. Don't believe him. He only wants to get his own back, because he's no longer alive.

POKORNY: (*To Anna.*) Be quiet!

ANNA: (*To Hudetz.*) I won't be quiet. Believe me, it's dreadful where we are! Stay alive, stay alive!

POKORNY: (*To Hudetz.*) Don't listen to her! The train's coming!

ANNA: (*Suddenly clings to Hudetz.*) Stay alive, stay alive! (*She screams.*) Officer! (*The 9:05 Express passes by, thundering and whistling—there is complete darkness. When it becomes lighter Hudetz is standing by the side of the railway line. Left foreground the Policeman, Landlord, Ferdinand and Alfons. All the others have become invisible.*)

ALFONS: Thomas!

HUDETZ: (*Slowly going towards Policeman.*) Officer, here I am.

POLICEMAN: In the name of the law.

HUDETZ: (*To Alfons.*) I've thought it over—(*Smiles at him.*)

LANDLORD: (*His hand on his heart.*) At last! It's the gallows next—the gallows—

HUDETZ: Maybe. The main thing is not to find yourself guilty or not guilty— (*He smiles.*)

FERDINAND: (*Screams suddenly.*) Handcuff him, handcuff him!

HUDETZ: No need for that.

FERDINAND: What nerve! Just you wait, I'll beat the daylights out of you— (*Wants to attack him.*)

ALFONS: Stop! Do me a favor and leave him in peace!

HUDETZ: (*To Alfons.*) Thanks.

POLICEMAN: (*To Hudetz.*) Come on—(*Sound of wind as before.*)

HUDETZ: (*Listens.*) Quiet! (*He listens.*) Weren't those trumpets?
ALFONS: It was only the wind.
HUDETZ: (*Nods and smiles at Alfons.*) Don't you believe that—

END

Faith, Hope and Charity

a satire on throwing the book at petty criminals

translated by
Paul Foster and Richard Dixon

AUTHOR'S NOTE:

In February 1932, on a stopover in Munich, I met a friend, Lukas Kristl, who's been a court reporter for some years. He said to me, "I don't understand dramatists. When they dramatize a crime, why do they prefer only capital crimes which are seldom committed? Dramatists almost never bother with the small crimes which we see committed a thousand times more often all over the country. The facts in these cases are almost always wrapped in tantalizing mystery and are similar in many ways to those crimes which carry a penalty of life in prison or a penalty of death."

Kristl told me of a case out of his own experience. From this ordinary case I developed my little dance of death, *Faith, Hope and Charity*. The characters of Elisabeth, the Cop, the Judge's Wife and the Head Undertaker were personally known by Kristl. So you see, I have to thank him, not only for his telling of the story, but also for his encouragement.

Kristl's intention was to write a play about the legal traps which ensnare the little guy, the hooks baited with the fine print of the law dangled by certain bureaucrats. The fine print, of course, is in every system which society has ever created, but Kristl hoped that the little guy would get a little more compassion in the future.

This was my intention too. This attack against the letter of the law gave me the material to show once more the larger stuggle between the Individual and Society, this eternal battle which will never end. If there is a cease-fire, beware, for it will be only a life-threatening deception.

As in all my plays, I've made it a point with this little dance of death, to focus on man's animal instincts. If his acts are brave or meek, if his choices are fight or flight, it's up to the animal instinct in him to choose the action. Good and evil don't enter into it at all.

I haven't improved on anything, but then I haven't made facts any worse than they really are, either. Emotional responses can be faked. Anyone can beg for sympathy to win you over to their side. It's easy to parody this glib sentiment. I avoid parody simply because it's not an accurate mirror of emotions.

I've always tried to set lies and stupidity up on a tee and give them a good whack, and, I assume, I've convinced myself that I'm being terribly noble to fuss so much over people's foibles. Well, it won't hurt any of us to be set up now and then for some self-examination and a hard squint at ourselves.

Faith, Hope and Charity could be the title of any of my plays, for any one of them this biblical epigram could fit:

"And the Lord smelled a sweet savour; and the Lord said in his heart, I will not again curse the ground anymore for man's sake; for the imagination of man's heart *is* evil from his youth; neither will I again smite anymore every thing living, as I have done.

"While the earth remaineth, seedtime and harvest, and cold and heat, and summer and winter, and day and night shall not cease."

Genesis, 8:21-22

CHARACTERS:

Elisabeth
Cop
Undertaker
Head Undertaker
Baron
Assistant Undertaker
Miss Prantl
Wife
Invalid
Worker's Wife
Accountant
Maria
Detective
Precinct Judge
Chief Inspector
Second Cop
Third Cop
Bookkeeper
Joachim

FIRST TABLEAU

SCENE 1

(*Spring. The milky glass windows of the Anatomical Institute. Elisabeth paces in front of them. She wants to go in, but looks up and down the street once more. In the distance an orchestra plays Chopin's* Trauermarch. *A young Cop walks past Elisabeth slowly. He doesn't notice her.*)

SCENE 2

ELISABETH: (*She walks to the Cop. The music dies away.*) Excuse me, I'm looking for the Anatom . . .
COP: The Anatomical Institute?
ELISABETH: Where they cut up the cadavers.
COP: This is it.
ELISABETH: Aha, so this is where they do it.
COP: Better watch out. In there they put the heads all in a row.
ELISABETH: I'm not afraid of the dead.
COP: Me neither!
ELISABETH: Nothing's scared me in a long time.
COP: Well, in that case I guess you can take care of yourself. (*He salutes her and exits.*)

SCENE 3

(*Elisabeth tosses her head at the departing Cop and braces herself to ring the bell. An Undertaker in a white coat comes to the door and stares at her. She's indecisive.*)

SCENE 4

UNDERTAKER: And what can I do for you, my pretty?
ELISABETH: I want to talk to somebody in charge.

UNDERTAKER: What business could you have here?

ELISABETH: Urgent business.

UNDERTAKER: Do we have a body that belongs to you?

ELISABETH: There's only one body that belongs to me. I'm wearing it.

UNDERTAKER: You sure are, and it's a perfect fit.

ELISABETH: Look, are you one of the guys in charge here?

UNDERTAKER: You might say I am. I prepare the bodies. Come on, you can tell me, what's this all about?

ELISABETH: (She waits a minute.) Somebody told me you could sell your body here.

UNDERTAKER: I say, I say, I say, look, my pretty, this is a respectable place . . .

ELISABETH: Take it easy! I mean sell it after it's dead. (He's disappointed.) Then they bring my body here so it can serve science, or whatever they serve in here. It's not such a bad deal. I get paid to use it while I'm still alive, and they get it when I'm done. It's like I'm selling it but then I rent it back.

UNDERTAKER: How'd you hear of all this?

ELISABETH: Let's say it was brought to my attention.

UNDERTAKER: Who brought it to your attention?

ELISABETH: Let's say a friend.

UNDERTAKER: Oh, yeah? Well, let's say I'd like to know just what you do for a living.

ELISABETH: You would, huh? Let's say I don't do anything for a living.

UNDERTAKER: So, let's say you don't have a job.

ELISABETH: Yeah, let's say, you could say, but I don't let it get me down.

UNDERTAKER: Selling your body . . . what'll they think of next?

ELISABETH: I haven't a clue. I can't think there's much more than that.

UNDERTAKER: And I think you are the victim of a diabolically clever deception. (He feeds the pigeons birdseed. The pigeons perch on his shoulders and eat out of his hand.)

SCENE 5

(The Head Undertaker enters from the Anatomical Institute with a stiffly formal Baron who holds a funeral wreath.)

HEAD UNDERTAKER: It will be done quickly, Herr Baron, and again my deepest sympathy.

BARON: Thank you. I can only blame myself.

HEAD UNDERTAKER: But the court has cleared Herr Baron of any of those groundless charges against him and proved conclusively that we are all in God's hands.

BARON: I was at Verdun and the Somme in 1915, but nothing shook me so much as that accident yesterday. We were only married three months, and I was at the wheel of the car at the fateful curve between Lechbruch and Steingarden. Ah, well, at least her corpse will serve science.

HEAD UNDERTAKER: (*He sees the Undertaker.*) Excuse me a moment, Herr Baron. (*To the Undertaker, very loudly.*) Idiot! You're out here feeding the pigeons again?! It's a pigsty in there. Fingers and throats lying around. Two hearts sliding around in the sink, and what the hell is that old liver doing in the corner?! There will be order in there, mein Herr, order or else. Now get busy and file that stuff away, schnell!

UNDERTAKER: Yes, sir, but this woman wants to sell her corpse.

HEAD UNDERTAKER: Her corpse?! Not again.

BARON: Sell her corpse, that's incredible.

HEAD UNDERTAKER: We've said it time and time again, but people just don't believe it. We do not buy cadavers. Never. Why do some people think that the governments will just give them money for their bodies? Why? It's always what my country can do for *me*.

BARON: It's irresponsible to think that everything is the responsibility of the government.

HEAD UNDERTAKER: It won't always be like this, Herr Baron.

BARON: Let us hope not, mein Herr. This kind of thinking leads to drastic action on the part of superiors in charge.

SCENE 6

(*The Assistant Undertaker suddenly enters with the hat of the Head Undertaker.*)

ASSISTANT UNDERTAKER: Telephone, sir.

HEAD UNDERTAKER: Who? For me?

ASSISTANT UNDERTAKER: It concerns your testimony in the Leopoldine Hachinger case from Brünn, sir. You are to go at once to the clinic, and Professor . . . (*He hands the hat to the Head Undertaker.*)

HEAD UNDERTAKER: Right away! (*He quickly takes off his white coat and gives it to the Assistant Undertaker who disappears again into the Institute. To the Baron.*) Excuse me, Herr Baron. It seems that the authorities cannot figure out how this Sudeten-German died. Well, duty calls!

BARON: Oh, of course. Mustn't keep the authorities waiting.

HEAD UNDERTAKER: And once again, my deepest sympathy.

BARON: Thank you.

HEAD UNDERTAKER: Now, if you will excuse me please, Herr Baron. (*Exits stage right.*)

BARON: Goodbye. (*Slowly exits stage left. In the background a few bars of Chopin's Trauermarch. It slowly begins to be twilight.*)

SCENE 7

UNDERTAKER: (*Watching the Baron leave.*) A bad man. Ahh, the poor pigeons. Believe me, Miss, the best thing for them is to just jump out of the window and die.

ELISABETH: Oh, come now, you're a friendly man for an undertaker.

UNDERTAKER: Let me be frank with you, miss. Who would buy a corpse today?

ELISABETH: Maybe they will tomorrow.

UNDERTAKER: It won't be any different tomorrow.

ELISABETH: I don't believe that.

UNDERTAKER: Whom can you believe? Do you think that maybe you're going to . . .

ELISABETH: (*Smiles.*) No, I won't take that sour diagnosis. My luck will get better. Look, suppose I had just sold my body for a hundred and fifty marks . . .

UNDERTAKER: A hundred and fifty marks!?

ELISABETH: Yes.

UNDERTAKER: (*He smiles and is silent.*) Child . . .

ELISABETH: Yes?

UNDERTAKER: What does your father do?

ELISABETH: Inspector.

UNDERTAKER: An Inspector! Well, that's something.

ELISABETH: But he can't help me to get back on my feet because my mother passed away in March and there were so many expenses with the funeral.

UNDERTAKER: Well, still, what's a lowly Head Undertaker compared to an Inspector?

ELISABETH: If I just had a hundred and fifty marks then I could get my vending license. The world would open its doors again, because I could get a self-supporting job in my old line of work that I gave up because of the hard times.

UNDERTAKER: What was your old line of work?

ELISABETH: I sold girdles, corsets and brassieres wholesale.

UNDERTAKER: Interesting, very interesting.

ELISABETH: (*Silence.*) Ahh, whatever happened to the affluence of yesterday?

UNDERTAKER: (*Silence. He searches through his wallet and takes out a photo.*) Here, look at this.

ELISABETH: (*She looks at the photo.*) A nice dog.

UNDERTAKER: It's my Doberman.

ELISABETH: He looks alert.

UNDERTAKER: And smart! But he's dead, unfortunately.

ELISABETH: That's too bad.

UNDERTAKER: (*Whistles.*) That's how I used to call him. (*He talks to the photo.*) Burschi, Burschi, you're gone now, and your romping days are over. (*He puts the photo back.*) I'm glad that you share my feelings for Burschi. What's your name?

ELISABETH: Elisabeth.

UNDERTAKER: The Empress of Austria. Now that was a great lady. But she was assassinated in Geneva. The League of Nations had something to do with it. Vicious! You know, I have a butterfly collection and a canary, and yesterday a cat followed me home. Are you interested in aquariums?

ELISABETH: Am I interested in what?

UNDERTAKER: I have a terrarium too.

ELISABETH: Oh, well, that's better.

UNDERTAKER: Then you must come and visit me, my little Fraulein-Inspector's-Daughter.

ELISABETH: Hmmm, maybe.

SCENE 8

(*The Head Undertaker comes out of the clinic. His index finger is bandaged. He is surprised to see the Undertaker. He glares at him. Elisabeth and the Undertaker slowly move away.*)

SCENE 9

(*The Head Undertaker sneaks up behind the Undertaker and stops right behind him. He shouts.*)

HEAD UNDERTAKER: Aha! Caught you! Feeding the pigeons again, right? Am I right? Of course, I'm right! (*To Elisabeth.*) Look, you, why don't you beat it? Understand?!

ELISABETH: Alright, alright . . . if that's how you want it. (*She exits.*)

SCENE 10

HEAD UNDERTAKER: (*He watches until Elisabeth leaves.*) This is a fine way to run a business. I told you to make a catalogue of the tumors, but instead you spend your time out here getting steamed-up over Lili Marlene. Nice. Don't you like tumors, mein Herr?

UNDERTAKER: You're mistaken, sir. That young lady is the daughter of an impoverished Customs Inspector.

HEAD UNDERTAKER: Don't make me laugh, a Customs Inspector. Hah! Look, I'm laughing.

UNDERTAKER: Sir, if this Customs Inspector's daughter only had one hundred and fifty marks she could get her very own vending license and the world would open its doors to her again. I realize that you think I'm inept, sir, because I have an aquarium and because I feed pigeons and because I have a soft heart and . . .

HEAD UNDERTAKER: Oh, get to the point!

UNDERTAKER: The point is, sir, that I'm going to take this pretty Customs In-spector's daughter under my wing. That is my resolution. Only a hundred and fifty marks.

HEAD UNDERTAKER: A hundred and fifty marks! That's a very big wing, mein Herr.

UNDERTAKER: I believe the young lady will pay me back, sir.

HEAD UNDERTAKER: Sure, and I believe elephants can fly, Herr Rothschild. Hah! I told you, don't make me laugh! If you were my wife, I would beat and beat you, and I would beat you some more. I'd beat some sense into that sponge you call a brain. (*He threatens him with his thickly bandaged index finger.*)

UNDERTAKER: Of, sir, what happened? Did you cut your finger?

HEAD UNDERTAKER: (*Petulant.*) It's infected.

UNDERTAKER: Oh, sir, not from one of the cadavers?

HEAD UNDERTAKER: (*Pouting, babyish.*) Yes . . . from one of them, from that bad cadaver in Brünn.

UNDERTAKER: No! Now you ought to be more careful, sir.

HEAD UNDERTAKER: It doesn't hurt, not much anyway. That can be suspicious.

UNDERTAKER: Could be. When I look at my collection of butterflies, I always think that there's somebody up there who makes certain things happen.

HEAD UNDERTAKER: Get to the point. Come on, get to work. (*They go inside.*)

SECOND TABLEAU

SCENE 1

(*The office of Irene Prantl & Company. Miss Prantl sits at her desk, busy with paperwork. On the other side of her desk sits the wife of the precinct jugde. In the background are mannequins with corsets, girdles and brassieres. They are lined up like the heads in the Anatomical Institute.*)

PRANTL: Congratulations! That's seven girdles, six corsets and eleven pairs of garters in only three days. That's better than a career saleswoman. You've got a real talent for sales.

WIFE: We have a wide circle of business friends. They wouldn't dare refuse the wife of a precinct judge.

PRANTL: You're too modest. Selling in these hard times isn't easy. People will just slam the door right in your face.

WIFE: If anybody asks you, of course, you say that I'm selling just to use my spare time. Tell them it's my hobby, understand?

PRANTL: Of course! Would Macy's tell Gimbels?

WIFE: Listen, my husband makes only 600 marks as it is, and they're laying off everybody, judges, government lawyers, everybody. These are hard times, so, when the going gets tough, the tough sell girdles. Right? (*The telephone rings.*)

PRANTL: (*On the telephone.*) Alright, tell her to come in. One second, please. Alright, Madam, we're all set now.

SCENE 2

(*Elisabeth enters.*)

PRANTL: Come in, Elisabeth. Let's take a look at your order book.

ELISABETH: (*Gives her the order book.*) Here you are, Miss Prantl.

PRANTL: (*Looks through the book.*) A pair of garters, one girdle and one corset.

Why, that's nothing!

ELISABETH: Selling in these hard times isn't easy. People just slam the door in your face.

PRANTL: Oh, come off it with the excuses. It's your job to give customers a sense of beauty. Everybody goes to the gym these days. Naked women are everyplace you look, and that's why our products should sell . . . if you have *any* talent at all. You've got to get to the men. It's men who appreciate the naughty little teasers we sell. Tell me, what happened in Kaufbeurgen?

ELISABETH: Nothing happened in Kaufbeuren.

PRANTL: What do you mean, nothing happened in Kaufbeuren? Corsets and Kaufberen go together. Kaufbeuren's the kitchy-koo capital of the country!

ELISABETH: I didn't go to Kaufbeuren.

PRANTL: Would you listen to this? She didn't go to Kaufbeuren.

ELISABETH: I tried to save time, so I went by car, but the fuel line was on the fritz and I had to spend the night in a shed in the woods.

PRANTL: I don't believe this. Who *could* believe this? (*Yelling at her.*) The woods?! Do you mean to tell me after I advanced you one hundred and fifty marks to get a vending license that instead of selling a hot territory like Kaufbeuren, you spend the night in the woods?! With your system you won't pay me back until the Messiah comes!

ELISABETH: I . . . I couldn't help it. It was an act of God!

PRANTL: Listen to me, sweetheart, and listen good. The business of Irene Prantl and Company cannot afford the luxury of your peculiar sales method. I don't know what you're doing in the woodshed, but believe me, it ain't an act of God!

ELISABETH: I couldn't help it. My hands were tied. It wasn't my fault.

PRANTL: I told you, I don't want to know what kinky things you do in that woodshed, so don't give me that little Miss Act-of-God story. Look at the judge's wife. She doesn't even need the job and look at the turnover she does. Four times yours! Four times!

SCENE 3

(*The enraged Undertaker rushes in. At once, he shouts at Elisabeth.*)

UNDERTAKER: Here you are, you little cheat! You little liar! Your father's not a Customs Inspector at all. If you told me in the beginning that he wasn't a customs inspector instead of only an insurance inspector, do you think I would have gotten you this job?!

ELISABETH: I never said that he was . . .

UNDERTAKER: You certainly did!

ELISABETH: I did not.

UNDERTAKER: (*He slams his cane on Miss Prantl's desk and the papers fall all over.*)

Customs Inspector, hah! Customs Inspector, double hah! Customs Inspector, triple hah!

PRANTL: (*Trying to catch her papers.*) Wait a minute! Wait a minute!

UNDERTAKER: (*He bows to Prantl and the judge's wife.*) Ladies, excuse me for roaring in like a madman, but compared to an Insurance Inspector, even a crummy Head Undertaker is higher in the pecking order. This hustler tricked me out of my hard-earned money . . .

ELISABETH: That's not true!

PRANTL: Quiet!

UNDERTAKER: Quiet!

PRANTL: (*Poking her with her finger.*) Now, young lady, whenever anybody raises her voice, she's usually in the wrong!

UNDERTAKER: (*Fairly screaming.*) You bet she's in the wrong!

ELISABETH: (*Silence for a moment.*) Alright, I won't say another word.

UNDERTAKER: That would suit you just fine, wouldn't it?

PRANTL: Please sit down, sir.

UNDERTAKER: Thanks. People like me, I like people, but when somebody lies to me I lose control.

ELISABETH: I didn't tell a lie.

PRANTL: Will you be quiet, young lady! (*Offers the Undertaker a cigarette.*)

UNDERTAKER: Thank you. (*He lights up and relaxes.*) Well now, ladies, this . . . person comes to my apartment, worms her way into my confidence and I, ah . . . show her my aquarium. I even lend her a book on Tibet, and then I buy her an expensive vending license. Then I sort of ask around, just curiosity, you understand, but I bought her the license. You see, people always laugh at me. I'm a soft touch, I'm a sucker for a hard luck story. Then I find out her father is not Customs Inspector at all!

PRANTL: Wait a minute, just a minute. A vending license? She got that from me.

UNDERTAKER: What?! She took you too!?

PRANTL: That's common in this business. The company pays for the license and the employee works off the debt. A hundred and fifty marks.

UNDERTAKER: (*Blows up.*) A hundred and fifty marks!

PRANTL: (*Silence. Then taps her finger on the desk.*) Honey, that's fraud.

ELISABETH: No, no, I'm not a swindler, I'll work it off.

WIFE: That's not how it works, my dear. The real question is, does the evidence *suggest* a fraud. Guilt, innocence, a mere piffle. I mean, otherwise, the whole legal system would come to a grinding halt. I wouldn't want that, would you?

PRANTL: No, I wouldn't, would you?

UNDERTAKER: No, I wouldn't, would you?

WIFE: It's really none of my business, even though my husband is a judge, but you did buy your license with this gentleman's money. Why, I can hear my August on the bench now, "Taking money under false pretenses is intent to fraud."

UNDERTAKER: (*As though already in the witness box.*) I'm just a poor undertaker who tried to do a good deed . . .

ELISABETH: You'll get your money back, don't worry.

UNDERTAKER: I don't think so.

ELISABETH: Yes, you will. All of it.

UNDERTAKER: When?

ELISABETH: I'll work it off. I didn't lie to you.

PRANTL: (*Reads from Elisabeth's order book.*) How're you gonna do that? Not with these orders. (*Reads.*) Two pairs of garters, one girdle, a corset, and one Act of God.

UNDERTAKER: She's a fraud! Give me my money back right now!

ELISABETH: I don't have it now.

PRANTL: But you got your license from me!

ELISABETH: That's right.

UNDERTAKER: Well, then, where's my money?

ELISABETH: I needed your money for something more urgent.

PRANTL: What could be more urgent than him?

ELISABETH: Me. I used the money to pay a fine.

UNDERTAKER: So! You're an old hand at having trouble with the law. You're a second offender. Well, this time you're going in the slammer. I was your last victim, my pretty. (*He exits quickly.*)

SCENE 4

PRANTL: Now that's what I call an honest man.

WIFE: If he testifies about all this with the Customs and Insurance Inspector, you'll be convicted for sure.

PRANTL: You mean, prison?

WIFE: It'll only be a reformatory, you know, minimum security. About ten days.

ELISABETH: Now everybody will say that I'm a big criminal.

PRANTL: Well, you can't blame them, can you? You didn't even tell us you're a second offender.

ELISABETH: I don't have to tell you that!

PRANTL: Of course, you didn't. As far as the public is concerned you're as pure . . . as pure as the driven slush! You're fired, but you're going to stay right here until the police come for you. (*She exits.*)

SCENE 5

WIFE: Of course, I'm not a judge . . . but I am a judge's wife, and from where I sit, which is right behind the judge, I would say that a second offense is serious business.

ELISABETH: (*She speaks like a little girl.*) They fined me 150 marks for working without a vending license. It was supposed to be in installments, but it all came due at one time. If they sent me to jail, I'd be all washed up. So, I took the Undertaker's money and paid the fine.

WIFE: Now, listen to me, my girl. Don't deny anything and don't think you can outsmart the judge. My husband is patient, but don't let your defense get too drawn out. Have some consideration for us. I sit home and wait for him, but he's stuck in court with case after case and all he can think about is lunch. Just because you're accused and might go to jail, doesn't mean you can't have a little consideration, you know. After all, the judge is only human.

THIRD TABLEAU

SCENE 1

(*A small garden in front of the Welfare Office with people: Elisabeth, a worker's wife, an older accountant, a young woman named Maria. Elisabeth leans on the garden fence and suns herself in the afternoon sun. An invalid hobbles out of the office.*)

INVALID: Great! Now they tell me in the Welfare Office that I don't belong in their department, that I have to go to another office. That's what we get for letting the government take over our lives.
WORKER'S WIFE: You have to go to the Invalid's Benefits Office.
INVALID: The Invalid's Benefits Office told me I'm not their problem. I should go to the Vocational Association. The Vocational Association says that my feet were in bad shape before the accident. I had varicose veins and flat feet. Their lawyer told me I couldn't't've walked without my cane a long time ago if I really wanted to.
ACCOUNTANT: Did you go to the Special Claims Office?
INVALID: They told me the Vocational Association dropped my benefits from sixty percent to forty percent. They decided I couldn't get more than that because when I worked I couldn't get any more than forty percent.

SCENE 3

(*Everything is still. A Cop goes by very slowly and doesn't notice anybody. Gradually it becomes twilight.*)

SCENE 4

WORKER'S WIFE: (*She watches the Cop.*) The big General.
ACCOUNTANT: Give us this day our daily bread.
MARIA: I wish He would.
INVALID: You'd be happy with just bread?
MARIA: You bet I would. I've got seven mouths to feed and the eighth is on the

way. But since my father brings home forty marks a week, they take more out of my check.

INVALID: You'd think they could run the country without your help.

ELISABETH: They didn't want to give me anything either because my father works too.

ACCOUNTANT: What's your father do?

ELISABETH: He's an insurance claims inspector. (*She laughs.*)

WORKER'S WIFE: Why're you laughing, you jerk? (*Elizabeth stops laughing.*) Go home.

ELISABETH: No!

WORKER'S WIFE: It's your own fault. She's got an inspector for a father.

ELISABETH: He's an insurance claims inspector!

WORKER'S WIFE: Same difference, sister!

ELISABETH: (*Smiles.*) It is?

ACCOUNTANT: She just went up in the world.

WORKER'S WIFE: You've got a home, that's more than most. Why don't you go to it.

ELISABETH: I've got a good reason for not going home right now.

WORKER'S WIFE: You do? Do you have a job?! (*Silence.*)

ACCOUNTANT: All that glitters is not gold. (*He exits.*)

SCENE 5

MARIA: Look, just let it be for now.

ELISABETH: I don't want to talk about it anymore.

SCENE 6

INVALID: (*Counting to himself.*) The Welfare Office, the Employment Office, the Vocational Association, the Invalid Benefits Office, The Special Claims Office . . . oh, shit, if all of this comes through, I'll be a millionaire in a pauper's grave.

SCENE 7

WORKER'S WIFE: Don't spend the money yet. I'm betting on the pauper's grave for you, lover. (*Exits.*)

SCENE 8

MARIA: Have they got anything?

ELISABETH: Nothing.

MARIA: They closed for a while, didn't they. (*Elisabeth is quiet.*) Oh, you can tell me! If they get me for dishing them, so what? You can always get caught for something and you never know what you're caught for. They threw my father in jail for ten days because he swiped some boards from a construction site. They were just lying there, and it was raining in, right on our bed, so . . . I say, if you're gonna steal, don't bother taking a few boards, steal the whole damn house. (*Elisabeth sits quietly. It is now dark. The two women sit alone on the edge of the garden fence in the light that comes out of the Welfare Office windows.*)

MARIA: Are you married?

ELISABETH: No. (*Silence.*) When I was born, my father was so mad that I was a girl. He's held it against me ever since. He wanted a boy so he could, you know, puff himself out. The big macho honcho. My mother just let him get away with it, but she should have busted him in the head with a frying pan before she died to wake him up.

MARIA: You haven't met the right guy yet?

ELISABETH: Maybe I have, and maybe I haven't.

MARIA: He'll come along when you're not thinking about it.

ELISABETH: (*Silence, then.*) Out of ten thousand men, there's at least one who understands.

MARIA: You think so.

ELISABETH: I want to be independent, my own person.

MARIA: That's tough to do. (*Silence.*) I wouldn't mind being asked to get married, long as he doesn't beat me. Where're you working now.

ELISABETH: No place.

MARIA: (*Silence.*) What're we doing? We could call each other by our first names. They can't forbid that.

ELISABETH: I guess so.

MARIA: (*Silence. She gets up.*) Come on, Elisabeth. Look, there's a guy sitting over there. He's good for a sandwich, come on.

ELISABETH: I'm not going to start that.

MARIA: (*Silence.*) You're not? Why not?!

ELISABETH: Principle, that's why!

MARIA: Principle?! Principle!? What's that, something between starvation and suicide?!

SCENE 9

(*The Baron enters with the funeral wreath. He is tired and bitter. Maria sees him and stares at him, fascinated.*)

SCENE 10

BARON: (*Exaggerated chivalry.*) Ahh, guten abend, Madonna! I was afraid that you wouldn't appear.

MARIA: Me? Sure I would. It's a matter of . . . "principle."

BARON: (*Silence. He recognizes Elisabeth.*) Ah! (*He takes off his hat and smiles maliciously.*)

MARIA: You two've met before, I guess. That's my luck. They always prefer the mysterious ones.

BARON: Yes, she is mysterious. She wanted to sell her valuable corpse.

MARIA: Her corpse?

BARON: (*He pats his limp wreath a bit.*) Yes, but that was in better times. I still had my consulting firm then.

ELISABETH: (*She smiles at him.*) For corsets, maybe?

BARON: No. Liquers. Ah, but now I'm down on my luck.

MARIA: (*Checks herself out in her pocket mirror by the light that comes out of the Welfare Office windows.*) Hugo, do you notice anything different about me?

BARON: Well, let me see . . . off-hand, I'd say . . .

MARIA: Look. (*She shows him her teeth.*) Since yesterday I've had two new caps in front. Both of those teeth were broken off and all black. The nerve was dead.

BARON: (*Smiles cunningly.*) Yes, what a smile, like sunshine after a storm.

MARIA: Thanks. I thought you'd like it.

SCENE 11

(*A police detective enters behind Maria who is still checking out her front teeth in her pocket mirror. The Baron fades back, and the detective waits for Maria to turn around. She seems him in her mirror and is startled.*)

SCENE 12

DETECTIVE: You come with me. You know why.

MARIA: (*Quietly.*) I don't know what you mean.

BARON: What about my shirt studs?

MARIA: (*Silence, then quietly.*) Do you believe this?

BARON: Well, someone stole them.

DETECTIVE: Police're involved now. Come along.

MARIA: (*Stares at the Baron.*) For a couple of shirt studs I'll have a police record!

DETECTIVE: I told you to be quiet and come along.

MARIA: And to think I loaned you my last three marks.

DETECTIVE: I told you to button it up, sister.

BARON: I am always at your service, liebchen! (*He exits.*)

MARIA: You pig!

DETECTIVE: (*He snaps handcuffs on her.*) Let's go. (*Exits, pushing her off.*)

MARIA: Ouch!

SCENE 13

(*The Cop hears Maria shout. He comes running onstage. He stops short when he sees Elisabeth. They stare.*)

SCENE 14

COP: Hellow, hellow, hellow. What's going on here?

ELISABETH: (*A perfectly evil smile.*) Oh, nothing at all. A woman was just handcuffed and dragged off to prison for nothing. Nothing at all.

COP: Impossible.

ELISABETH: Impossible? Said the little Dutch boy when he pulled his finger out of the dyke. (*Silence.*) Why're you looking at me like that?

COP: (*Smiles, really a smirk.*) Is it against the law?

ELISABETH: (*Silence.*) Well, since you're the law, I must be talking to an echo.

COP: (*Silence.*) You know, you remind me of someone. The way you're standing like that. We used to be lovers. But she's dead now.

ELISABETH: Whew, are you weird!

COP: (*Silence.*) Where're you headed?

ELISABETH: Why? You wanna head me off at the pass?

COP: Well, I am off duty.

ELISABETH: Oh yeah, well I'm on duty.

COP: What's the matter? Don't you like cops?

ELISABETH: Me? I don't like rat poison. I don't like gangrene. I don't like lung cancer, but cops? How do I know you don't just want to . . . blow me away?

COP: There have to be cops. There's some of the rapist and some of the murderer in everybody.

ELISABETH: Not in this body there ain't.

COP: Are you sure?

ELISABETH: No, I'm not sure. But then I'm not sure that a brick falling off a building won't feel as soft as a pussy cat either.

COP: (*Smiles.*) You're acting guilty already.

ELISABETH: Seen through your eyes I'm sure I'm guilty of a lot of things.

COP: Maybe you're not. Don't give up hope.

ELISABETH: That's your style. Take a homely old saying and give it a new twist, a new hook.

COP: (*Silence.*) If you don't have faith, hope and charity, there's just no reason for living. Everything links up sooner or later, doesn't it?

ELISABETH: How would you know? You've got a steady job. I could starve.

COP: We all have to die sometime.

ELISABETH: Thanks. Are you trying to make love to me?

COP: (*Silence.*) Listen, you little fool! I've watched you walk up and down, up and down with that walk of yours. For days I've watched you stalking in

front of the welfare office. You . . . remind me of someone who's dead now
. . . I loved her and . . .

ELISABETH: Who was she?

COP: A girl. I was going to marry her. (*Silence.*) We were like one heart and soul.
But she had problems with her liver and . . . Why are you laughing?

ELISABETH: Mister, the sphinx would laugh at that line.

COP: (*Silence.*) You're bitter.

ELISABETH: What do you want, I lead a fast life.

COP: Oh yeah, I'm pretty fast myself. (*In the distance a shot is fired, then another
and another. Someone moans. Silence as the Cop listens.*) Did you hear that? The
street gangs are at it again. You can't let them out of their cages. I'm gonna
have a look. I'll be back. Wait for me . . . please?

ELISABETH: Sure, what else have I got to do? (*The Cop exits stage right.*)

SCENE 15

(*The Wife and then the Precinct Judge enter stage left.*)

WIFE: August, I told you to come on! Now go in that welfare office and tell
whoever runs it that he has to make an appointment if he wants to see you.
You're going to start spending more time with me or else!

JUDGE: Oh, I don't like going to the movies. Two hours without a cigar, liebchen.

WIFE: Don't call me liebchen! Smoking's bad for your lungs.

JUDGE: The doctor warned me about them only yesterday, my little snitzel . . .

WIFE: Don't call me a snitzel! He warned me too. He said I shouldn't climb stairs
with my swollen glands.

JUDGE: Then why do you have to sell those tight corsets? It's ridiculous, poop-
sie!

WIFE: Watch it! I sell corsets so I don't have to beg you for every penny I get, my
little dumpling!

JUDGE: Don't call me a dumpling! You don't know what real poverty is. Day in
and day out I have to sentence those poor people and put them in the slammer because they don't have a roof over their heads, my little blockhead!

WIFE: Who're you calling a blockhead, blockhead?! Then if I were you, I just
wouldn't sentence them at all.

JUDGE: (*Shocked.*) Hermine! Have you gone crazy? (*Silence.*) I'll go and tell the
Welfare head we won't be playing cards tonight. I'll tell him I want to spend
a romantic evening with my little honeypot. (*Exiting into the welfare office.*)
God, I hope it's not going to be another one of those schticky musicals.

SCENE 16

(*The Judge's Wife notices Elizabeth. They stare at each other. Elisabeth just turns around and stalks back and forth but the Wife is not about to be snubbed.*)

SCENE 17

WIFE: Just one moment, Fraulein. Don't we know each other?
ELISABETH: (*She looks around, frightened.*) Sure we do, but please act as if we don't.
WIFE: You don't have to worry about me. How much time did you get?
ELISABETH: Fourteen days.
WIFE: There, you see?! What did I tell you?!
ELISABETH: But no suspended sentence.
WIFE: Nothing at all?
ELISABETH: No, I was already fined once before. (*Grins.*) If I only knew what I did wrong.
WIFE: You don't have to tell me about injustice. I'm pretty close to the source of it. Since then, I don't suppose that you found another job.
ELISABETH: No, but I just met a man who told me about his lover who died. (*She smiles again.*) Who knows how my fortunes could change.
WIFE: The best thing you could do now is to get married.
ELISABETH: (*Without expression.*) I wouldn't say no.
WIFE: Well, I'm in there pushing for you.
ELISABETH: Funny, how he and I just met by accident.
WIFE: A love affair can start any place. The birds, the bees, the bunny rabbits, you know. They don't need an ocean cruise with moonlight and full orchestra. No, not the birds, the bees and the bunny rabbits. They do it anyplace . . . in the park, on the ground, up in the trees.
ELISABETH: It could be the biggest coincidence in my whole life.
WIFE: What does he do, the bridegroom-in-waiting?
ELISABETH: Civil servant.
WIFE: Civil servant? Not bad. Does he know about the "fourteen days."
ELISABETH: No, and I ain't gonna tell him either.
WIFE: Hmm. You really ought to. It might eventually damage his career.
ELISABETH: Oh, come on.
WIFE: No, really, it could happen.
ELISABETH: There he is. He's coming back again.
WIFE: What?! A cop! Well, God, couldn't you do a little better than that? (*She moves away.*)

SCENE 18

COP: (*Enters.*) They shot an innocent bystander. Today, you've got to wear armor plate just to go shopping. (*Sees the Judge's Wife.*) Say . . . what's she want with you?

ELISABETH: How should I know. Never saw her before.

COP: She's looking at us.

ELISABETH: I'm sure she thinks we're somebody else.

COP: I'd never confuse people for somebody else. I'm trained that way. And it's tough training too.

ELISABETH: Like a bloodhound, right? And kept on a tight leash.

COP: Are you cold? You're shivering.

ELISABETH: Yes.

COP: Very cold?

ELISABETH: Well, pretty cold.

COP: I'd offer you my coat, but it's against regulations.

ELISABETH: (*Smiles.*) And your coat is always on-duty.

COP: I'm trained that way, and . . .

ELISABETH: . . . and it's tough training. Let's go somewhere, it's drafty here.

SCENE 19

(*The Judge comes out of the welfare office.*)

WIFE: August, look! That's the girl. You remember the case of fraud with the Insurance Inspector and the Customs Official?

JUDGE: What're you talking about?

WIFE: Don't you remember? You sentenced her to . . .

JUDGE: I don't remember.

WIFE: (*Silence.*) It wasn't right that you didn't give her a suspended sentence.

JUDGE: (*Angrily.*) Hermine, mind your own injustices and you'll have enough to keep you busy!

FOURTH TABLEAU

SCENE 1

(*Elisabeth's furnished room. The Cop lies in bed in his shorts and takes a nap. Elisabeth makes coffee and looks at the autumn asters in a vase by the alcohol stove. Outside, the October sun is shining, but the blinds have been lowered down halfway. The scene is a pleasant picture of two people relaxed after hours in bed together.*)

SCENE 2

ELISABETH: (*She reaches over the white asters.*) How fresh these still are, after five days. At first, I didn't think you would buy me white asters.

COP: Something told me to.

ELISABETH: Yes, but still . . .

COP: Maybe you thought that a handsome, dashing police officer would come empty-handed? Maybe you thought he'd like only women with lots of loot? Wrong. I like a woman to depend on me, not the other way around. Do I still get a kiss?

ELISABETH: Yes.

COP: Is the coffee almost ready?

ELISABETH: In a minute. (*He takes the earphones from the night table and puts them on and hums the* Radetzky March *on the radio.*) Yesterday they played *Aida* on the radio, Alfons.

COP: (*Puts the earphones back on the table.*) Then you didn't miss me at all.

ELISABETH: Oh, Alfons!

COP: Do I still get a kiss?

ELISABETH: Here, you can have coffee now, and here is your kiss. (*She gives him coffee and kisses him lightly, then sits on the edge of the bed.*)

COP: (*Sipping from his cup.*) I'm so glad the elections are over, and there's no more emergency duty. Last night they shot another buddy of mine.

ELISABETH: A lot of good people believe those elections will change things.

COP: But you can't have violent changes in a country based on law and order.

ELISABETH: I can understand that some violent things have to happen just to get even a little change.

COP: Aha, she likes it when I talk about big issues. What else do you like about me?

ELISABETH: Most things.

COP: How would you describe me if you had to?

ELISABETH: I don't know.

COP: Go on, just one word.

ELISABETH: Hmm, you've changed a little. You used to be . . . well, sadder.

COP: What do you mean?

ELISABETH: Kind of melancholy.

COP: I'm still like that. (*He laughs.*) That's supposed to be funny.

ELISABETH: Excuse me. (*She gets up.*)

COP: Now where're you going. Just don't bind up how you feel.

ELISABETH: "Bind up." What a funny word. It's like "girdle."

COP: Say, are you alright?

ELISABETH: (*Silence. She smiles.*) I'm just a little nervous today. (*She exits.*)

SCENE 3

COP: (*He sits alone.*) Sad? What's she mean by that?

SCENE 4

(*Elisabeth enters again.*)

COP: Well, that took a long time.

ELISABETH: Long?

COP: Not too long.

ELISABETH: What do you want to say?

COP: I was keeping track.

ELISABETH: Oh, I see.

SCENE 5

(*There is a knock at the door. The two lovers listen. Then, there is another knock. This time, it's louder and more forceful.*)

COP: No one's home!

ELISABETH: Who do you think it is?

SCENE 6

VOICE: (*From outside the door.*) Police!

ELISABETH: Oh, my God!

COP: Police?! And me lying here . . . of all the . . . (*He quickly grabs his clothes and hides in the closet.*)

SCENE 7

(*The knocks at the door become more forceful. Elisabeth opens the door and a man enters the furnished room. It is a Chief Inspector of the Vice Squad.*)

SCENE 8

CHIEF: Ah, my patience is rewarded at last. (*He looks around and points to the un-made bed.*) Have I disturbed your nap?

ELISABETH: Why?

CHIEF: I think you know why, don't you?

ELISABETH: I wasn't feeling well.

CHIEF: I see. And some people have night duty and have to sleep during the day.

ELISABETH: What do you mean?

CHIEF: (*He holds up Alfons's stocking hung over the chair.*) Do women wear men's stockings these days?

ELISABETH: (*Silence.*) What do you want from me?

CHIEF: You received an advance from the Police Commission that you find *legitimate* employment within three weeks. But, you don't have any job and you have shown that you don't really intend to get one.

ELISABETH: Why don't you worry about those people who don't have a roof over their heads?

CHIEF: Your sympathy is touching. It is not against the law to be without a roof over your head, it is only against the law when, beneath that roof, you en-danger the public order.

ELISABETH: I have not endangered the public order.

CHIEF: As long as you cannot tell us how you get the rest of your money . . . it leaves open a legitimate question about your legitimate employment.

ELISABETH: I'm well taken care of.

CHIEF: That is exactly why we are here, Fraulein.

ELISABETH: I've already told you. I get twenty marks a week from my fiancé. I live off that.

CHIEF: And just who is this fiancé? (*Silence.*) So you won't tell us his name?

ELISABETH: No. I won't.

CHIEF: And why not?

ELISABETH: Because it will harm his career.

CHIEF: (*Smiles.*) That is indubitably correct. It is also very funny because I am wondering how many fiancés you need to collect twenty marks.

ELISABETH: You have a rotten mind.

CHIEF: You must excuse me if I am a trifle indiscreet. (*He yanks open the closet door and is not surprised to find a man inside, but when he sees it is a police officer in his shorts and cap, he is surprised.*)

SCENE 9

(*The Cop stands at attention in the closet.*)

CHEIF: What are you doing here?!

COP: Everything she told you is true, Inspector.

CHIEF: (*Silence. To Elisabeth.*) Please leave us alone. (*Elisabeth hesitates.*)

COP: Please.

ELISABETH: Excuse me. (*She exits.*)

SCENE 10

CHIEF: So! This is where you spend your off-duty time.

COP: (*He dresses quickly.*) If you'll let me explain, Inspector, it's not what it looks like.

CHIEF: Not what it looks like? Man, how did you get involved with this woman. We suspect her of being a, uh, businesswoman.

COP: Businesswoman?

CHIEF: Of course.

COP: (*Silence. He smiles.*) Oh, no, Inspector.

CHIEF: Do you know her at all?

COP: Of course I do.

CHIEF: And you want to marry her?

COP: I intend to, Inspector.

CHIEF: How old are you?

COP: Twenty-four, Inspector.

CHIEF: Same old story.

COP: (*Now completely dressed.*) It's true about the twenty marks, Inspector.

CHIEF: And you with only eighty marks a month. That's not very much.

COP: My folks help me out, sir.

CHIEF: What does your father do?

COP: He's a carpenter, sir.

CHIEF: You should have become a carpenter too.

COP: I don't understand, sir.

CHIEF: (*Silence.*) I'm sorry to have to tell you this, but you don't seem to realize just who it is you're going to marry. She's served time for fraud.

COP: She spent time in jail?

CHIEF: For fraud. Plus she was fined once before that. She's trying to establish connections with the police. It won't look good on your record.

COP: I had no idea!

CHIEF: There, you see? (*He opens the door and motions Elisabeth to come in.*) You may come in now.

SCENE 11

(*Elisabeth enters.*)

COP: (*Silence.*) Fraud? Is that true?

ELISABETH: Well, it's all out in the open.

COP: Jail?

ELISABETH: Yes. (*Silence.*)

COP: Elisabeth, why didn't you tell me about this?

ELISABETH: Don't be so stupid. (*Silence.*)

COP: (*Snapping to attention.*) Thank you very much, Inspector!

CHIEF: No need to thank me. (*Cop salutes and makes a motion to go.*)

ELISABETH: Wait! (*Silence.*)

COP: You lied to me, and that's all I need. That decides it.

ELISABETH: No, your career, that decides it.

COP: Oh no . . . but duty comes first and then nothing after it . . . nothing at all.

ELISABETH: (*Silence.*) Alfons, when you were in the closet, I wanted to protect you.

COP: Me?

ELISABETH: Us.

COP: Yourself! Just you against me. I'm not a total fool. My eyes are open now. (*Silence.*)

ELISABETH: (*Smiles sadly.*) I just didn't want to lose you, Alfons.

COP: (*Salutes again.*) Inspector! (*Exits quickly.*)

SCENE 12

CHIEF: It wasn't necessary for you to endanger the career of that young man so thoughtlessly . . .

ELISABETH: What about my career?

CHIEF: You aren't still insisting on your innocence, are you?

ELISABETH: Oh no, I got rid of that habit a long time ago. Excuse me, but I just have to laugh. (*She sits on the edge of the bed and laughs silently.*)

CHIEF: Laugh about it now, while you still can. (*Exit.*)

FIFTH TABLEAU

SCENE 1

(*Police station, after midnight. The Cop plays chess with a Second Cop. It is raining outside and in the background an orchestra plays* Trauermarch *of Chopin. The music continues until Scene 3.*)

SCENE 2

COP: (*Listening.*) Who's that playing?
SECOND COP: It's a radio.
COP: After midnight?
SECOND COP: Maybe it's from America. It's still daytime there. Your move.
COP: Just a minute. (*Silence. The Cop moves the rook.*)
SECOND COP: (*Deliberating.*) If I go here, then he'll move there. If I go over there, then he'll move here. It was dark that night and the moon shone bright, when, like lightning, the ship of state moved out of the harbor gate . . . and check!
COP: Not you too! (*Silence.*) Whose turn?
SECOND COP: You always have to ask. (*Silence.*)
COP: (*Standing up.*) I give up. Checkmate.
SECOND COP: Checkmate? In this position?
COP: It's not worth it. I'm finished.
SECOND COP: Look, move your knight here, and it's no problem!
COP: It might work.

SCENE 3

SECOND COP: (*Still looking at the chessboard.*) That you could give up now, when before you played every game to the bitter end . . . even when it was hopeless for you.
COP: I think I might be sick. When I go to bed I can't sleep, and when I get up, I

can't stay awake.

SECOND COP: It's nerves.

COP: (*Smiles painfully.*) I've just had a bad experience.

SECOND COP: On duty?

COP: No, a personal matter. A woman. You do everything for her, you show her your best side, you spend your free time with her, your money, you'd lay down your life for her—and what does it get you? In the end you lose anyway.

SECOND COP: Most broads are ingrains. (*Silence.*) I think I mean ingrates. Yeah, I think I do.

COP: All I can do is think about her.

SECOND COP: You eat yourself up doing that. Better you should eat her up.

COP: The first girl I really loved, died. Then I found her. Yeah, my first girl dies and my second lies. Somebody up there likes to dump on me. Maybe there's nobody for me after all.

SCENE 4

(*A Third Cop enters the station. He brings the Undertaker who is drunk. Trailing behind is the Assistant Undertaker, and he's drunk too.*)

THIRD COP: So! Here we are.

ASSISTANT UNDERTAKER: Officer . . . May I say something . . .

THIRD COP: Quiet. (*To the other two cops.*) Disturbing the peace and insulting an officer.

ASSISTANT UNDERTAKER: Who said he insulted an officer?

THIRD COP: Didn't he yell out to the whole neighborhood and bang his cane on the store shutters and wake everybody up? Didn't he call me an old buffalo, a wheezing old walrus? Or am I deaf too?

ASSISTANT UNDERTAKER: (*Silence.*) We were just going to celebrate his six-ty-second birthday. Quietly of course. Well, that's fate for you.

SECOND COP: (*Smiles.*) Oh, fate is it now?

UNDERTAKER: It's the Head Undertaker's fault, I guess.

THIRD COP: Sssh! (*Points to chessboard.*) Who won?

SECOND COP: I did.

THIRD COP: You won? Against him? Impossible!

COP: I'm not up to my usual form today.

UNDERTAKER: The Head Undertaker hates me!

THIRD COP: All right, pipe down.

SECOND COP: What about the Head Undertaker?

ASSISTANT UNDERTAKER: Look, I'm the Assistant Undertaker, and he's the Head Undertaker. He was promoted last month, but when he drinks he forgets his promotion. The Head Undertaker before him died from an infection from a corpse in Brünn.

THIRD COP: That's enough out of you. Sit down. Where's the report?!

SCENE 5

(*The Bookkeeper rushes in.*)

BOOKKEEPER: Help! Officer, there's a young woman lying out in the street near the canal!

SECOND COP: Near the canal!

THIRD COP: What kind of a young woman?

BOOKKEEPER: She attempted suicide. A daring young man dove into the water, swam out to her and pulled her to shore. I think she's still alive. There she is.

SCENE 6

(*Two men, one in a tuxedo, enter with the daring young swimmer. They carry Elisabeth in. She is dripping wet. They place her on a bench. Joachim, the daring young swimmer, is soaked. One Cop hands him a blenket which he throws around himself. All, except the Undertaker, gather around Elisabeth. Alfons, her Cop, recognizes her and stares at her.*)

BOOKKEEPER: There's still a spark of life . . .

THIRD COP: Quick, artificial respiration.

ASSISTANT UNDERTAKER: I know her. Let me help. I studied medicine for a year.

SECOND COP: Quick! Quick!

UNDERTAKER: Get some whiskey!

JOACHIM: Get some for me, too!

UNDERTAKER: (*To Joachim.*) You were brave to jump into the water on a dark night in November! You're a hero!

JOACHIM: I did what anybody else would have done. (*He drinks from the whiskey bottle.*)

UNDERTAKER: You're much too modest! (*He takes the bottle and turns to the Cop.*) Am I right, General?

COP: I'm not a General.

UNDERTAKER: A toast to the hero, this young swimmer! Toast! (*He drinks.*)

JOACHIM: (*To Alfons.*) I was walking past and heard a splash. I looked into the water and saw a silvery reflection. It was her face. At once, I jumped in and swam toward her. It was my duty, that's all. Anyone would've done it, even you.

COP: Sure.

UNDERTAKER: It'll make all the papers. With pictures. Long live the daring young swimmer! Hip-hip-hooray! (*He drinks again.*)

THIRD COP: (*At Elisabeth's side.*) Where's the whiskey?

UNDERTAKER: Here.

JOACHIM: (*To the Cop.*) Can I use your phone?

COP: Sure, it's over there.

SECOND COP: She's got no ID on her. Only an invalid vending license.

UNDERTAKER: Vending license?

SECOND COP: Yeah. (*Undertaker turns to Elisabeth and scrutinizes her very carefully.*)

SCENE 7

(*While everyone, except for Alfons and the two men, who have left the station now, busies himself around Elisabeth with artifical respiration, Joachim telephones his mother.*)

JOACHIM: Hellow, mom? Is that you, mom? No, nothing's wrong. I just saved this girl's life. She tried to drown herself. Pretty brave, huh? It was my duty. It'll be in all the papers, with pictures. It'll be in every edition! Do I get the motorcycle now? But, mom, you promised! Bye, mom. (*Hangs up angrily.*) The old camel!

SCENE 8

COP: Is she dead?

SECOND COP: I think she's still breathing.

ASSISTANT UNDERTAKER: We'll see. Give it time.

SCENE 9

UNDERTAKER: (*He recognizes her at last.*) It's her. I'm sure of it. The same one who . . . (*He turns to the Cop.*) The public prosecutor . . .

COP: (*Interrupts him.*) Leave me alone!

UNDERTAKER: You have to make time for me, officer. I have a confession. This young lady was murdered.

COP: Murdered?

UNDERTAKER: And I know the murderer.

COP: What are you talking about, man?

UNDERTAKER: (*Silence.*) It's got to do with a Customs Inspector and an Insurance Inspector. I was wrong, officer. So, an eye for an eye, and a tooth for a tooth. You'd better arrest me and get it over with. I killed her.

ASSISTANT UNDERTAKER: Laying it on a bit thick, ain't he?

COP: (*To Undertaker.*) You son-of-a-bitch!

UNDERTAKER: (*Sitting in a corner.*) I'll have to pay for what I did. I can see it now . . . I climb the scaffold. In full control I say, "Hangman, do your duty!" Don't anybody weep for me, just make sure none of you are tempted to do the same thing. Think of what it costs me. My life! (*He buries his head in his hands.*)

SCENE 10

THIRD COP: She's coming to!

SCENE 11

(*Elisabeth slowly becomes conscious, but still distant. She sits on the bench and looks around, dazed. Gradually, she starts to realize where she is.*)

SCENE 12

ELISABETH: (*To Bookkeeper.*) Who are you?
THIRD COP: (*Silence. He holds the bottle to her.*) Here, drink now.
ELISABETH: (*Staring at the Bookkeeper.*) Who are you?
ASSISTANT UNDERTAKER: (*To the Bookeeper.*) Why don't you tell her?
BOOKKEEPER: Me, I'm nobody.
ELISABETH: (*She smiles sadly.*) He's nobody. How sad. (*She looks around the room anxiously.*) Am I still alive?
SECOND COP: Of course you are.
THIRD COP: Here, take a drink.
ELISABETH: (*She stares horrified at the Second Cop.*) What are you wearing?!
SECOND COP: My uniform . . .
ELISABETH: Green, grey, silver. Do you people have me in your clutches again? What new crime did I commit?
THIRD COP: There, there, take it easy. We're here to help you.
ELISABETH: (*Distant.*)! Who breathed on me just now?
SECOND COP: Come on, snap out of it. Nothing's as bad as it seems. Certainly not bad enough to jump in a canal about.
ELISABETH: Did you people pull me out?
JOACHIM: I did.
ELISABETH: (*Silence.*) You shouldn't have bothered.
JOACHIM: And that's the thanks I get.
ELISABETH: I'd be gone now if you didn't interfere. But now it's just the same as always. Nobody's responsible for me, and I still don't have any reason to live.
ASSISTANT UNDERTAKER: (*He touches her shoulder.*) Don't give up hope. Everybody's got a reason to live. If not for yourself, then for others.

ELISABETH: I don't.

ASSISTANT UNDERTAKER: Yes, you do.

ELISABETH: No.

ASSISTANT UNDERTAKER: (*To Second Cop.*) It drives me to despair when someone talks like that. My work is around the dead, so automatically I think
about the reasons for living. As an Assistant Undertaker . . .

ELISABETH: You're the Assistant Undertaker? (*Shrilly.*) How's the other undertaker? Does he still feed the pigeons?

SCENE 13

UNDERTAKER: Yes. (*He rises full of self-importance, swaying a bit.*) The pigeons
perch on my shoulders and eat out of my hand; the canary sings, and I have
tamed my wild snake. I have a cage full of white mice and my three goldfish
are named Anton, Joseph and Herbert. And I must ask you all for a little
more respect, if you please. It is apparently still not clear who I am. I am the
Head Undertaker, if you please. And if I do take a person's life, then I have
already cleared it ahead of time with myself. With myself and with my God!
Officers, gentlemen, good day. (*He exits grandly.*)

ALL: (*Everyone except Elisabeth clicks their heels and salutes.*) Good day, Sir!

SCENE 14

(*Elisabeth sees her Cop for the first time. She raises herself up and bites her hand.*)

ASSISTANT UNDERTAKER: Now, now, now! Stop that.

BOOKKEEPER: (*Silence.*) She's hallucinating.

JOACHIM: To jump into ice-cold water in the middle of night at this time of
year, well, that's just not a piffle, you know.

ELISABETH: (*Raising her hand slowly over her eyes.*) Is that you, Alfons?

SECOND COP: (*Silence.*) Do you know each other, Klostermeyer?

ELISABETH: Do we know each other? (*Silence.*) Tell them if we know each other.

COP: We know each other.

ELISABETH: (*Smiles.*) Good, good . . . what about your career?

THIRD COP: (*To Alfons.*) What's all this?

COP: Later.

ELISABETH: Why later?

COP: (*Silence. He puts on his white gloves.*) I'm on duty now. I've got to march in
the parade.

ELISABETH: Oh, the parade.

COP: In front of town hall. It'll be daylight soon.

ELISABETH: It's still pitch dark, Alfons.

COP: It's over between us.

ELISABETH: You think so, do you?

COP: It is over, I said.

ELISABETH: (*Silence.*) And you think you can leave just like that?

COP: Don't try to talk anymore.

ELISABETH: (*An angry smile.*) And why not?

COP: (*Silence.*) Look, this is no place to talk about it. Am I to blame that your past caught up with you? I offered you a helping hand.

ELISABETH: Your helping hand should be cut off. (*Silence.*) I'm going to go now. Do you hear me, Alfons?

THIRD COP: (*Standing in front of the door.*) Hold it.

ELISABETH: (*Surprised.*) Good night.

THIRD COP: You're not going anyplace.

ELISABETH: (*Silence.*) Let me go.

THIRD COP: Where do you think you're going?

ELISABETH: That's no concern of yours.

THIRD COP: We cannot allow you to go anyplace . . . in your condition, of course.

ELISABETH: (*Smiles sadly.*) So. You have me once again.

SECOND COP: Not arrest, mind you, just protective custody.

ELISABETH: Ah, lovely word. It sounds so warm and cozy.

THIRD COP: For your own good.

ELISABETH: Sure. (*She smiles weakly.*) With this many people standing around you'd think you might manage to get somebody a vending license.

ASSISTANT UNDERTAKER: My child . . .

ELISABETH: I'm not talking about myself, I'm talking about things more important than me. (*Angrily, she turns to her Cop.*) You don't have to stare at me! Oh, I could just knock you senseless, knock those eyes right out of your head! Do you think I jumped into the water because of you?! You're a conceited ass! I jumped in that water because I didn't have anything to eat. And if I did have something to eat, do you think I'd take the time to spit on you?! Don't look at me like that! (*She throws the bottle at his face and misses.*)

SECOND COP: Hey, watch it, sister!

ELISABETH: Let me go!

THIRD COP: Calm down!

JOACHIM: Oww, damn. She bit me.

ASSISTANT UNDERTAKER: Oh, so you bite do you? (*Elisabeth retreats timidly.*)

BOOKKEEPER: Now she's biting the hand that saved her life. (*Elisabeth bares her teeth, cornered.*)

SCENE 15

(*In the distance a parade formation marches by to the accompaniment of the march* Ich hatt' einen Kamaraden. *As the music dies away, Elisabeth sits sunken, ex-*

hausted in a chair.)

SCENE 16

COP: That's my parade. (*He puts on his helmet.*)

SECOND COP: We still have time, Klostermeyer. Wait for us. (*He puts on his white gloves.*)

THIRD COP: We have to go, too.

ASSISTANT UNDERTAKER: What's that noise?

BOOKKEEPER: Her stomach is growling, you fool.

THIRD COP: (*To Second Cop.*) Don't you have anything for her to eat?

SECOND COP: Maybe. (*He reaches into his coat pocket and brings out a roll. He gives it to Elisabeth. She takes it apathetically and chews it a bit.*)

THIRD COP: (*He puts on his gloves.*) There. How's that taste? (*Elisabeth smiles weakly. Suddenly she lets the roll fall from her hand and collapses on the table.*)

ASSISTANT UNDERTAKER: Oh, my, oh, my, oh, my.

THIRD COP: Hold it right there! (*He and the Assistant Undertaker help her.*)

SECOND COP: She only fainted.

BOOKKEEPER: I'll bet she hasn't had anything to eat in a long time.

ASSISTANT UNDERTAKER: Or she has a weak heart.

BOOKKEEPER: Whatever it is, she dropped like she had been hit.

JOACHIM: To jump into ice cold water in the dead of night in November, well, it's not just a piffle, you know. Hey, is anybody listening?

ASSISTANT UNDERTAKER: Take it easy now. Keep quiet.

ELISABETH: (*She wakes and smiles weakly.*) Could I speak with someone in charge?

THIRD COP: Someone in charge?

ELISABETH: It's urgent business. They say things could get worse, but I don't let it get me down. (*She brushes away imaginary flies.*) Oh, why are all these black worms flying about so? (*She dies quietly.*)

SCENE 17

BOOKKEEPER: (*He knocks softly on the table.*) Can you hear me? Miss? Miss?

THIRD COP: I fear the worst. (*Her Cop takes off his helmet.*)

ASSISTANT UNDERTAKER: She couldn't take the strain. Her heart. Well, we'll take a look at her tomorrow.

JOACHIM: It was all for nothing. (*He exits.*)

SCENE 18

COP: For nothing. (*He runs his fingers through her hair.*) I never have any luck, I just don't.

BOOKKEEPER:
  I'll live until I don't know when,
  And I'll die, but until then
  I'll wander from dawn to dawn
  It surprises me, but I still go on. (*He exits.*)

SCENE 19

ASSISTANT UNDERTAKER: A poet.
THIRD COP: It's still raining.
SECOND COP: The parade'll be rained out.
COP: Yeah.
ASSISTANT UNDERTAKER: If you gentlemen will excuse me. (*He exits.*)

SCENE 20

(*A formation marches past outside to the time, Ich hatt' einen Kamaraden. The three policemen put on their helmets and leave the police station to go back to the parade ground. Only her Cop looks back at his beloved Elisabeth.*)

END

Figaro Gets a Divorce

a comedy in three acts

translated by Roger Downey

TRANSLATOR'S NOTE:

Horváth was himself an émigré when he wrote *Figaro Gets a Divorce*, and its first public performance took place in shortened form and under very modest conditions in 1937, under the auspices of a German-language cultural society in Prague, Czechoslovakia. He died in Paris in 1938, and no full-scale production of the play took place until 1960.

The standard published text comprises only nine of the play's thirteen scenes. A few lines from the four omitted scenes were incorporated, presumably by the author or with his consent, into the nine-scene version. In addition there is a lengthy additional passage providing an alternative ending for one of the nine scenes of the published text. There are also a number of indications (notably the letter dropped by Susanna in Act II, Scene 1, of which we never hear again) that the play never was edited in detail during the author's lifetime.

Hence there can be no question of a "definitive" version of the piece; and until the translation has been through the testing process of rehearsal and performance, it would be unwise of me to attempt by cutting or conflation to produce a "performing version." With the exception of the variant ending to Act II, Scene 4 (included as an appendix), this translation is the available published text of the play in its appropriate chronological order. Overlappings and repetitions between scenes are indicated where they occur by footnotes. Notes also indicate which scenes were omitted in the nine-scene version of the play. Words and phrases added by the translator for clarification are indicated by brackets [ ].

A final word of caution: Horváth's texts are sprinkled with carefully-notated "silences" and "pauses." These should be seen as the equivalent of phrase and breath markings in a musical score: certainly not as fermatas or double-bars. Horváth's dialogue is full of the subtle hesitations and accelerations produced in human speech by the parallel but not always harmonious progress of thought and articulation. The labeled pauses and silences are only the most prominent.

The same caution applies to his differentiation in stage directions between "smile" and "grin," "interrupting" and "cutting off." These too are only indications of the precise emotional tone of the moments they accompany, and are always colored by their environment. Any rigidity in their interpretation is antithetical to the spirit of this most graceful and musical of playwrights.

CHARACTERS:

Count Almaviva
Countess Almaviva
Figaro, formerly a barber (of Seville), now a valet to Count Almaviva
Susanna, Figaro's wife, chambermaid to Countess Almaviva
Cherubino, nightclub owner, formerly a page to Count Almaviva
Forester
Midwife
Antonio, former gardener to Count Almaviva
Pedrillo, former stableboy to Count Almaviva
Barberina, Antonio's daughter, Pedrillo's wife
Border guards, shopkeepers, barbershop customers, foundlings, citizens of Haggelburg.

TIME: "Some time after the marriage of Figaro"

SETTING: Europe, in the 1930s.

ACT I

SCENE 1

(*Deep in the forest on the frontier. Count Almaviva, the Countess, Figaro and Susanna flee from the Revolution. One hears only their voices, as it is a pitch-dark night.*)

COUNTESS: Where are you?

COUNT: Here.

COUNTESS: I can't see a thing.

COUNT: This is the blackest night of my life. (*Susanna emits a short scream.*)

FIGARO: What happened?

SUSANNA: I stepped on something soft.

COUNTESS: I hope there aren't snakes here.

SUSANNA: Heaven have mercy! (*The moon breaks wanly through the clouds; [and] now one can see the fugitives.*)

COUNT: (*Looking upward; ironically.*) Our moon is on the rise.

COUNTESS: (*Looking about her.*) Do snakes bite at night, too? (*Susanna shudders fearfully.*)

FIGARO: [*To the Countess.*] Your Grace, with all respect, I beg you not to complicate the situation. It's complicated enough without snakes.

COUNT: We are in the hands of God.

SUSANNA: I'm covered with scratches from these bushes.

COUNTESS: And my clothes are in tatters . . . (*In the distance there is a shot.*)

SUSANNA: (*Fearfully.*) What was that?

FIGARO: A gunshot. But we're safe now.

COUNTESS: I have to rest . . . (*Sits on a [projecting] root.*)

COUNT: (*Softly and slowly to Figaro.*) Are you sure we've passed the frontier?

FIGARO: I know every clearing in these woods, your Grace. Lake on our right, ravine on our left: straight ahead is open country. The beloved Fatherland is that way — behind us.

COUNT: Let us hope so. In the last twenty-four hours I've asked myself over and over: why must I leave the land of my forefathers — in secret, like a common bandit running for his miserable life? What crime have I committed?

FIGARO: You're the Count of Almaviva: by right of birth and in the eyes of God you're custodian of the lands, peer of the realm. Isn't that crime enough, your Grace? (*He smiles ambiguously.*)

COUNT: The events of the past few days are incomprehensible. His Majesty murdered, the nobility put to flight, massacred, their estates plundered, the churches vandalized, the palaces looted. . . . A baker's helper is field marshal, a shoemaker is president! The ambassador to London is a petty clerk! Distinctions swept away, equal justice for all, prince or vagabond. Equal justice! How long can such injustice be maintained? It flies in the face of divine law. No one could have imagined such a thing.

FIGARO: Apart from those who made it happen. (*Count looks hard at him.*)

COUNTESS: (*Fearfully.*) I hear someone moving . . .

SUSANNA: Where? (*All listen.*)

COUNTESS: We're being followed.

FIGARO: There's no one there.

COUNT: One always hears footsteps in a forest at night.

SUSANNA: In autumn when the leaves are falling. (*Silence.*)

COUNT: (*To the Countess, tenderly.*) Come, we must keep going . . .

COUNTESS: (*Softly.*) I'd rather sleep.

COUNT: Here? On the bare earth? (*Countess gazes at him and hums a melancholy tune. Count covers his eyes with his hand.*)

FIGARO: (*To cheer the Countess up.*) Your Grace, I knew a man once the doctors had given up for dead. And he said: better a hunted animal above ground than a king beneath it. Better to sleep under heaven than go there. I swear, your Grace, the first village is no more than half an hour from here—I can smell it! Trust my instinct; my instinct is notorious!

COUNTESS: (*Laughs softly in spite of herself.*) My dear man, those instincts of yours, I must say . . .

SUSANNA: (*Interrupting, only to cheer her.*) Oh no, your Grace, I'd trust Figaro's instincts over anything! He's always making predictions, and everything that he predicts comes true.

COUNT: Oh? [Did he predict] the Revolution?

FIGARO: Predicting that required no special talent.

COUNT: (*Glaring at him.*) Indeed?

FIGARO: (*Avoiding an answer.*) All of us were deaf. Or blind.

SUSANNA: I see a light! There! (*All gaze in that direction.*)

COUNT: I see nothing.

COUNTESS: Where is my lorgnette?

FIGARO: It's true! A light! I can see it clearly—it's a house for certain, your Grace!

COUNTESS: God be thanked! (*She rises.*) I was ready to believe I was in Hell, and Hell was filled with trees.

SCENE 2

(*Four hours later; it is a still night. In the border-patrol station, a mile beyond the Revolution. An office-like room with writing desk, cabinet, an iron bedstead, etc. Four border guards have night duty. The first sits at the desk reading a newspaper; he is the oldest. The second and third are playing chess, and the fourth lies on the bed smoking and lost in his own thoughts.*)

FIRST GUARD: We're getting reinforcements. (*Reads from the paper.*) "The sanguinary occurrences in our sister realm cannot be ignored. In consequence, the Royal Ministry of War has, with the full agreement of the Ministry for Internal Affairs, taken steps to reinforce the Border Patrols with units of the military. The action is deemed necessary not only to prevent entry to undesirable elements but also to minimize the influx of inflammatory and destabilizing propaganda." (*He looks up from his paper.*) "Minimize the influx"—they can try, anyway. But anyone tries to stop the inevitable unfolding of the world-historical process, they got *my* sympathy. (*Grins.*)

SECOND: Check! (*Third Guard captures a piece.*) Damn! I forgot about my king!

THIRD: Can't take your eyes off them kings.

FIRST: They got a first-class report from the scene in here about how the King was murdered. By an eyewitness. (*Reads.*) "He died like a king." What kind of crap is that? You're a king, you *die* like a king; it don't take no special effort! (*He looks up for confirmation, but gets no reaction.*)

THIRD: Check!

FOURTH: (*Suddenly, to First Guard.*) Hey: you know Kitty?

FIRST: (*Confused.*) Kitty who?

FOURTH: If you don't know her you wouldn't be interested. She's a barmaid at the Wild Indian.

FIRST: (*Angrily.*) Please, I don't want to know! (*Silence.*)

FOURTH: Kitty's got the longest legs I ever seen.

SECOND: That ain't all she's got.

THIRD: Mate!

SECOND: (*Jumps up.*) What?

FIRST: Comrades, I don't understand you any more! A new world is giving birth to itself a mile from here, a fundamentally significant hurricane of historical events is blowing down whole centuries of dead wood, and all you can do is play chess and worry about a barmaid's legs!

(*An officer enters. All four snap to attention and salute. Officer takes off his greatcoat and gloves and sits at the desk.*)

OFFICER: Report.

FIRST: Sir, nothing to report, Sir!

OFFICER: (*Signing forms.*) Has that rabble fired on us again?

FIRST: Sir, a few shots in the air, Sir! Just celebrating.

OFFICER: Murder is all that makes their kind happy. Cannibals! Nothing new?

FIRST: Sir: apprehension [of fugitives]. Four of them. (*Officer looks up in surprise*).

SECOND: I was on post over by the ravine and walked right into them: two men, two women.

OFFICER: Refugees?

SECOND: So they say. They were lost, walking in circles. The older woman was worn out.

THIRD: Ready to drop.

SECOND: No passports or papers on them.

FIRST: The older man resisted arrest, so we went by the book and searched them. The female claiming exhaustion had this on her. (*Hands the Officer a jewel case.*)

OFFICER: (*Opens the case.*) Wheeh! (*Looking at the string of pearls.*) Well, sergeant, if these are real, your refugees must be in the Blue Book.

SECOND: Or burglars.

THIRD: Without passports it's hard to tell which. (*First Guard chuckles.*)

OFFICER: (*Looks sharply at him.*) What was that? (*First Guard snaps to attention. Officer glares at him, shouts suddenly.*) Silence! (*A silence: to First Guard, almost softly*) Bring them in. All four.

FIRST: Sir!

OFFICER: Any of you gentlemen acquainted with a girl named Kitty?

FOURTH: Sir: Kitty who, sir?

OFFICER: Kitty is going to have a baby. She says the father is a border patrolman, but she can't recall which one. You're on notice, gentlemen: the situation is going to be regularized. (*Points in turn at Second and Third Guards.*) One. Way. (*Points at Fourth Guard.*) Or another. (*First Guard returns with the Count and Figaro. To First Guard.*) What about the two women?

COUNT: My wife is in no condition to see anyone.

OFFICER: (*Gapes; looks round uncertainly.*) Ah. (*To First Guard.*) What about the other one?

FIGARO: (*Stepping in front of the First Guard.*) The other one stayed in the cell to look after her Grace the Countess.

OFFICER: (*Gapes again.*) Countess?

FIRST: Looks to me like she's not faking, Sir. Lies on the floor and can't move.

OFFICER: Get the doctor.

FIRST: Sir! (*Exits.*)

COUNT: (*Ironically.*) I am indebted to you, sir.

OFFICER: Step forward. (*Count does so.*) Name?

COUNT: Count Almaviva.

OFFICER: Occupation?

COUNT: Knight Commander of the Empire. Chief of Diplomatic Service to his unhappy Majesty the King. Ambassador to London, Lisbon and Rome.

OFFICER: Please, be seated. (*Count doesn't move. Officer points to chair.*) Please.

COUNT: I protest. I escape from Hell thanking Heaven for my salvation and find myself treated like a criminal.

OFFICER: You crossed an interdicted border without permission and without papers of identity. I have to follow established procedure. If your violation proves to have been in the act of bare survival, you have nothing to fear.

COUNT: They would have beaten me to death.

OFFICER: I'm sure that's true.

COUNT: My country is ruled by animals.

OFFICER: Cannibals.

COUNT: (*Nods slightly in acknowledgement.*) As to my identity: please note that I have the honor and privilege of including among those few I call my friends the permanent Undersecretary [of your department]. I met him in London, where he was trade attaché. He will be happy to identify me at your convenience.

OFFICER: I'll put you in touch with the Undersecretary as soon as possible and you can arrange matters between you. As for your wife—her Grace—I'll see to it she's transported to the hospital as soon as the doctor has had a look at her. Now will you please take a seat? (*Smiles obligingly.*)

COUNT: Will you permit me to return to my wife's side?

OFFICER: Certainly, your Grace! (*Count bows slightly and returns to the cell. To Figaro.*) Step forward. Your name?

FIGARO: Figaro.

OFFICER: Occupation?

FIGARO: Personal valet to his Excellency the Count of Almaviva.

OFFICER: Born?

FIGARO: Hard to say.

OFFICER: Meaning what?

FIGARO: I was a foundling.

OFFICER: Age? Approximately.

FIGARO: No idea!

OFFICER: That won't do. You surely can recall some important event that would help you reconstruct your age.

FIGARO: If I figure my age by the important events of my life I come to the obviously faulty conclusion that I'm about three hundred—that's how much living I have behind me. Gypsies steal me before I'm old enough to recognize my parents, I run away—I'm no vagabond—I look around me, try to get ahead, wrestle with fate: the paths are closed, the doors are barred. I go hungry, get in trouble—stop me if you've heard this one—before I get my chance; I take on any job that comes my way: journalist, bartender, politician, gambler, proxy, barber, giving orders one day, taking them the next, hard-working because I have to be, ambitious because I'm too proud not to be, lazy if I ever get a chance to be. Orator when opportune, poet for relaxation, musician when convenient, lover on impulse. I saw it all, did it all, enjoyed it all, no more illusions, too enlightened for my own good—till I got married. That was the milestone of my life, the great divide, the turning point. When Figaro married, he turned into somebody else . . . (*The Officer pounds the table to halt the torrent of words.*)

OFFICER: (*Immeasurably astonished.*) That's enough! (*To the guards.*) Has he been drinking?

FIGARO: Yes.

OFFICER: (*Grimly.*) It's noticeable.

FIGARO: I haven't eaten for twenty-four hours, and since my fellow fugitives didn't feel up to drinking a toast to our arrest, I put away the brandy we had with us myself—for safekeeping, in case your men were thirsty.

OFFICER: (*Sighs in frustration.*) A comedian too! Wife's name?

FIGARO: Susanna. She's her Grace's chambermaid.

OFFICER: Aha.

FIGARO: We've been married six years already.

OFFICER: That's of no interest to me. (*First Guard returns with the doctor.*)

DOCTOR: Someone dead?

FIGARO: Not yet.

OFFICER: (*Has to smile.*) A sick woman's all we can offer you. Come with me please . . . (*Exits with Doctor.*)

FIGARO: One of you gentlemen got a cigarette?

FIRST: No smoking.

SECOND: Come on, he's no murderer! (*Tosses him a cigarette.*) There you go, comedian.

FIGARO: (*Catching it.*) Thank you, General. (*Lights up.*)

SECOND: (*To First Guard.*) He's just glad to be alive. (*A silence.*)

THIRD: Is everything as upside-down over your way as the newspapers say?

FIGARO: It's not so bad. They're only burning down castles and killing the gentry.

FIRST: You see? I knew all those atrocity stories were exaggerated!

SECOND: Is it true they fired all the border guards? Without pension?

FIGARO: Nothing but propaganda! The Customs Service goes right on as usual.

FIRST: [To the others.] See?

FOURTH: What about alimony? I read where they're going to have Free Love so you can have any woman you want—I was just wondering, who takes care of the children?

FIGARO: According to the [Manifesto of the Revolution]: the State.

SECOND: Jesus! We could use something like that!

FOURTH: That's some manifesto.

FIRST: It's population policy, that's what it is.

FIGARO: The whole relationship of man and woman is going to be different—according to the platform. Take my own case: my wife and I are always arguing about having children. I'm against it. When you're a chambermaid and valet who can be let go any time with two weeks's notice, when your very existence depends on your boss's mood, children are no blessing from heaven: more like criminal frivolity!

FIRST: (*To the others.*) Now see? The boss gets moody, and here's a solid citizen (*pointing at Figaro*) suspected of who knows, being a revolutionary courier or what, when all the time he hates what's going on and ran because . . .

FIGARO: (*Interrupting.*) Wait: I've got nothing against this revolution. How could I? I understand completely why it happened, I know from close up how much our former bosses have to answer for. The scars on my back let me know the thunderbolt was coming: I felt the twinges, saw the lightning in the clouds, prophesied it.

THIRD: So you flirted with the revolution, did you?

FIGARO: I never flirt. Why, gentlemen, you're looking at the first servant who ever told his master the truth. (*Silence.*)

FIRST: If you're such a big one for the truth, what're you doing here 'stead of over there? (*Grins.*)

FIGARO: The grounds were highly personal, gents. When my wife and I were talking, should we stay home or run along with them, she said: there's such a thing as loyalty. You don't just have obligations to yourself but to your fellow man, even if it's only your boss. If we could live with them in the good times, we had no right to leave them when their luck ran out . . . My wife's a person with a heart, you see.

FOURTH: So actually you only ran on account of your wife?

FIGARO: (*Looks up; hesitates; softly.*) Could be. (*Figaro is lost in thought. Silence.*)

SECOND: Sometimes I ask myself, why do there got to be two kinds of people, men and women?

THIRD: Ask God: maybe he knows.

FIRST: [*Pedantic as ever.*] There is no God.

FIGARO: (*Suddenly.*) Can I go talk to my wife?

FOURTH: Anytime you like.

FIGARO: Thanks. (*Starts to cell, runs into Susanna in the door coming out.*)

SUSANNA: *There* you are . . .

FIGARO: I was just coming to see you.

SUSANNA: (*Smiling.*) That's funny. I must have been thinking about you for five minutes.

FIGARO: And me about you. Telepathy . . . (*He grins slightly.*)

SUSANNA: Where have you been all this time?

FIGARO: Enjoying a chat with these gentlemen here.

SUSANNA: (*Smiles.*) I was beginning to think you'd gone and left me sitting.

FIGARO: No. How's the Countess?

SUSANNA: Bad.

FIGARO: What does the doctor say?

SUSANNA: Not a word. (*Silence.*)

FIGARO: She'll be better soon.

SUSANNA: I don't know how you can be so detached . . .

FIGARO: I'm just a little jumpy at the moment.

SUSANNA: The poor Countess: she can't relax at all. She's had an injection, but she still hears footsteps and thinks she's being followed . . .

FIRST: (*With a sigh.*) No one'll follow her here! We still got law and order.

SUSANNA: Thank God! I'm just glad to be over the border, it's like Hell over there! You can't picture what it's like there, gentlemen, not in your wildest dreams! Pure wickedness: robbery and murder and . . .

FIGARO: (*Interrupting.*) Now, now, don't exaggerate so much!

SUSANNA: (*Confused.*) Exaggerate! Me?

FIGARO: They're only doing what every revolution does. It's even logical: from the standpoint of the revolution, what they're doing is right.

SUSANNA: Right!

FIGARO: Right cuts two ways, depending on where you stand. Look at us: we could have stayed home and never turned a hair. Why, by now, I might have been appointed bailiff of the castle.

SUSANNA: (*Interrupting.*) Bailiff?

FIGARO: Why not? (*Silence.*)

SUSANNA: (*Staring at him.*) I've never heard you talk this way before . . .

FIGARO: (*Looks hard at her.*) Is that so? Have you forgotten?

SUSANNA: (*Looking almost fearfully around; softly.*) I have to get back to the Countess . . . (*Exits to cell. Silence.*)

FIRST: Tell me, Comrade: why do you suppose your lady wife reacts so different to the world-historic process than you?

FIGARO: (*Grins.*) She still believes in God.

SCENE 3

[Omitted from 1936 version.]

(*A few days later, in a foreign capital. A small but exclusive jewelry shop. A door, flush with the wall and covered in the same fabric, leads to the private office of the Jeweler, a youthful, elegant man in eyeglasses. He is standing now in the doorway of his office, conversing with his Assistant. It is forenoon and the sun is shining.*)

ASSISTANT: You just have to see it, sir, this movie is one of a kind, a historic document. You see the whole thing: his head, the revolver—poof, down he goes. Fantastic.

JEWELER: Un-heard-of.

ASSISTANT: See it today if you can; I hear it's going to be banned because yesterday the audience clapped; and how often do you get to see a king actually
murdered?

JEWELER: When does it start?

ASSISTANT: The last show's at ten.

JEWELER: Reserve two tickets for me. I'll take Miss Mia. (*Exit to private office.*)

ASSISTANT: (*Telephoning.*) Hello? Hold two tickets for the last show under the
name Tenbroek. Yes, the jeweler. Nothing left but loges? That's fine. Wait,
hello? The murder still showing, isn't it? Still on? All right then. (*Hangs up.
Count enters with Figaro.*)

ASSISTANT: May I help you?

COUNT: Might I speak to jeweler Tenbroek?

ASSISTANT: What name shall I give?

COUNT: Count Almaviva.

ASSISTANT: At once. (*Exit through office door.*)

COUNT: (*Looking after him.*) I remember that door perfectly. The ring the
Countess lost last summer: do you recall?

FIGARO: Perfectly.

COUNT: I bought it here. That was on my honeymoon, but nothing's changed:
a conservative house.

FIGARO: You smell that right away.

COUNT: (*Smiling.*) Yes, [you do]. (*Jeweler enters followed by Assistant.*)

JEWELER: Your Grace: how may I serve you?

COUNT: I'd like to speak to jeweler Tenbroek.

JEWELER: I am he.

COUNT: You? Excuse me, but I recall you quite differently; with a white beard,
in fact . . . (*Smiles.*)

JEWELER: (*Quite seriously.*) That was my Papa.

COUNT: What!

JEWELER: When did you meet Papa?

COUNT: Oh! Ages ago, ages . . .

JEWELER: It must have been. After all, he's been dead eighteen years.

COUNT: Dead? (*Looks about him.*) But everything here is just as it was then . . .

JEWELER: [*Apologetically.*] Yes: it *is* all a little out of date. But next month I re-
model: from the ground up.

COUNT: Indeed? (*Silence.*)

JEWELER: Your Grace: to what do I owe the honor. . . ?

COUNT: Do you know who I am?

JEWELER: The name is familiar, but frankly, at the moment I am at a loss . . .

COUNT: (*Cutting him off.*) I am a refugee. (*During the ensuing speech, the Jeweler
becomes more and more reserved.*) Yes, the last few days have brought no small
upheavals in their wake. Due to the excitements of our escape, my poor wife
has fallen seriously ill; she is in the Park Convalescent Home, suffering from

a complete nervous breakdown.

JEWELER: (*With detachment.*) Dreadful.

COUNT: She will most probably have to remain there another month. Then we will go to the mountains. For the air.

JEWELER: I envy you exceedingly. I myself am a passionate skier. . . .

COUNT: (*Cutting him off.*) Excuse me: before the skiing starts we shall have returned home. I am certain that current conditions in my unhappy homeland cannot long endure. It is an outbreak of the basest instincts—a development therefore evil by nature, which must and shall shatter when it comes in contact with the [fundamentally] healthy character of our people, the farmers in particular.

JEWELER: (*Smiles detachedly.*) Let us hope so.

COUNT: Two months, at most, and it will all be over.

JEWELER: (*Exchanging a glance with his Assistant.*) And in what way might I be of service to you?

COUNT: (*Slightly embarrassed.*) It's rather confidential.

JEWELER: Of course. Then please, come with me! (*Exit with Count through door. Silence.*)

ASSISTANT: Are you a refugee, too?

FIGARO: Yes.

ASSISTANT: Do you know Prince Bisamsky?

FIGARO: The fat one, or the tall one who's simple-minded?

ASSISTANT: I only know the fat one.

FIGARO: He's simple-minded, too.

ASSISTANT: He brought in a tiara yesterday, but we didn't take it. (*Figaro becomes attentive.*) Every other refugee brings in a tiara at least. You can't keep them off you.

FIGARO: You don't say.

ASSISTANT: And the gentry out your way used to be our best customers.

FIGARO: I wouldn't expect them back.

ASSISTANT: (*[Self-] importantly.*) You've got that right. Instead of buying, they're actually competing with us! Prices have gone right through the floor, the market is flooded with diamonds . . .

FIGARO: (*Interrupting.*) What about pearls?

ASSISTANT: Oh, now pearls are different!

FIGARO: Glad to hear it.

ASSISTANT: (*Looking toward the door.*) Can't imagine he'll have much luck in there. You can't stop the wheel of fortune, much less roll it backward. Over in two months: fat chance! Or what do you think?

FIGARO: (*Grinning broadly.*) I'm not telling.

ASSISTANT: More like a thousand years!

FIGARO: By then I think I'll have lost interest. (*Jeweler enters with Count from office.*)

JEWELER: Come in here, and bring a contract. (*Sotto voce.*) A real find! Pearls! (*To Count.*) This will only take a moment, your Grace! (*Exit with Assistant through door.*)

COUNT: (*Looking after.*) Scoundrel.

FIGARO: But not a fool; so he must have bought them.

COUNT: (*Smiles.*) Yes, he bought them; for a sixth of what we hoped for . . .

FIGARO: (*Cast down.*) Only a sixth?

COUNT: It can't be helped. I never learned to dicker; only to buy.

FIGARO: Your Grace should have let me handle it . . .

COUNT: What's done is done; and they aren't gone forever. The Countess will wear her pearls again, and soon!

FIGARO: Knock wood, quick!

COUNT: I feel nothing but relief: to be free of this disgusting penny-pinching; at last we can begin to live properly again.

FIGARO: And even a sixth . . . We can live three years on that . . .

COUNT: (*Interrupting.*) Three years! Are you insane? Should I move into a boarding house perhaps? I'd end it all first! The Count of Almaviva must live with a certain style, in the luxury to which he is entitled by birth. For such a man, emigration is a mere pleasure outing; the mob must learn that it is incapable of inconveniencing me. This peddler here (*pointing to the door*) babbling about five hundred years. . . .

FIGARO: Only [five hundred]?

COUNT: (*Not hearing him.*) How shortsighted they are, every one of them! No, the future is quite clear before me: before the first snowfall we'll be home; and in the meantime I'll do everything in my power to make it sooner, set everything in motion to keep our cause incessantly before the public—oh, don't forget to remind me, my friend the Permanent Secretary's expecting me at the Ministry tomorrow at half past one.

FIGARO: (*In shock.*) The Ministry! Oh God!

COUNT: (*Surprised.*) What's wrong?

FIGARO: Forgive me, I completely forgot, your Grace, this letter, it came today before noon. . . . (*Takes letter from his pocket and gives it to Count.*) It's from the Ministry. (*Count opens letter, reads, stops, stares. Then passes it back to Figaro.*)

COUNT: (*Softly.*) Read it.

FIGARO: (*Reads.*) Hm. (*Silence.*)

COUNT: What do you think of that?

FIGARO: I expected it.

COUNT: Such fine words to veil such craven content. I must not visit my "friend" at the Ministry [*as if quoting*] for fear the appearance of such a prominent émigré might rouse suspicion of dishonorable intentions in regard to the commercial treaty . . . Hmph. (*Smiles.*) Very well, it seems I must write to the newspapers about this ominous trade contract with barbarians, letter after letter: I know my subject, and I accept the challenge.

FIGARO: I'm afraid no one's going to print your letters.

COUNT: Then I'll hold a press conference.

FIGARO: They won't let it happen.

COUNT: (*Alertly.*) You think so?

FIGARO: Or perhaps the press just won't come.

COUNT: (*Glaring at him.*) And why shouldn't they?

FIGARO: Because they don't want any trouble with the barbarians: some out of sympathy, others out of fear. (*Silence.*)

COUNT: Susanna said once you were a prophet. But I can prophesy as well. Pay attention.

FIGARO: What do you mean, your Grace?

COUNT: In times like these, a person who wishes to remain in daily converse with me should not be too free with his opinions, even if they happen to be sound ones; better to deceive me by unconditional agreement: for in times like these, truth, more often than not, is merely a form of covert disapproval. And I can provide that service for myself . . . . (*Nods to Figaro with a smile.*)

JEWELER: (Returning with Assistant and piece of paper.) The contract, your Grace!

SCENE 4

(*Three months later. High in the mountains, in one of the loveliest winter resorts in the world. Spacious terrace of Count Almaviva's hotel suite with a splendid view of Alpine majesties. Music rises from the hotel skating-rink below. Susanna is lacing up the skates of the Countess, herself again. Snow and sunshine.*)

COUNTESS: A few weeks ago I wouldn't have dreamed I'd ever go skating again.

SUSANNA: Even bad things pass, Countess. The skates are a beautiful fit.

COUNTESS: They're too tight for me.

SUSANNA: Oh, that'll pass too!

FIGARO: (*Entering.*) The skating instructor's waiting, your Grace.

COUNTESS: Coming! What's my husband up to?

FIGARO: His Grace is to be found in the Casino.

COUNTESS: (*Smiles.*) He should get some exercise like me, instead of gambling, gambling, gambling. He always loses.

SUSANNA: Enjoy yourself, your Grace!

COUNTESS: And you get some sun, Susanna! (*Exit.*)

SUSANNA: Come on, Figaro, now it's our turn to relax. (*Setting up two deck chairs in the sun.*) Do you know how high up we are? Nearly seven thousand feet above the ocean.

FIGARO: That's still lower than the prices. The most expensive winter resort in the world. And the most expensive hotel in it.

SUSANNA: But you and I aren't paying for it.

FIGARO: Think so?

SUSANNA: (*Offering him a seat.*) May I offer you a chair, your Grace?

FIGARO: This mountain sun's unhealthy. It's only healthy for sick people.

SUSANNA: Who says so?

FIGARO: I do.

SUSANNA: (*Smiles.*) Afraid of getting sick? Poor Figaro!

FIGARO: Go on, enjoy yourself.

SUSANNA: Oh, Figaro, how changed you are! What's the *matter* with you? We've [only] been away from home three months, and most of the time the poor Countess has been in the hospital . . .

FIGARO: (*Interrupting.*) That was no hospital, it was a madhouse—catering to only the best people, of course: the most expensive madhouse in the world. (*Silence.*)

SUSANNA: You didn't use to be so picky.

FIGARO: I've got problems.

SUSANNA: You're *making* problems! Since we've been refugees we've never had it so good: nothing but grand hotels, treated like paying guests!

FIGARO: Like paying guests. But the way our masters like to live, how long can we keep on paying? Till Easter, and what happens then? When we've used up the pearls, what are we going to pay the pigs with?

SUSANNA: (*Salving herself with a white suncream.*) Last night [I heard] the Count tell the Countess we'll be home in a month.

FIGARO: (*Jumps up.*) I can't listen to this nonsense any more! Three months ago he said it'd all be over in two months. That's just crap! Two months ago, he said six weeks would finish it. More crap! A month ago he said we'd be home by Christmas—and Christmas is the day after tomorrow! Crap again! It's all crap, I tell you, they're consolidating their position, resistance is fading, and the only end in sight is our own. Crap, crap, crap!

SUSANNA: The Count's a cultivated diplomat, you think you know better than him?

FIGARO: (*Stops abruptly and stares at her.*) Then choose between us.

SUSANNA: (*Thrown off balance.*) What's that supposed to mean?

FIGARO: Susanna, a world is coming to an end. That night we crossed the border, in the forest, when I tried to cheer the Countess up with that nonsense about a corpse that came back to life—remember?—right then I suddenly realized I was *talking* to a corpse; that I'm a liar if I play the fool and tell a terminal case that where there's life there's hope. The Count and Countess would be better off if they'd never made it across the border, if they'd stayed and been put out of their misery . . .

SUSANNA: (*Horrified.*) Figaro!

FIGARO: A world is coming to an end: an old, old world. The Count and

Countess are already dead, they just don't know it. They're lying in state in the Grand Hotel and think the mortician's a headwaiter and the gravedigger's a wine-steward. That's no manicurist bending over them; it's the woman come to lay the bodies out! They [can] change their outfits every day, but it's still the same old shroud; they [can] dab on the perfume but the smell is still of lilies withering on a grave! They're going under, Susanna! Do you want to go along? I don't.

SUSANNA: (*Fearful.*) I don't understand what you're saying, Figaro . . .

FIGARO: We got to leave them, Susanna.

SUSANNA: Leave them?!

FIGARO: Leave the Almavivas. Declare our independence. This is our Bastille Day.

SUSANNA: Are you crazy?!

FIGARO: I may not be a cultivated diplomat, but I know what I have to do. (*Pulls a newspaper out of his pocket.*) Here, in the little ads in the back: I see there's a barber shop for sale.

SUSANNA: Barber shop?

FIGARO: Yes. I'm going back to barbering again. (*Reading.*) "For sale due to re-marriage: highly-regarded hair salon. [Box 12,] Haggelburg." Haggelburg's not a big town, but it's growing. Thirty-four hundred people. Nice part of the country. Hilly. I looked it up. Lots of trees. (*Silence.*)

SUSANNA: (*Staring at him.*) Are you serious about this?

FIGARO: Absolutely. All we have to ask the Count for to settle our account is as much as we spend to live in a week in this place, never mind what he throws away at the roulette table every day. But the game's over for me, we're going to break loose and save ourselves. Why are you looking at me that way?

SUSANNA: Because I just remembered something . . .

FIGARO: What?

SUSANNA: You won't like it.

FIGARO: There's nothing you can't tell me. (*Silence.*)

SUSANNA: When we got married, you always said that people in our position, completely dependent, shouldn't have children, and I had to admit you were right . . .

FIGARO: Well?

SUSANNA: But you also used to say that if we ever managed to break free, then right away — "right away," that's what you said . . .

FIGARO: True. But we have to wait and see which way the frog jumps first.

SUSANNA: Which frog is that?

FIGARO: Wait until we know that we can *stay* free!

SUSANNA: (*Smiles strangely.*) How timid you've become . . .

FIGARO: I'm not frightened: I just want to anticipate every problem. (*A silence.*)

SUSANNA: (*Suddenly.*) The Count will look out for me.

FIGARO: I'm the one who looks out for you!

SUSANNA: I'm staying.

FIGARO: So now you're going to leave me all alone? After I only came along because of you?

SUSANNA: That's not true, you're just as devoted to the Count as I am to . . .

FIGARO: (*Interrupts.*) Maybe so, but I would have stayed home if you had! What it comes down to is that I'm a refugee because of you, because I'm a faithful husband, nothing else! (*Silence.*)

SUSANNA: What will it be like when we're old and there's no one that belongs to us? To never hear anybody call us "Mother" and "Father." Our lives won't have made any sense.

FIGARO: Life doesn't make a lot of sense one way or the other. And what makes you think we'll ever *get* old, in times like these?

SUSANNA: When you talk that way I feel like dying here and now.

FIGARO: (*Tenderly.*) You know how much I love you.

SUSANNA: Love's not enough for me.

FIGARO: Not enough?

COUNT: (*Entering, to Susanna.*) Where is the Countess?

FIGARO: Skating. On thin ice. (*Count looks at Figaro in surprise and sizes him mistrustfully, hearing a certain disrespect in his tone.*)

SUZANNA: (*Covering for him.*) Figaro's so edgy today . . .

COUNT: (*Faintly ironic.*) Ah: the sultry weather? Or have you two quarreled again?

FIGARO: No, your Grace: we're in complete agreement.

COUNT: That *would* be grounds for celebration. (*He sits. Susanna turns away weeping. Count looks at her in surprise.*)

FIGARO: (*Girding himself.*) Your Grace, you've written article after article attacking the revolutionaries, you've made speeches . . .

COUNT: (*Interrupts.*) No point to it: I saw that. The so-called leaders of the people will destroy each other [with no help from me]. I give them another month at most . . .

FIGARO: (*Cutting him off.*) But your Grace, what if they don't? (*Count rises, furious.*) Excuse me. (*Silence.*)

COUNT: Susanna told me once you were a prophet. But I can prophesy as well. Pay attention.

FIGARO: What do you mean, your Grace?

COUNT: In times like these, a person who wishes to remain in daily converse with me should not be too free with his opinions, even if they happen to be sound ones; better to deceive me by unconditional agreement, for these days truth, more often than not, is merely a form of covert disapproval. And I can provide that service for myself. (*Nods to Figaro with a smile.*)

FIGARO: I would never have spoken so carelessly if I didn't have the future to worry about, but unfortunately I have a wife to consider, whether she likes it or not, that's my number one obligation. Your Grace, if I were you I'd buy a share of a first-class coffee house; there's still time.

COUNT: You *must* be ill! What an obscene suggestion!

FIGARO: One dictated by circumstances.

COUNT: You're suffering in your present circumstances?

SUSANNA: (*Weeping.*) He's lost his mind, Sir; he wants to give notice: give *you* notice! (*Sobs.*)

COUNT: Notice? (*Stares hard at Figaro. Silence.*)

FIGARO: (*Embarrassed and uncertain.*) Your Grace, the first of the month is . . .

COUNT: (*Cutting him off.*) No matter. Anyone not wishing to remain with me may go immediately. Accepted.

FIGARO: Thank you, your Grace. (*Silence.*)

COUNT: (*To Susanna.*) Where will you go, then? Back *there*, perhaps?

FIGARO: (*Stepping between them.*) I can make my own arrangements, your Grace.

COUNT: (*To Figaro.*) Careful: go back after leaving as you did and they'll chop off your head!

FIGARO: And they'd be right to.

COUNT: (*Stupefied.*) Right?

FIGARO: There are two kinds of right, your Grace, depending on where you stand. Unfortunately.

SUSANNA: (*Flaring up suddenly at Figaro.*) And two kinds of wrong, too!

FIGARO: That's the way things are. (*Silence.*)

COUNT: (*To Susanna.*) Then you don't want to go back . . .

SUSANNA: (*Weeping.*) He wants to go back to being a barber . . .

COUNT: Back to the scissors! (*He laughs involuntarily.*)

FIGARO: I plan to settle in Haggelburg, your Grace . . .

COUNT: (*Interrupting him.*) The place does not concern me.

FIGARO: [*Stiffly.*] Very well, your Grace. (*Silence.*)

COUNT: How long were you in my service?

FIGARO: Nine years, sir.

COUNT: Hm. I'm sorry to part with you, but I expected it. For some time I've felt in you . . . passive resistance.

FIGARO: Excuse me; [what you feel is] only a lively instinct for self-preservation.

COUNT: I could bear anything but this: you've turned bourgeois, my friend . . . (*Smiles faintly.*)

FIGARO: Your Grace, I've gone hungry so often in my life that even the word "bourgeois" has lost its terror.

COUNTESS: (*Returning from skating, seeing the Count.*) What, back from the Casino already? What have we lost today, then?

COUNT: Figaro and Susanna.

ACT II

SCENE 1

(In Haggelburg. A year later. Figaro has taken over the top-rated hair salon. Left a door to the living quarters. It is the end of December, round about midday or so. Susanna is in the salon just now, waiting on the Junior Forester, a crafty child-of-nature type. She is lathering him.)

FORESTER: But friend husband'll do the actual shaving, won't he?

SUSANNA: (Smiles.) No. Does that make you nervous, Sir?

FORESTER: Well, frankly, a razor in a dainty little hand . . . But I'd get my revenge quick enough. (He laughs. Silence.) What are you doing Thursday, milady Barber?

SUSANNA: How do you mean, Sir?

FORESTER: Thursday's New Year's Eve: time for new beginnings. (Silence.)

SUSANNA: I'm going to [the dance at] the Post House. With my husband.

FORESTER: Then I'm going to the Post House, too. You like to dance?

SUSANNA: Yes.

FORESTER: But no one ever sees you at parties or dances . . .

SUSANNA: Haggelburg's not much of a town for dancing.

FORESTER: How true! But then, personally, I don't come from Haggelburg. I'm only stationed here.

SUSANNA: (Smiles.) Me too.

FORESTER: Companions in suffering, so to speak. When I'm not actually out on on patrol, I'm bored to death here.

SUSANNA: (Shaving him.) You're the only man who's ever let me shave him.

FORESTER: What about the husband?

SUSANNA: He shaves himself. (Silence.)

FORESTER: What's he up to at the moment?

SUSANNA: He's asleep. Every day after lunch.

FORESTER: But not you?

SUSANNA: We take turns.

FORESTER: But never at the same time, hum? (*Susanna stops, jolted, stares fearfully at him for a moment, and then goes on shaving him as if she hadn't heard anything. Silence.*) So I'm the one—the only one who lets you shave him . . .

SUSANNA: Yes.

FORESTER: I'm not afraid. I wouldn't mind having my throat cut if it was you that did it. (*Grins.*)

SUSANNA: (*With a forced laugh.*) What a thought! All that blood! What would your fiancée have to say if you came courting with your throat cut!

FORESTER: She'd just have to get used to it, wouldn't she?

SUSANNA: (*Finished shaving.*) Warm towel? Or hot?

FORESTER: Hot, the hotter the better . . . I like it hot. (*He grabs hold of her brutally and steals a kiss. Susanna tears herself free.*)

SUSANNA: (*Holding herself in.*) Stop it! What do you think you're doing?

FORESTER: Just what comes naturally . . . (*Rises and approaches her slowly.*)

SUSANNA: Leave me alone, you . . . Look out, I really will cut your throat . . .

FORESTER: (*Breaking in.*) Try it. (*Swiftly catches her by the wrist and twists.*)

SUSANNA: Ow! (*She lets the razor fall.*) Now look, my husband: if he wakes up . . . I'll call him . . . I'll call . . .

FORESTER: (*Backing her into the corner.*) Go ahead and shout, no one'll hear you, only me . . . (*Grabs her again and kisses her.*)

SUSANNA: You animal . . . you animal . . . Get out of here, or I'm leaving . . . (*The Forester doesn't move. Silence. He slowly turns from her and pulls on his fur coat.*)

FORESTER: Another time.

SUSANNA: Not a chance.

FORESTER: Tomorrow. After the movie. (*Susanna doesn't answer.*) I haven't paid yet.

SUSANNA: Forty.

FORESTER: (*Giving her the money.*) There you are.

SUSANNA: Thank you. (*Exit Forester. In the doorway he meets the Midwife, just coming in carrying a little bag.*)

MIDWIFE: Good day to you, dearie. Just a quick wave, my day isn't over yet . . . How's business?

SUSANNA: (*Taking care of her.*) We're getting by, thanks.

MIDWIFE: I've got so much on my hands I don't know if I'm coming or going. Five calls in a week, and two of them pairs of twins. Samson couldn't keep it up. If things go on this way little old Haggelburg will be the size of Paris, and look at my hair: like the stork's been nesting in it! It's an invasion! I just came from the schoolmaster's wife: he brought her a baby girl, a teeny bit too early, but she'll be happy with it just the same, and the stars are favorable: Mercury in Capricorn.

SUSANNA: Do you understand the stars?

MIDWIFE: I understand everything.

SUSANNA: What's May?

MIDWIFE: Venus rules May in the sign of Taurus. Who might that be?

SUSANNA: Me.

MIDWIFE: I see. And what's your husband?

SUSANNA: No one knows. He was a foundling.

MIDWIFE: No! Oh, well. The stars aren't so important when it comes to our lords and masters. Men change their ways oftener than their socks, but it's always the same old swindle. Sometimes you'd think a man doesn't have a star to his name. How long have you been married, dearie?

SUSANNA: Seven years.

MIDWIFE: Really? You don't look it.

SUSANNA: I was [just] eighteen.

MIDWIFE: You be careful, seven's a naughty number. Every marriage takes a beating every seven years, that's a rule of higher metaphysics, sad but true. Why haven't you had children? The best barbershop in town, you could have managed several by this time.

SUSANNA: I wanted to. It's my husband. (*Silence.*)

MIDWIFE: But you still share a bed, don't you?

SUSANNA: Not often. I've told him and told him, without children I know I'll go to pieces. But he won't come round. Absolutely not.

MIDWIFE: But you can bring him round. I've been through this situation a thousand times, believe me! Listen dearie: all you have to do is walk up to the lord and master and lie in your teeth. Tell him the worst has happened: what's he got to say for himself then? Nothing!

SUSANNA: That's what you think.

MIDWIFE: But what can he do about it? An act of God! He'll feel like Nature got the best of him, stop worrying and start shopping for a crib. There's your solution: anticipate the consequences! (*She rises, her wave complete.*) What do I owe you, dearie?

SUSANNA: I don't know how to thank you. Eighty, please.

MIDWIFE: I'll be seeing *you* in September. Mars in Libra: congratulations! Farewell, Mother Figaro! (*Exit.*)

SUSANNA: Goodbye, Ma'am! (*Figaro enters in dressing gown and slippers from the living quarters; he's still a little sleepy, yawns, slips out of his robe, dons his barber smock, and checks the contents of the till.*)

FIGARO: One shave, one set . . . (*To Susanna.*) That's all?

SUSANNA: Yes.

FIGARO: Funny how in the holidays everybody [decides to] get his hair cut at four-thirty in the afternoon on New Year's Eve. Then they all come in at once and you have to send half of them to the competition. Thank you, come back soon! I'm going to bring it up again at the Chamber of Commerce. And it wouldn't hurt the teachers to let the parents know that Saturday afternoon's not the only time a kid can get a haircut—have to turn down a full-beard trim because some sticky brat's taking up the chair, and kids' haircuts don't bring anything in anyway. What's a razor doing on the floor? (*Picks it up.*) A used razor! (*Fires a punishing glance at Susanna.*) How sloppy can you get? (*He turns to Susanna almost solemnly.*) It's time we had a serious talk, Susanna. We've had this salon just nine months, and because I know my business, all the top people come here: everyone from the minister to the midwife, shaves, haircuts, permanents, manicures—I've [even] introduced them to pedicures, et cetera, et cetera . . . But the real trick isn't finding customers, it's holding on to them, and you don't do that just by providing first-class shaves, haircuts, et cetera; no, it takes certain psychological skills, diplomacy, the way you approach people, take an interest in their problems, agree with their opinions, flatter their little vanities, share their concerns, answer their questions, laugh when they laugh, cry when they cry . . .

SUSANNA: (*Interrupting.*) And that's what you call freedom?

FIGARO: Don't distract me, please, let me finish. Freedom means I'm free to play the hypocrite if I want to, and hypocrisy is necessary if we don't want to find ourselves in the gutter some day! You don't realize the seriousness of the situation. At the dance at the gymnasium not long ago, you practically turned your back on the mayor's wife . . .

SUSANNA: She was telling me the whole story of her rupture, who can put up with that kind of thing?

FIGARO: Rupture or no rupture, you can listen! You have a responsibility! [And that reminds me,] you'll have to go to the Arts Club drama festival tomorrow night: the baker's wife is one of our best customers, and her daughter Irma's in the play.

SUSANNA: I'd rather stay home and read a book . . .

FIGARO: Your job is going to see Irma, not reading books!

SUSANNA: The ugliest little girl in the world! A squinting dwarf with a head like a squash . . .

FIGARO: Squash or no squash, you're going to find the little monster adorable and clap till your hands are sore, understand me?

SUSANNA: I can't stand these nobodies!

FIGARO: Like them or not, those nobodies pay the bills!

SUSANNA: The smell of a roomful of them is more than I can bear . . .

FIGARO: Our days of titles and perfume are over; over and done with.

SUSANNA: Just don't pretend you're not as sorry as I am.

FIGARO: I work at not being sorry, I've broken the habit. I concentrate on one day at a time.

SUSANNA: (*Darkly.*) This hole will get me yet . . . (*Suddenly flaring up at him.*) I wasn't born to curl a baker's wife and praise her nasty little girl: I learned about music listening to the greatest artists in the world. I wasn't born to swill beer in smoky taverns, I've drunk the finest champagne in my time. I wasn't born to talk ruptures at the card table, I've been the confidante of a great lady . . . (*Stops suddenly and begins crying.*) I wish we'd never left the Almavivas!

FIGARO: You think things are rosy for them? Be glad we haven't heard.

SUSANNA: (*Weeping.*) They're beter off than I am anyway.

FIGARO: Don't tempt fate. (*Silence.*)

SUSANNA: Sometimes you sound just like our customers . . .

FIGARO: You have to play the cards you're dealt: otherwise you're out of the game, and it's the only one around . . . (*Grins.*)

SUSANNA: Haggelburg is Hell.

FIGARO: It's not my fault we ended up here.

SUSANNA: (*Suddenly attacking.*) Then whose fault is it? Mine, of course! If it hadn't been for me and my stupid loyalty we never would have emigrated and gotten in this mess, we could have stayed peacefully at home like Uncle Antonio and Pedrillo and Barberina*—and by now you might be in charge of the castle, is that how it goes? I ought to have it right by now, I've heard you say it three times every day since we came here!

FIGARO: That's not true! Just once I said . . . something like that!

SUSANNA: But I hear it even when you don't say anything! I hear it when you read the paper, I hear it when you're looking out the window, I hear it at night when you're beside me, in your dreams . . .

FIGARO: (*Ironically.*) Is that all you hear?

SUSANNA: . . . that it's no good between us any more, Figaro. (*Silence.*)

FIGARO: In what way?

SUSANNA: When we left the Countess I'd said I'd go anywhere with you, because I was yours—remember?—even to Haggelburg—because I love you: but I had to be your wife to do it, really your wife.

FIGARO: What's that supposed to mean? I'm not your husband?

SUSANNA: Then you don't remember? (*Silence. Night is falling.*)

MIDWIFE: (*Returning in a rush.*) Did I leave my little bag here? Thank God, there it is. (*Picks it up.*)

FIGARO: Nothing gets misplaced here, Madam!

MIDWIFE: That would have been a nice surprise: what a look the stork would have given me! Speaking of nice surprises: have you heard yet, Figaro?

FIGARO: [Heard] what?

SUSANNA: (*Suddenly.*) I haven't told him.

FIGARO: Clear as mud.

SUSANNA: (*To Figaro.*) I couldn't say it to you.

FIGARO: What kind of remark is that? There's nothing you can't tell your husband, nothing in the world, day or night—except right after dinner: I don't like surprises then. (*To Midwife.*) Has she broken something?

MIDWIFE: On the contrary, my friend! A blessed event!

FIGARO: Blessed event?

---

*"Fanchette" in the original; changed for uniformity with Da Ponte's libretto.

MIDWIFE: (*To Susanna.*) Courage! (*To Figaro.*) Listen: (*Whispers to him. Figaro's eyes widen as he keeps staring at Susanna. Susanna turns her back on both of them and cleans the used razor, lost in thought.*) There. (*To Susanna.*) Now it's out. (*To Figaro.*) Congratulations, congratulations! Goodbye, little mother! (*Exit.*)

FIGARO: (*Stares petrified at Susanna: softly.*) Is it true?

SUSANNA: (*Tonelessly.*) Yes.

FIGARO: But how . . . when . . .

SUSANNA: (*Turns.*) Where did it come from? Is that what you're saying? You think I'm capable of betraying you?

FIGARO: No, of course not. Why would you do something like that to a person who's done everything for you? I'm sorry, I'm just a little shaken. What a disaster.

SUSANNA: Disaster?

FIGARO: Should I be cheering? (*Silence.*)

SUSANNA: You're not human.

FIGARO: How often do I have to tell you: I'm human, all right – but I also have a sense of responsibility, and you know that I'm a prophet. Have I got to look down from heaven and watch my son die in the next war?

SUSANNA: You're much too responsible for heaven. You'll go to Hell.

FIGARO: Spare me that, please! Who can bear a child in times like these with a clear conscience? Don't you read the papers? Every other day a new [kind of] death! A blind man could see it! Here in Haggelburg there's a chance we'll survive quite a while: no fortress in the neighborhood, no transfer points, nothing worth the trouble of destroying. But they'll get around to destroying the worthless too, and the earthquakes will finish the job. Rome is falling, Susanna; no one has more right than us to say: after us, the Deluge! Bring a child into this world, go ahead: let him live in a landscape like the moon, craters and poisonous haze . . . I've got to have a talk with the midwife, she's smart, she'll know some way out of th . . .

SUSANNA: (*Breaking out.*) Go ahead and talk to her! I don't *want* a child of yours any more – if you gave me one I'd crawl away like a stray bitch to keep you from knowing where he saw the light of day, to keep his father's curse off him, because you won't even grudge him a life! I'd never let you see him, never! You don't deserve better, you're Death, Death!* (*Figaro looks round concerned: goes to door, opens, closes it.*)

FIGARO: Not so loud, Susanna! Let's keep appearances at least. People are whispering already . . .

SUSANNA: (*Interrupting, with loathing.*) People again!

FIGARO: And again and again and forever! That's right!

SUSANNA: (*Staring, hate in her eye.*) And you want peace and quiet?

---

*Following section to asterisk on p. 157 incorporated from Act II, Scene 3 for 1937 world premiere, in which that scene was omitted.

FIGARO: Now you've got it.

SUSANNA: (*Slowly, with hate in her voice.*) Then there's nothing more to fight about. I lied to you just now, Figaro. I'm not carrying your child . . .

FIGARO: (*Jumps up.*) What?! No baby?!

SUSANNA: I only said it to win your sympathy. It was just a trick . . .

FIGARO: Trick?

SUSANNA: Your wife tried to trick her Lord and Master into giving her a child. But that's all over with. The man whose child I want doesn't live in Haggelburg.

FIGARO: Thank you so much!

SUSANNA: I dreamed about him last night. He was bending over me, and his shadow was three times as big as the world. I knew him right away.

FIGARO: Who?

SUSANNA: The love of my life. (*Silence.*)

FIGARO: And who's that?

SUSANNA: He's dead. (*Silence.*)

FIGARO: Who was he, then?

SUSANNA: His name was Figaro.

FIGARO: Figaro?!

SUSANNA: Yes. My Figaro took pleasure in the future: when the thunderheads gathered he ran to the window to watch the lightning strike, but you? You won't leave the house without an umbrella if there's a cloud anywhere in the sky! My Figaro went to prison for writing what he believed: you'd be afraid to read what he wrote! My Figaro was the first man to stand before his master and tell him the truth to his face; and you keep up appearances in Haggelburg! He was a citizen of the world, you're a petty bourgeois! he was a man; and *you*!

FIGARO: After seven years with me, you've got no right to say that! I'll tell you something though: you're not fit to be a mother. You're a fraud, you're still a chambermaid at heart, not an independent woman: always looking in the mirror and still come to work a mess, conceited, flirtatious, self-pitying, superficial . . .

SUSANNA: (*Interrupting.*) Superficial? *Me* superficial?

FIGARO: (*Grinning.*) [Yes]: [At last] we know each other, inside and out.

SUSANNA: You used to catch a glimpse of yourself from time to time; but today you've forgotten it all.*

SCHOOLMASTER: (*Enters.*) Haircut, please! Good day to you, Madam! (*Susanna runs sobbing into the living quarters. Schoolmaster looks after her, perplexed.*)

SCHOOLMASTER: What's the matter with her?

FIGARO: You know women.

---

*See note on p. 156.

SCENE 2

(*In a large foreign city. Cheap furnished room. The Countess is sitting in the only easy chair reading novelettes from the lending library. Her hair has gone white. The Count stands at the window. It is snowing.*)

COUNT: It's snowing.
COUNTESS: (*Smiles.*) Soon it'll be winter again. A mild one, I hope, firewood's gone up.
COUNT: Has the mail come yet?
COUNTESS: Are you expecting something?
COUNT: Yes. Word from the editor.
COUNTESS: It's certainly time.
COUNT: We'll pay today.
COUNTESS: Every time someone knocks I'm frightened, it's been two weeks since we've paid them anything . . .
COUNT: An Almaviva remains no man's debtor. (*Knock at the door.*) Come in.
MAID: (*Entering with two letters.*) The mail, your Grace. (*Exit.*)
COUNT: For you. And from the editor. (*He opens his letter and scans the contents. She opens hers and reads the signature; with an exclamation she buries herself in the contents. Count finishes reading his letter and sticks it in his pocket apathetically.*) Who's it from?
COUNTESS: Susanna.
COUNT: Susanna? But I asked you not to correspond with them.
COUNTESS: And I haven't done so, here, look at the envelope! It was sent to the Esplanade and they forwarded it.
COUNT: (*Reading the addresses on the envelope.*) [Grand Hotel] Esplanade, [Hotel] Carlton, [Pension] Regina . . .
COUNTESS: (*Smiles.*) Step by step.
COUNT: Down and down. (*Silence.*)
COUNTESS: Still dreaming of the [Grand Hotel] Esplanade?
COUNT: (*Still staring at the addresses.*) Fourth floor. Furnished. Care of Therese Bader . . . (*Lays the envelope on the table.*)
COUNTESS: Mrs. Bader is a fine person.
COUNT: Yes. She pities us. Horrible.
COUNTESS: You haven't learned yet.
COUNT: I completed my studies some time ago.
COUNTESS: [No:] we're still in the schoolhouse, even though we're in a higher grade: perhaps we're in the university by now . . . (*Smiles.*) Look at poor Susanna, learning to read and write for the first time and frightened of being left alone in the dark, like all children. We're not frightened any more, are we?
COUNT: You're grown so brave . . . (*Smiles gently.*)

COUNTESS: I've managed to change. Thank God. (*Silence.*)

COUNT: What does Susanna have to say?

COUNTESS: She wants to leave Figaro.

COUNT: (*Surprised.*) Leave him? Why?

COUNTESS: Because *he's* changed.

COUNT: Has he betrayed her?

COUNTESS: No, but he seems only to care about his hair salon and doesn't return her affection . . . (*Looks at the letter.*) Poor Susanna! She asks if she can come back to us . . .

COUNT: To us?

COUNTESS: As chambermaid. (*Count grimaces.*) She longs for what's past. (*Silence.*)

COUNT: (*Rises and walks up and down.*) Oh, by the way: the editor says my memoirs aren't suitable for the literary page *or* the Sunday Supplement. Count Almaviva puts himself on the market and no one cares to buy! His name is to be obliterated, his life-work dissolved into mist . . . (*Pulls the letter from his pocket and scans it once more.*) Insolence! My style is antiquated, according to these vulgarians: and not one of them competent to construct a decent sentence . . . hacks, all of them! Look . . . (*Gives her the letter.*)

COUNTESS: (*Reads, looks large-eyed at the Count.*) Don't you feel like going to the café today?

COUNT: I have no money.

COUNTESS: I have some . . . Here: go!

COUNT: And how are we to dine this evening?

COUNTESS: I've already arranged for your supper. I won't eat.

COUNT: You can't starve yourself!

COUNTESS: It's healthy to skip a meal now and then . . . Go along now, play some chess, take your mind off things . . .

COUNT: (*Smiles.*) These days I feel like your little boy . . . (*Draws on his coat, starts to leave, stops in doorway.*) What will you tell Susanna?

COUNTESS: I'll tell her to keep her spirits up.

COUNT: And as for our temporary situation, just pass over all that . . .

COUNTESS: I shall, I shall . . . (*Nods goodbye to him smiling.*)

COUNT: Adieu! (*Exit.*)

COUNTESS: (*Getting letter-paper and writing.*) Dear Susanna: a woman belongs with her husband . . .

SCENE 3

[Omitted from 1936 version]

(*The New Year's Eve gala at the Post House. Susanna has withdrawn [from the ballroom] into a neighboring empty room. Next door in the hall, music is playing. On the wall hang a clock and a poster for the New Year's charity raffle. The Junior*

Forester comes in from the hall. He is in full dress.)

FORESTER: I've been looking all over for you, what are you doing alone in here? In twenty minutes it'll be midnight.

SUSANNA: *(Tonelessly.)* Shall we dance?

FORESTER: No. *(Susanna looks at him wide-eyed.)* I came to tell you I can't dance with you any more. Someone overheard us last night after the movies. I just this minute found out. They know you were with me. We have to deny it all.

SUSANNA: *(Tonelessly.)* Is that so?

FORESTER: Doesn't that bother you?!

SUSANNA: I knew it would happen.

FORESTER: *Knew?*

SUSANNA: I expected—that we wouldn't dance again. *(Rises.)* He doesn't deserve any better.

FORESTER: *(His attention alerted.)* Who?

SUSANNA: Figaro. Yes, I've got to go.

FORESTER: *(Suspiciously.)* Go where?

SUSANNA: Away from Figaro. *(Pause.)*

FORESTER: Now just a minute here! You looking for grounds for divorce? *(Susanna flinches and stares at him.)* So you come to the movies with me, just because you want loose from him? Just casually use me to break up your marriage, is that it, means to an end?!

SUSANNA: *(Screaming at him.)* That's not true!

FORESTER: Don't scream at me! You get me in more hot water here, you'll find out, you're not the first [to try it] . . .

SUSANNA: *(Interrupting, but quietly.)* [Just] kill me.

FORESTER: Now you want to make a murderer out of me?

SUSANNA: You might enjoy it . . . *(Smiles.)*

FORESTER: *(Shaking her.)* Get hold of yourself! *(Silence.)*

SUSANNA: *(Unnaturally cold and clear.)* I went out with you because I liked you. *(Forester stares at her. Still coldly.)* That was all.

FORESTER: That's all? You're going to wreck my marriage prospects, what decent person is going to give his daughter to a known adulterer . . . you call that nothing? But I'll deny it all! Everything! *(Exit rapidly to hall. Susanna alone. She stares darkly into space, then takes a little mirror from her purse and powders herself. Figaro enters from the hall in an elderly tail-coat. Susanna ignores him.)*

FIGARO: Come [with me].

SUSANNA: No.

FIGARO: And may I ask why not?

SUSANNA: That place is full of smoke.

FIGARO: It's twenty minutes until New Year's.

SUSANNA: I'll have choked to death by then. *(Pause.)**

---

*Following section to asterisk on p. 162 moved to Act II, Scene 1 in 1937. See note on p. 156.

FIGARO: Susanna, we have to consider other people. Let's at least keep up appearances.

SUSANNA: The hell with appearances.

FIGARO: Don't get on my nerves again, all right? People are talking already . . .

SUSANNA: People again!

FIGARO: And again and again and forever! That's right!

SUSANNA: (*Fixing him with a hate-filled look.*) What are we fighting about really?

FIGARO: You know why. And you also know I don't want to fight . . .

SUSANNA: (*Sneeringly.*) You just want peace and quiet?

FIGARO: (*Grimacing.*) Now you've got it.

SUSANNA: (*Slowly, with hate in her voice.*) Then there's nothing more to fight about. I lied to you the day before yesterday, Figaro. I'm not carrying your child . . .

FIGARO: (*Jumps up.*) What?! No baby?!

SUSANNA: I only said it to try to win your sympathy. It was just a trick . . .

FIGARO: Trick?

SUSANNA: Your wife tried to trick her Lord and Master into giving her a child. But that's all over with. The man whose child I want doesn't live in Haggelburg.

FIGARO: Thank you so much!

SUSANNA: I dreamed about him last night. He was bending over me, and his shadow was three times as big as the world. I knew him right away.

FIGARO: Who?

SUSANNA: The love of my life. (*Silence.*)

FIGARO: And who's that?

SUSANNA: He's dead. (*Silence.*)

FIGARO: Who was he, then?

SUSANNA: His name was Figaro.

FIGARO: Figaro?!

SUSANNA: Yes. My Figaro looked forward to the future, when the thunderheads gathered he ran to the window to watch the lightning strike, but you? You won't leave the house without an umbrella if there's a cloud anywhere in the sky! My Figaro went to prison for writing what he thought: you'd be afraid to read what he wrote! My Figaro was the first man to stand before his master and tell him the truth to his face; you keep up appearances in Haggelburg! He was a citizen of the world, you're a petty bourgeois! he was a man; and *you*!

FIGARO: After seven years together, you've got no right to say that. But I'll tell you something; you're not fit to be a mother; you're a fraud, you're still more chambermaid than independent woman, always looking in the mirror and still come to work a mess, conceited, flirtatious, self-pitying, superficial
. . .

SUSANNA: Superficial? *Me* superficial?

FIGARO: (*Grins.*) [Yes]: at last we know each other, inside and out.

SUSANNA: You used to catch a glimpse of yourself from time to time; but today you've forgotten it all.* (*Schoolmaster enters from the hall with Adalbert (pastry-baker) and Basil (butcher).*)

FIGARO: (*Softly, to Susanna.*) Someone's coming! Get hold of yourself. (*To the men.*) Happy New Year, gentlemen!

BASIL: Same to you. Figaro, you only cut my hair this afternoon, and look at it!

FIGARO: What's wrong with it, Basil?

ADALBERT: S'what happens when your mind's not on your work . . . (*Throws a pulverizing glance Susanna's way.*)

FIGARO: [*To Basil.*] Naturally I'll correct it free of charge.

BASIL: You can fix up just about anything, even a broken marriage: but not a rotten haircut! All you can do about that is let it grow out! (*Laughs unpleasantly, joined by Adalbert: only the Schoolmaster remains serious. Figaro confused, bows to Basil, turns to Susanna, speaks under his breath.*) Move! (*Aloud, to her.*) May I offer my arm? (*Under his breath.*) Now I can't cut hair! (*Leads Susanna into the hall.*)

ADALBERT: Alone at last! (*Puts the cognac bottle and three glasses he has hidden under his frock-coat on the table and pours drinks all round.*) My lady wife is always afraid I'll have a stroke if I drink — I'm afraid, yes, I'm afraid if she came in right now, *she's* the one that'd have the stroke . . . (*Grins.*)

BASIL: (*Grinning.*) Knock wood, my friend! Who are we drinking to, gentlemen?

SCHOOLMASTER: To your dear daughter, Basil!

ADALBERT: Hear, hear! (*All drink.*)

BASIL: You think the hairdresser suspects anything yet?

ADALBERT: Not likely. He's still speaking to his wife.

BASIL: If my wife ever pulled that on me, I'd let her have it with my cleaver . . . but a gypsy barber like him, he lets wifey cheat him up down and sideways and takes her out dancing afterwards.

SCHOOLMASTER: He's keeping up appearances.

BASIL: Appearances! That one? People like that don't know what honor is: the hell with them!

SCHOOLMASTER: And if *he* went after Susanna with his razor, I'd hate to hear what you'd say! You can't please us Haggelburgers. [But] we have our little weaknesses too.

BASIL: Well, teacher, if we do we can afford them, and they're nobody's business but ours; but a johnny-come-lately like that had better watch his step if he wants to get ahead round here!

ADALBERT: I always say it's all the women's fault: first they bring you into the world, and then they help you out of it again. (*Josepha enters from hall with Midwife.*) Christ, my wife! (*He acts as if he doesn't see her and whispers with Basil and the Schoolmaster.*)

JOSEPHA: (*To Midwife.*) There he sits, master of all he surveys! I can't let him out

---

*See note on p. 160.

of my sight or he gets falling-down drunk and has a heart attack and leaves me to pick up the pieces . . . What a way to start the New Year! (*Men laugh loudly and then whisper again.*)

MIDWIFE: The gentlemen are telling jokes.

JOSEPHA: Now it's mine's turn. I know the joke. He only has the one and he's told it since the beginning of time. No one laughs at it [any more]. (*The men laugh disagreeably.*)

MIDWIFE: Maybe he knows one you haven't heard.

JOSEPHA: (*After a devastating look at the Midwife, calls.*) Adalbert! Adalbert!

ADALBERT: (*Sighs and comes up to her.*) What is it now, Josepha?

JOSEPHA: (*Reproachfully.*) You told a joke just now and everybody laughed!

ADALBERT: That was no joke! We were talking about the barber's wife!

BASIL: She cheated on Figaro last night!

MIDWIFE: (*Horrified.*) What?!

ADALBERT: It's quite true.

BASIL: After the movies!

MIDWIFE: But that can't be!

JOSEPHA: Why not? It wouldn't surprise me in the least! Her with her nose in the air, I wouldn't put anything past her, she's nothing but a bundle of depravity! (*To Basil.*) Who did she betray him with?

ADALBERT: With the Junior Forester.

JOSEPHA: (*Outraged.*) With that fine, upstanding young man? That's a scandal! She led him astray, that trollop!

SCHOOLMASTER: (*Standing, seriously concerned.*) I shouldn't think it took much leading, Ma'am . . .

JOSEPHA: But you don't understand her kind of woman, teacher. I know that young man well and I've seen how shy he is around women: he's always proper and correct and from a very good family! I always said we never should have let these foreigners settle here, they'll just undermine our moral character!

BASIL: Quite right!

JOSEPHA: He's presentable at least, but she's a pestilence!

BASIL: He's as worthless as she is: look how he cut my hair!

FIGARO: (*Enters beside himself but controlled: to Adalbert.*) Adalbert, I want to speak to you. You have stated [in public] that my wife betrayed me yesterday . . .

ADALBERT: (*Cowardly.*) Me? I didn't say anything!

MIDWIFE: Oh yes, he did . . .

JOSEPHA: (*Interrupting brusquely.*) I beg you not to involve yourself in affairs that are none of your concern! (*To Figaro.*) My husband never says anything whatsoever, neither yesterday not today nor tomorrow: is that clear? How dare you use that tone with us and excite my husband into a heart attack—us, your oldest customers!

FIGARO: That has nothing to do with it! My wife's honor has been attacked and I demand satisfaction . . .

BASIL: (*Interrupts, roaring.*) Demand nothing! You sneaking foreigner! Demand! Demand! Did you ever hear anything like it! You should be grateful we took you in at all here like generous people and give us bad haircuts, you refugee you . . . if we hadn't supported you you'd have starved by now!

JOSEPHA: Quite right! The nerve of him!

BASIL: Come on, teacher!

SCHOOLMASTER: (*Breaking out suddenly at Basil.*) Stop calling me "teacher": my title is "Assistant Principal": understand? (*Exit rapidly to hall.*)

JOSEPHA: (*To Adalbert.*) Come, Adalbert! (*Exit with him to hall.*)

BASIL: I could buy five like him—teacher! (*To Midwife.*) As for you: you wouldn't dare speak up for trash like that if you had any competition! It would serve you right if we let the race die out! (*Exit to hall. Figaro stares stonily into space.*)

MIDWIFE: Figaro, don't let them bother you, they're dreadful people, I know them all. Trust your wife. But you have to change your ways.

FIGARO: What's wrong with my ways now?

MIDWIFE: Everything. She loves you so much . . .

FORESTER: (*Entering from the hall.*) Excuse me. I just heard about something that took place here. Man to man, now: I've had many adventures in my time, but never with a married woman. I have a certain sensitivity to the feelings of other men, and I have no taste for hanging round married men's houses. I met your wife quite by chance after the movies—that is all.

FIGARO: Word of honor?

FORESTER: [And prepared to defend it] at any time.

MIDWIFE: There now! (*The lights go out and the New Year is greeted with noise and cheering. Twelve chimes. Cries of "Toast! A toast!" As the lights come up, [the band] strikes up a lively march in the hall; in the room next door stand Figaro and Susanna, no one else.*)

SUSANNA: Happy New Year, Figaro.

FIGARO: Happy New Year . . . Susanna, I suspected you: please forgive me.

SUSANNA: I have nothing to forgive, Figaro: I betrayed you.

SCENE 4

(*Six months later, in the land of the revolution; on the former country estate of émigré Count Almaviva, in fact. Sitting in the sun before the noble Baroque portal of the castle are Antonio, the elderly castle gardener, and Pedrillo, formerly the Count's groom, now castle bailiff. The former smokes, the latter reads the newspaper. It is high summer.*)

ANTONIO: So: what's in the paper?

PEDRILLO: Progress.

ANTONIO: Where?

PEDRILLO: Here. Everywhere else things are going downhill fast, but we're on the upswing.

ANTONIO: Be nice to see some evidence.

PEDRILLO: Grumbling is subversive. If you weren't my father-in-law, I swear I'd have hauled you in front of the Revolutionary Tribunal long ago.

ANTONIO: Haul away, son-in-law, I'm an old man and haven't got long to live anyway, I'd tell your pals on the Tribunal [same as I tell you], things'll never be like they were when his Grace Count Almaviva was still in charge, never again!

PEDRILLO: Thank the Lord!

ANTONIO: Things were better then.

PEDRILLO: Is that so? And what about his dear Grace's licentious lawlessness? I guess you don't remember the kind of vicious outrages that highborn criminal of yours used to perpetrate every day of the week, huh? Let me remind you of the cynical, arrogant way he used to exercise his so-called "seigneurial rights"! The daughters of the Poor were nothing but wild game for him to sate his low appetites on, look at Susanna, the wife of his own trusted servant, even *she* came near to giving in to him back in your Good Old Days—and I wish she had, it's all that dirty traitor Figaro deserves, turning his back on the People! Helping the Count across the border, an aristocrat totally dedicated to his bestial lusts! [Openly!] Sneeringly!

ANTONIO: If we two'd been aristocrats, I bet we'd have done the same . . .

PEDRILLO: But we weren't, remember that! You were nothing but a pitiful slave when you were castle gardener . . .

ANTONIO: (*Interrupts him.*) How's that? A slave?

PEDRILLO: [*Going right on.*] . . . growing fancy baby vegetables for her Ladyship's table, and what was on *your* table? Greens! Day in, day out: greens!

ANTONIO: (*Grins warningly.*) Greens keep you young.

PEDRILLO: (*Yelling at him.*) Well I don't like greens, understand? Or turnips neither! (*Children run past laughing and screaming; they are playing with a ball, which hits Antonio.*)

ANTONIO: (*Looking angrily after them.*) Dirty little animals . . .

PEDRILLO: And those aren't animals, they're wards of the State Foundling Home, and your dear Count's castle now belongs to them, get that straight for once. Where Painted Relics of the Past pursued their Brainless Pleasures, a New Race is growing up Joyous and Free and Strong!

ANTONIO: That New Race of yours has stolen every apple in my orchard . . .

PEDRILLO: You are [nothing but] a malicious old Nihilist!

ANTONIO: I won't take that from you! Castle Bailiff! What kind of Bailiff are you? All you can see is "the Future": "the Future," while all the beautiful things rot in the cellar, the paintings, the furniture, the tapestries: you don't give a damn about them! When I think abou the cellar I feel like my heart is going to break.

PEDRILLO: A single human being means more to me than all the dead art in the world.

ANTONIO: Which of your pamphlets you get that one out of?

PEDRILLO: I'd be ashamed to be illiterate as you!

BARBERINA: (*Running excitedly past.*) Pedrillo! Pedrillo!

PEDRILLO: Where's the fire?

BARBERINA: You'll never guess what I saw . . . I was in the park just now, over by the Neptune Fountain . . .

PEDRILLO: (*Interrupting.*) Will you get it through your head, that's not the Neptune Fountain any more, it's the 27th of September Memorial.

BARBERINA: What difference does it make?

PEDRILLO: I see! That's how my wife talks! (*To Antonio.*) *Your* daughter!

ANTONIO: Kiss my ass!

PEDRILLO: Ass-kissing's more your style, [old man]! (*To Barberina.*) Get on with it.

BARBERINA: Don't order me around, I'm not one of your underlings! Well, anyway: there I was standing by the 23rd of Neptune, and who should I see coming over the big meadow, my heart stopped cold, for a second I thought it was a ghost!

ANTONIO: A ghost?

BARBERINA: (*To Antonio.*) In broad daylight!

PEDRILLO: (*To Barberina.*) Supernatural beings do not exist. Get on with it.

BARBERINA: Well so it wasn't supernatural, just a perfectly natural flesh-and-blood person—an old friend of ours!

PEDRILLO: Who?

BARBERINA: You'll never guess!

PEDRILLO: Then tell me!

BARBERINA: Figaro.

ANTONIO: Figaro?!

PEDRILLO: What?! That miserable runaway dares to come back here? Now that is the absolute limit, that's insolence personified, that is the most shameless presumption of the century!

BARBERINA: I wish you wouldn't talk so hoity-toity!

PEDRILLO: (*Glares at her.*) How'd it suit you if I lock him up in the dungeon?

BARBERINA: Are you *still* jealous?

PEDRILLO: Of a dirty fugitive? What do you think I am?!

FIGARO: (*Enters, stops.*) Oh! There you are. (*Smiles. None of the three move a muscle.*) Hello, Barberina!

PEDRILLO: (*Darkly.*) Good day.

FIGARO: And good day to you. How's everything?

ANTONIO: Not so hot. (*Silence.*)

PEDRILLO: (*Grimly.*) We weren't expecting you.

FIGARO: (*Smiling.*) Quite a surprise, hm?

PEDRILLO: (*Smiles nastily.*) And such a nice one . . . (*Flaring up at Figaro.*) You filthy emigrant camp-follower, this is all we needed! (*Silence.*)

FIGARO: (*Suddenly.*) So long! (*Starts to leave.*)

PEDRILLO: Halt! You know what's coming to you!

FIGARO: (*Smiling.*) Can't amount to much . . .

PEDRILLO: Oho!

FIGARO: After all, I only left on account of my wife; an émigré for love . . . (*Grins.*)

PEDRILLO: Love is a private problem of the Individual in a state of Anarchy and all things individual are devoid of political significance, so screw that!

BARBERINA: Where's Susanna?

FIGARO: No idea.

BARBERINA: What do you mean?

FIGARO: We've separated.

BARBERINA: Separated?!

FIGARO: Bed and board. It's already been six months.

BARBERINA: Did she catch you cheating?

FIGARO: On the contrary. More the other way around.

BARBERINA: (*Can't comprehend it.*) She . . . betrayed *you?*

FIGARO: Yes.

PEDRILLO: (*A quick look at Barberina; to Figaro, grimly grinning.*) Well what do you know!

BARBERINA: (*To herself.*) Poor Susanna!

PEDRILLO: Who'd she go off with? (*Another quick look at Barberina.*) The Count?

FIGARO: (*Smiles.*) No, just a Junior Forester, an ordinary mortal . . .

PEDRILLO: There are no ordinary or extraordinary mortals, there's only The People, you can get that straight right off, you johnny-come-lately!

FIGARO: (*Looks hard at him.*) Who are you talking to? Listen, I'm no immigrant, you know, I can't say for sure I was born here but I know damn well I was found here . . .

PEDRILLO: Our tough luck!

FIGARO: [*Going right on.*] . . . I'm just as much at home here as the trees, the fields, the water, the air, have *you* got *that* straight?

PEDRILLO: (*Threateningly.*) Don't yell at me, you. A runaway is always a johnny-come-lately, and this isn't your home because you betrayed it.

FIGARO: Betray nothing! You clown! I remember a kid named Pedrillo, he was the Count's stable-boy, and if it hadn't been for a certain man he'd still be the Count's stable-boy! Who showed you a book where it said in black and white that a slave didn't have to stay a slave?! Who taught you revolution? Me, that certain Figaro!

PEDRILLO: And if it wasn't for the certain Figaro the Count would never've got away from me—who got him across the border? You! Traitor! If I didn't have so much revolutionary discipline I'd knock you flat here and now!

BARBERINA: Oh, stop it!

PEDRILLO: Don't you get involved or you'll be sorry!

FIGARO: (*To Pedrillo.*) What did the Count ever do to you?

PEDRILLO: He raped my wife.

FIGARO: (*Puzzled.*) Raped? (*Gives Barberina a questioning look; she smiles, embarrassed, indicates covertly it wasn't that bad.*)

PEDRILLO: If I'd caught that Count of yours, I'd have given him something to remember . . . (*Punching the air.*) Pow! And pow and pow! (*Gives Figaro a withering look.*) I'm going to call the guards.

BARBERINA: (*To Figaro.*) Go, get away, please! My husband's got no sense of humor when his conscience gets going. You wouldn't believe how he can hate!

ANTONIO: He's a vicious animal . . .

BARBERINA: (*Attacking Antonio.*) That's enough "animal" talk out of you, Papa! Pedrillo has his good side; at least *he* believes in the Revolution! (*To Figaro.*) Please Figaro, for old times's sake, get away while you can! He'll put you in prison, they'll cut off your head yet!

FIGARO: My head? No, the head-chopping days are over. Heads are back on top where they belong, and [the new bosses] only pass death sentences in order to commute them. Heads with prices on them sit in the stock exchange and give the executioner bad tips . . . (*Smiles.*) No, Barberina: Figaro's here to stay. He's back from Haggelburg—by way of Damascus. But Damascus turns out to be as much like Haggelburg as the negative is the photograph . . .

PEDRILLO: (*Enters with guards: to Figaro.*) Figaro: in the name of the People, you're under arrest!

FIGARO: Just a minute. (*To the Sergeant of the watch.*) Before you go to the trouble of throwing me in irons, I advise you to have a look at this. (*Hands him a document.*) See, I'd like to spare you any embarrassment that I might owe . . . (*Indicating Pedrillo*) someone else.

PEDRILLO: (*Perplexed.*) What's going on? (*Sergeant reads document; his eyes widen.*)

FIGARO: (*To Pedrillo.*) I wouldn't have gone through with this if you weren't such an ungrateful bonehead . . . (*To Sergeant.*) Well, Sergeant, got it deciphered yet?

SERGEANT: Sir! (*To Guard.*) Ten-Hut! Pree-sent: Harms! Hyeees: H'left! (*Guards and Sergeant salute Figaro.*)

PEDRILLO: (*Beside himself.*) What are you doing?! Saluting him?!

SERGEANT: (*To Pedrillo.*) Silence!

PEDRILLO: "Silence"?! I'm losing my mind!

FIGARO: (*To Pedrillo.*) Hold on. It's no use, Pedrillo. [There it is in] black and white . . . (*Hands him the document.*) You just retired.

PEDRILLO: (*Thunderstruck.*) Retired?

BARBERINA: Who?!

PEDRILLO: Me?!

FIGARO: You.

ANTONIO: (*Aside.*) High time!

BARBERINA: Give me that . . . (*She tears the document from his hand and reads it hastily along with him.*)

FIGARO: (*To Sergeant of the Watch.*) Thank you, Sergeant: [that'll be all.]

SERGEANT: (*Commanding the Guard.*) Ten-hut! Leff . . . Hayce! . . . Hoarrd . . . Howrch! (*Exit with Guard.*)

PEDRILLO: (*Has mastered the document: screams.*) What?! I really have gone crazy . . . You're the new bailiff!? You?!

FIGARO: (*To Barberina, who's staring open-mouthed at him.*) Yes. Why play the barber-hairdresser in Haggelburg when all it takes is a little brains to be bailiff back home? No! I ran away in the dead of night like an aristocrat, not a servant; oh, yes, love had me in its spell, I was dead to the world and dreaming—but now I'm back again and wide awake. Been back three weeks in fact; putting my experience at the disposal of our new masters, atoning for my counterrevolutionary sins, getting absolution—though the penance wasn't all that bad . . . (*Grins.*) Yes, the Revolution's got a human face, now: there's plenty of opportunity for an independent type with an ace or two in the hole . . .

PEDRILLO: Some type! Criminal type you mean!

FIGARO: You're a fine one to talk!

PEDRILLO: What did I ever do to get cast off this way?! Maybe I was *too* revolutionary, was that it?!

FIGARO: Maybe. (*Softly, so the Guard doesn't hear.*) But you also have problems with your math.

PEDRILLO: What kind of problems?

FIGARO: You're looking after forty-eight children in the orphanage; but [in your reports] you always seem to get the number backwards—eighty-four. And you can thank me you're not in a cell right now, Noble Hero [of the Revolution].

BARBERINA: (*To Pedrillo.*) I always told you they'd find out some day!

PEDRILLO: Shut up! Who bought the piano on time-payments, me or you?

BARBERINA: And who drinks up the payments in the tavern: you or me?

FIGARO: Don't get worked up, friends. You only did what all bailiffs do. I only wish I *could* report it!

ANTONIO: (*Aside.*) I could've told them, but I know when to keep my mouth shut.*

BARBERINA: And what about Susanna?

FIGARO: Susanna? Who's that? She didn't want it any other way, she betrayed me.

BARBERINA: And you deserved it.

---

*For additional text relevant to this scene, see appendix.

FIGARO: Oho!

BARBERINA: If you don't even care if she's begging for her living or not, then you certainly do deserve it. Justice cuts two ways, depending on which side you're on. (*Figaro is struck, stares at her wide-eyed. She continues, slowly and almost threatening.*) Why do you think your wife betrayed you, anyway?

FIGARO: What do you mean, why? We just drifted apart . . .

BARBERINA: I see, "drifted apart": and whose fault was that?

FIGARO: Not mine.

BARBERINA: You were completely innocent, is that right? (*Pedrillo laughs, briefly and grimly.*)

FIGARO: I was always faithful to her.

BARBERINA: I don't see much sign of it.

FIGARO: (*Sharply.*) What! (*Silence.*)

BARBERINA: And still no children I suppose?

FIGARO: [*Shakes his head "no."*] Thank God.

BARBERINA: Poor Susanna! A woman without children makes no sense to herself!

FIGARO: The way the world is, lots of things make no sense . . .

BARBERINA: But becoming bailiff here, that makes sense, doesn't it, you innocent lamb, you? (*Silence.*) Aren't you ever ashamed? You're more corrupt than we are. Yes, corrupt: through and through.

FIGARO: Really?

ANTONIO: (*To Barberina.*) Leave him alone!

FIGARO: (*To Antonio.*) Let her speak! (*To Barberina.*) Go ahead.

BARBERINA: I'll go ahead with or without your permission, Mr. Castle Bailiff! (*Silence.*)

FIGARO: (*To Barberina.*) Listen to me for a minute. I learned something important when Susanna threw me over; nobody in the world is more hated and despised than an intelligent man who's honest, too. You have to choose: honesty or brains. An honest man always ends up paying the piper. If you're smart: *you're* the piper. I've made my choice.

ANTONIO: Bravo!

PEDRILLO: You listen for a minute, Figaro. I'm going down to the tavern now, but before I do I just want to tell you one thing, and this is serious. I fought for a great idea—all right, I faked my account book: but that doesn't rub off on the idea. It'll keep on marching forward if all the stewards in the country fake their books!

ANTONIO: (*Contemptuously.*) "Forward!"

FIGARO: (*Attacking Antonio.*) Don't think our dear Count Almaviva wasn't corrupt, too; he enjoyed [the game] as much as we do; it just didn't show up as much on him, because we'd had generations to get used to it—corruption was his customary right!

PEDRILLO: That's better!

FIGARO: Who was this great Count, anyway? A rich man who managed to convince himself he was rich in spirit too. "In two months it will all be over." Crap! Birth, wealth, rank, custom made him proud! And what did His Grace do to earn all those advantages? He took the trouble to be born, and it was the last time he took any trouble in his life, the rest of it was luxury, posing and waste!

PEDRILLO: Oh, how true! (*Attacking Antonio.*) I'll keep my ideals, retired or not, understand?!

ANTONIO: Go to hell, all of you! (*Exit furiously.*)

FIGARO: (*To Pedrillo.*) You still have ideals?

PEDRILLO: (*Seriously.*) Yes. (*Silence.*)

BARBERINA: (*To Figaro.*) If he didn't, why did he fight in the revolution?

FIGARO: To better himself.

PEDRILLO: That's not all. (*To Barberina.*) You tell him.

BARBERINA: We wanted to better ourselves so we could *be* better.

PEDRILLO: (*To Figaro.*) Hear that, Bailiff?

FIGARO: Yes.

PEDRILLO: Then remember it . . . (*Nods sadly to him and exits.*)

FIGARO: (*To Barberina.*) Your husband is a fool.

BARBERINA: (*Flares up at him.*) You can't take everything decent away from me! Not you!

FIGARO: You still haven't grasped the way the world works. And these days, it's the works that count; not the people. Unfortunately.

ACT III

SCENE 1

[Omitted from 1936 version]

(*Six months later, in the offices of the International Refugee Relief Fund. The General Directress is a fortyish chain-smoker with a Doctor of Laws degree. Her face is gray as the piles of case-folders awaiting disposition stacked on the floor-to-ceiling shelves. She is presently dictating an appeal to her Secretary, who takes it down in shorthand.*)

DIRECTRESS: Where was I?

SECRETARY: "Humanity."

DIRECTRESS: Oh, yes. Ummm: "In the name of Humanity, the International Refugee Relief Fund appeals to you; without regard for Party, Class, Race or Religion, appeals to your generous heart. Help to relieve the plights of the Refugee, exposed and defenseless, deprived by a stroke of fate or Faith, Hope and Charity. How many already have despaired, succumbed, taken their own lives! May every one of you who still rejoices in the security of a peaceful homeland, unable to conceive the misery of losing it: help us with a small contribution! Become a member of the International Refugee Relief Fund. Help us; help us; help now!" Box number so and so, et cetera. There. Is there any aspirin left?

SECRETARY: No, Doctor.

DIRECTRESS: My head is like a buzzsaw again today.

SECRETARY: You shouldn't smoke so much.

DIRECTRESS: Without a cigarette I'm not human. Is anyone out there?

SECRETARY: A man and a woman.

DIRECTRESS: Looking for financial assistance?

SECRETARY: I told them both right off we couldn't help them that way. They're not after money . . .

SECRETARY: (*Interrupting.*) Then send them right on in! (*Secretary exits. Directress nervously lights another cigarette. Count enters with Susanna.*)

COUNT: (*Bowing slightly.*) Madame: Count Almaviva . . .

DIRECTRESS: (*Pointing to chairs.*) Please. (*They sit.*) What brings you to us?

COUNT: It's about the girl, that is, this young woman; I've known her for ten years and would vouch for her under any circumstances . . .

DIRECTRESS: Excuse me, who are you?

COUNT: Count Almaviva.

DIRECTRESS: (*Smiles.*) I'm afraid the name means nothing to me . . .

COUNT: Please don't apologize: I'm used to that by now . . . In brief: I once was a very rich man. This young woman was my wife's chambermaid. When we fled my homeland she accompanied us; later we separated, and by the time she decided to return to our service we were living elsewhere . . . (*Smiles: to Susanna.*) You had quite a job finding us, didn't you? (*Susanna nods affirmatively. To the Directress.*) Yes. But of course one is no longer in the position to employ a chambermaid, but thanks to my earlier connections I was able to secure my protégé a good situation. She is presently a waitress, her employer is another refugee, a Signor di Cherubino, my page in the gray dawn of time . . .

DIRECTRESS: (*Impatiently.*) Then if your protégé has work, there's no problem, is there?

COUNT: Wrong. Quite wrong, for the young lady is a stateless person and requires a work permit . . .

DIRECTRESS: I see. The old story. (*To Susanna.*) Are you married?

SUSANNA: We're separated. Divorced.

DIRECTRESS: Ah. And where does your former husband reside?

SUSANNA: I've no idea.

COUNT: He abandoned her.

DIRECTRESS: Has your husband a profession?

SUSANNA: I don't know what he does now. He's been everything.

COUNT: He was at one time my valet.

SUSANNA: When we separated he was a hairdresser in Haggelburg, but he sold out right after we broke up. The townspeople wouldn't have anything more to do with him.

DIRECTRESS: Why not?

SUSANNA: A divorced man there can't make a go of it; not if he's a foreigner.

DIRECTRESS: Does he support you?

SUSANNA: No.

DIRECTRESS: Am I to understand that he left you and is therefore the guilty party? (*Silence.*)

SUSANNA: No; I'm the guilty party. (*Silence.*)

DIRECTRESS: Have you children?

SUSANNA: (*Shakes her head "no" and grins.*) Thank God.

DIRECTRESS: Yes: I suppose so. (*Silence.*)

COUNT: (*To Directress.*) Now about the work permit . . .

DIRECTRESS: (*Interrupting.*) There's hope for it, there's always hope: perhaps for a limited period.

COUNT: Bravo!

DIRECTRESS: (*Defensively.*) A work permit is often issued only to be called in again . . . (*She passes a form to Susanna.*) Fill out this questionnaire: conscientiously, please! (*Susanna sits at a table and fills it out.*)

COUNT: (*To Directress.*) Excuse me, there is also a private matter . . . Does the Fund have a legal bureau?

DIRECTRESS: Are you in need of legal counsel?

COUNT: Yes.

DIRECTRESS: I am a Doctor of Laws. Well?

COUNT: (*Looks shyly toward Susanna.*) Please, may we speak more softly?

DIRECTRESS: If you wish.

COUNT: Recently I have been passing time as a [customer's] representative: real estate, buying and selling, but I seem to have gotten into difficulties . . . (*He breaks off and passes letters and documents over to her.*) Here: if you would be so kind . . . (*Directress looks over the documents: stops cold, and looks at the Count wide-eyed.*)

DIRECTRESS: (*Softly.*) Did you sign this?

COUNT: Yes. (*Silence.*)

DIRECTRESS: Hm. And this?

COUNT: Certainly. (*Silence.*)

DIRECTRESS: So you sold something which did not belong to you?

COUNT: Excuse me: I sold it under strict contract, I was merely a representative and had so to speak very limited freedom of action . . .

DIRECTRESS: (*Interrupting.*) Freedom or no freedom: it's still fraud.

COUNT: You think so?

DIRECTRESS: Embezzlement and plain fraud.

COUNT: Indeed? But the man in whose interest I was acting expressly assured me that there was nothing illegal . . .

DIRECTRESS: Oh, come now! A child could see it!

COUNT: He gave me his word of honor [as a gentleman].

DIRECTRESS: And you believed him?

SUSANNA: (*Suddenly, to the Directress.*) Excuse me, but am I supposed to cross out the answer that doesn't apply or underline the one that does?

DIRECTRESS: Whichever suits you . . .

SUSANNA: I'll cross them out. (*Does so. Silence.*)

DIRECTRESS: (*To Count.*) Is this a first offense?

COUNT: Yes. (*Silence.*)

DIRECTRESS: I advise you to give yourself up voluntarily.

COUNT: (*Smiling strangely.*) What can one expect?

DIRECTRESS: Hm. One to three years.

COUNT: Three years?

DIRECTRESS: (*Holds a letter in each hand, weighing them.*) Your need versus gross negligence: aggravation outweighs mitigation. (*Silence.*)

COUNT: My wife always says we're still sitting in the schoolroom, waiting for the long holiday. (*Looking upward.*) Tell me, teacher: will it be much longer?

SCENE 2

(*A year later, abroad again, in Cherubino's Night Owl Club, a small café/nightclub catering to émigrés. Bar, piano, booths, At rear the entrance, right a door to the kitchen. It is evening, but the club is still empty. Susanna is the bar-waitress here, and is just setting out flowers and glasses on the tables. A Customer enters; he could be from Haggelburg. Dim lighting.*)

CUSTOMER: (*Doesn't sit down.*) I seem to be your only customer.

SUSANNA: This is a nightclub, Sir, we don't open until ten.

CUSTOMER: It only gets lively here later?

SUSANNA: Yes, toward midnight. (*Silence.*)

CUSTOMER: (*Gazing at Susanna.*) Are you a princess?

SUSANNA: Me?

CUSTOMER: I hear everybody in these places where émigrés hang out is an aristocrat. The chef is a duke, the piano player's a baron, and the barmaid's a Ladyship at least . . . (*Grins. Cherubino enters, unnoticed by Susanna and the Customer; he is a chubby, still youngish gentleman with a rosy countenance full of amorphous brutality. He eavesdrops.*)

SUSANNA: (*Smiles.*) I'm no princess.

CUSTOMER: Then what are you?

SUSANNA: A nobody. (*Silence.*)

CUSTOMER: Too bad, too bad. Well, maybe I'll come back round midnight. See you, pretty nobody! (*Exit.*)

SUSANNA: Goodbye, Sir, you remember to come back, now!

CHERUBINO: (*Coming forward.*) Susanna.

SUSANNA: (*Jumping a little.*) Yes, Boss?

CHERUBINO: How often have I impressed it on you, if someone asks if you're a princess, make him happy and say yes—or at least smile ambiguously, life's too short to spend it robbing decent folks of their illusions and spoiling business . . . (*He smiles.*) And speaking of illusions; I plagiarized together another song today: it's about a great love that isn't reciprocated. Can you help me with a title?

SUSANNA: I'm no poet, Mr. Di Cherubino.

CHERUBINO: How do you like "Susanna" for a title?

SUSANNA: That's not much of a name [for a song].

CHERUBINO: Who knows? Maybe it'll turn out to be an international hit . . . (*He sits down at the piano.*)

SUSANNA: Not if you call it "Susanna," it certainly won't be.

CHERUBINO: We'll see! (*He plays and sings softly and with sticky sentimentality.**)
Susanna, I love you, why won't you love me?
Hear the little birdies singing in the trees,
They know each He needs his peachie
That's Love's mystery.

Spring-time is ring-time:
Susanne, my heart is sore—
My blood is aching
Till you're mine once more

When you left I couldn't sleep,
I went half insane,
Till I started taking
Pleasure in the pain . . .

So come on, Susanna, say you know it's true
It's not just spring fever drawing me to you,
It's the song of true love calling
Say you hear it too.

Well?
SUSANNA: I like the tune.
CHERUBINO: Is that all? (*Silence.*)
SUSANNA: Mr. Di Cherubino, I'm sorry, but please don't name your song after me.
CHERUBINO: You know what you are?
SUSANNA: Yes. Ungrateful.
CHERUBINO: No, no . . .
SUSANNA: If it hadn't been for you I would have starved.
CHERUBINO: No, no, no!
SUSANNA: It's true! (*Silence.*)
CHERUBINO: (*Gazes hard at her but friendly.*) Incorrigible.
SUSANNA: I'll never marry again.
CHERUBINO: Was it that bad?
SUSANNA: Just don't bother with me, I'm a hopeless case; I'm fond of people I despise and the ones I respect I can't help laughing at and it's just no good either way.
CHERUBINO: I'm not entirely unfamiliar with the feeling, but I got over it when we had to emigrate. I used to be quite the romantic type myself, way back when . . . (*Stops abruptly.*) Good God: how long has it been since we left home?
SUSANNA: (*Smiles.*) Two hundred years.
CHERUBINO: At least! (*Silence.*)
SUSANNA: Do you know what today is? He gets out today.
CHERUBINO: Who?

---

*Lyrics set to fit the first three strophes of Mozart's "Voi che sapete."

SUSANNA: The Count. He was sentenced just a year ago today. (*Silence.*)

CHERUBINO: Will he come here?

SUSANNA: I've been expecting him any minute. (*Silence.*)

CHERUBINO: Will you answer me one question frankly?

SUSANNA: Of course, if I can.

CHERUBINO: (*Slowly.*) Did you have something going with the Count?

SUSANNA: Me? What makes you think so?

CHERUBINO: Well, he was always after you before you married Figaro . . .

SUSANNA: But you know nothing came of that. *Everybody* knows that!

CHERUBINO: But what about now? Since the Revolution?

SUSANNA: Since then, really, nothing's happened. Everything the Count did for me, bringing me here to work for you, it was pure compassion.

CHERUBINO: A word you don't hear often.

SUSANNA: But that's how it was. (*Silence.*)

CHERUBINO: Is it true that the Countess died of worry over what was going on between you and the Count?

SUSANNA: Who says that? That is nothing but a filthy slander! The poor Countess dying on account of me! Listen, I swear to you by everything's that's still holy to me, the poor Countess died of influenza, may she come through that door as she lay on her deathbed, mouth wide open [to accuse me] and carry me off [to hell], I had nothing to do with the Count, nothing, nothing, nothing, because I loved somebody else who ruined my life and wouldn't give me a baby and I hate him like the plague!

CHERUBINO: Figaro?

SUSANNA: Yes. The last man on earth. (*The stage darkens. Cherubino's song is heard, sung and hummed over piano accompaniment; as the lights come up again, the club is functioning. A pianist sings and plays the song, and the customers hum along, including the Customer who was there before, who has come back and is now sitting at the bar.*)

SUSANNA: (*To Cherubino, behind the bar.*) Has he had anything to eat?

CHERUBINO: He's still sitting in the kitchen.

CUSTOMER: (*To Susanna.*) Who's in the kitchen?

SUSANNA: A casual acquaintance . . . (*Turns her back on him and serves [others].*)

CUSTOMER: (*Looking after her, to Cherubino.*) Well, how do you like that: pretty snippy, isn't she?

CHERUBINO: (*Smiles.*) She's a princess. She just won't admit it, out of shame. (*Pause.*)

CUSTOMER: (*Suddenly drunk.*) So who's that sitting in the kitchen?

CHERUBINO: Nobody.

CUSTOMER: Don't try to kid me, mister!

CHERUBINO: Sir, there's no one in the kitchen but the staff and a beggar!

CUSTOMER: If he's a beggar, take this cognac to him (*Points to his own large, brimming glass*). Right this minute, if you please!

CHERUBINO: At your service . . . (*Exit with glass to kitchen, furious.*)
CUSTOMER: Hey, Princess! Who's that you got in the kitchen? A prince? (*Grins.*)
SUSANNA: Yes. (*Turns her back on him.*)
POLICE DETECTIVE: (*Entering.*) May I speak to the manager? Police.
SUSANNA: (*Startled, frightened.*) Right away. (*Runs to the kitchen and calls inside.*) Mr. Di Cherubino! (*Cherubino appears: Susanna points at the Detective.*) This gentleman would like to speak to you . . . (*Softly.*) Police . . . (*Glances fearfully into kitchen.*)
CHERUBINO: (*To Detective.*) Yes?
DETECTIVE: I'm following up a case; you have a waitress here, a displaced person, no passport, her work permit ran out a month ago . . .
SUSANNA: (*Interrupting, relieved.*) Oh, it's only me you're worried about?
DETECTIVE: (*Sizing her up with a glance.*) Yes, only you . . . (*Turns back to Cherubino.*) She's got to stop working here immediately, if she doesn't she'll be penalized, and the same goes for you, sir, you could still lose your license . . .
CHERUBINO: But I can't just throw the girl out on the street . . .
DETECTIVE: Sorry . . . ! (*Count appears in the kitchen door, the empty cognac glass in his hand; he has become a ruin, but traces of former elegance remain: since he can no longer hold his liquor, he is fairly affected by the single glass he's had. Continuing.*) . . . I'm just doing my duty, and individual [problems] have nothing to do with it, the law's the law.
COUNT: (*Overhearing.*) The law?
CHERUBINO: (*To Count.*) Quiet, please!
COUNT: Always the law!
DETECTIVE: (*To Count.*) This is official business, don't get involved!
COUNT: Oh, I know all about your official business, it's about time someone got involved with those laws of yours: high time!
CUSTOMER: Let's hear it for the Prince!
DETECTIVE: (*To Count.*) Shut your mouth!
COUNT: I won't shut my mouth: understand? Not a chance!
CHERUBINO: He's an old man, he's drunk . . .
DETECTIVE: He'd better be, for his own good.
COUNT: (*Screams at the Detective.*) My good does not concern you in the least, I forbid you to take an interest in me! And I've only had one drink, and I can hold my liquor well as ever, see?! And if you want my opinion . . .
DETECTIVE: (*Interrupting.*) We have no use for your opinions here!
COUNT: . . . I tell you that . . . (*Stops, lets the glass fall, clutches his heart, sways.*)
SUSANNA: Oh God, Your Grace!
COUNT: (*His voice thick.*) I'll tell the world what I think, the teacher too . . . (*He collapses onto a chair. Susanna busies herself over him. The customers leave the club.*)
DETECTIVE: What's that? A count?
CHERUBINO: Count Almaviva. (*Detective goes to Count and takes his pulse.*)

SUSANNA: Is he dead?

DETECTIVE: Not a chance. Drunk, that's all . . . (*Takes the Count's wallet out. Leafs through the papers in it: stops.*) Number eighty-seven: released on . . .

CHERUBINO: Yes, yes, it's a sad story; he sold something that didn't belong to him . . .

DETECTIVE: Embezzlement?

CHERUBINO: (*Nods affirmatively.*) Embezzlement and plain fraud . . . A child could have seen it, but not him. Yes, yes, poverty and dissipation: the aggravating circumstances outweigh the mitigating ones.

COUNT: (*Coming to.*) Where's my hat?

CHERUBINO: In the kitchen.

SUSANNA: I'll get it . . . (*Exit to kitchen.*)

DETECTIVE: (*To Count.*) You can go any time. I was just finding out who you were . . . (*Indicates wallet.*)

COUNT: (*Recognizing it.*) I see. (*Silence.*)

DETECTIVE: Everything's in order.

COUNT: Did you look at the castle?

DETECTIVE: (*Puzzled.*) What castle?

COUNT: My castle. Look . . . (*He takes some photographs from his wallet and shows them to the Detective.*) The grounds stretched all the way to the edge of the forest. And these, these are family pictures, mementos, my wife and so on . . . (*Smiles.*)

DETECTIVE: If I were you I'd go on home now.

COUNT: And where might that be?

DETECTIVE: Just where do you live?

COUNT: Are you familiar with the Hotel Esplanade? And the Carlton? I know them all; all of them . . . my respects, Commissioner! Good night! (*Exit. Susanna enters from kitchen with the Count's hat, looks around perplexed.*)

SUSANNA: Where is he?

CHERUBINO: Gone.

SUSANNA: (*Fearful.*) Without his hat?

DETECTIVE: Drunks never hurt themselves.

CHERUBINO: Just one glass . . .

DETECTIVE: He can't handle it any more.

CHERUBINO: Yes, yes, a sad story.

DETECTIVE: Hm . . . (*To Susanna.*) You, miss: come on into the station tomorrow, God knows, maybe you'll get another extension . . . Good night! (*Exit.*)

CHERUBINO: My compliments, Commissioner! (*Silence.*)

SUSANNA: I'm not going to the station!

CHERUBINO: Are you insane?

SUSANNA: To hell with their extension!

CHERUBINO: Without a work permit how can you survive?

SUSANNA: I'll answer a letter . . .

CHERUBINO: What letter?

SUSANNA: A letter I've been carrying around with me for two weeks. I'd just like to know how he got my address . . .

CHERUBINO: (Glowering.) Who?

SUSANNA: (Ignores the question.) He wrote to say I ought to come back to him. He said he's lonely . . . (She grins.)

CHERUBINO: Who?

SUSANNA: Figaro. (Silence.)

CHERUBINO: What's he been up to?

SUSANNA: He's become bailiff of the castle: and his conscience is bothering him.

SCENE 3

[Omitted from 1936 version]

(Some time later, again at the former estate of Count Almaviva. Figaro and all the foundlings are sitting at a long, laden table and eating. It is noon, and Barberina is serving. Carlos, Cesar, and Maurizio are three foundlings aged thirteen, twelve, and eight resepctively. Elvira and Rosina are two foundling girls of thirteen. Old Antonio squats on a box to one side fiddling with an old-fashioned radio, then puts on earphones, listens to the music of a foreign station, sometimes conducting to himself.)

FIGARO: Fork on the left, knife on the right! (To Carlos.) Hold on there, that's Rosina's bun! Don't be such a pig! (Pause.)

ROSINA: Uncle Figaro, is it true you used to be married?

FIGARO: (Puzzled.) Me? Yes.

ROSINA: (To Carlos.) Nyah! I was right!

FIGARO: Why "nyah"? What's it got to do with you I've been married or not? (Pause. To Rosina.) How did you find out, anyhow?

ROSINA: Auntie Barberina told me.

FIGARO: (To Barberina.) Now look here! My private life is not educational material, keep that in mind, will you? (To Maurizio.) Fingers out of the plate! (Pause. Listens.) Where's that slurping sound coming from?

CARLOS: Me.

FIGARO: Then stop it, would you please? Future Leaders of the People don't slurp.

ELVIRA: Uncle Figaro, where's your wife now?

FIGARO: None of your business. Don't be so saucy! (Elvira cries.)

BARBERINA: (Comforts her.) The child was only asking.

FIGARO: The child had no business asking. (To Maurizio.) Finger out of the nose! (Pause. Elvira has quieted down.)

ELVIRA: (Sullenly.) Is it true your wife was so bad?

FIGARO: (*Perplexed.*) Bad?

ELVIRA: Yes, because when Auntie Barberina was fighting with Uncle Pedrillo a while ago he said she was as bad as your wife . . .

FIGARO: (*To Barberina.*) Please don't quarrel in front of the children!

BARBERINA: I don't start it.

ELVIRA: (*To Figaro.*) Uncle Pedrillo said he was just as innocent as you, too . . .

FIGARO: (*Grimly cutting in.*) Is that right? Well, he should know. (*Pause.*)

ROSINA: Uncle Figaro, I don't believe it.

FIGARO: What?

ROSINA: That you're so innocent.

FIGARO: (*Perplexed.*) Why? Why not?

ROSINA: (*Saucy.*) Because you don't look like it.

FIGARO: And what's *that* supposed to mean? How *do* I look? Good grief, take a look at yourself, before you go looking at me . . . Miss Smartypants! (*Pause.*)

CARLOS: Oh, Mr. Bailiff, Sir . . .

FIGARO: What now?

CARLOS: (*Hypocritically flattering.*) I believe it.

FIGARO: What?!

CARLOS: That you're completely innocent . . . (*He can't keep a straight face and breaks out laughing; all the children laugh with him, laugh at Figaro. Figaro looks at them a moment helplessly, but catches sight of Barberina trying to keep from laughing too; she doesn't succeed, and he smiles in spite of himself.*)

FIGARO: Just wait! I'll show you who's innocent, you miserable rabble, you . . .

ANTONIO: (*Suddenly roars at the children.*) Quiet! (*Children fall silent.*)

FIGARO: (*To Antonio.*) Quiet yourself! (*As he stands, to the children.*) That's it, lunch is over! Stand up! Say your prayers!

CHILDREN: (*Standing: in chorus.*) Death and Destruction to the Enemy!

ROSINA: (*Points at Cesar.*) Uncle Figaro, he didn't say it, I heard him!

FIGARO: Did you now? Off with you, now, everybody. (*To Cesar.*) You stay. (*Children except Cesar rush off shouting. Barberina clears the table.*)

FIGARO: Why didn't you say your prayer?

CESAR: Because I don't have any enemies.

FIGARO: You think so?

CESAR: I don't want to have any enemies. (*Silence.*)

FIGARO: But when someone gives you a poke, you poke him back, don't you?

CESAR: No.

FIGARO: And why not?

CESAR: Because nobody *gives* me a poke, because I don't like it.

FIGARO: (*Smiles.*) You're a philosopher . . .

CESAR: What's a philosopher?

FIGARO: One of the forbidden occupations. (*Silence.*)

CESAR: Someone *did* hit me a little while ago . . .

FIGARO: Oh? And what did you do?

CESAR: I didn't hit him back.

FIGARO: (*Grins.*) Because he was too big for you, huh?

CESAR: No. Because he was too little. (*Silence.*)

FIGARO: Are you new here?

CESAR: No.

FIGARO: Why can't I remember you . . .

CESAR: We see each other every day. (*Silence.*)

FIGARO: Hm. Well, goodbye for now, Cesar my boy . . . (*Exit Cesar.*)

ANTONIO: Figaro, I just been listening to the news on a foreign station. Lordy, lordy, it looks like we're goners!

FIGARO: Goners? (*Looks off in the direction Cesar departed.*) On the contrary, things are looking up!

ANTONIO: Up?!

FIGARO: Thanks to that kid there, who doesn't hit somebody back because the other kid's too little, I think I see the point of this revolution of ours: this revolution which makes such a handy target for my more or less witty remarks with no point to them but to irritate people or make them feel ridiculous and drive any decent person away from me . . . Yes, maybe if a revolution had landed *me* in a foundling home I might have turned out better . . .

ANTONIO: (*Grumpily.*) You were talking about a point: what point?

FIGARO: I can't say.

ANTONIO: It's a riddle, is it?

FIGARO: Yes, a riddle, a hard one: what is it we always look for, never find, and keep on losing just the same? (*Antonio shrugs. To Barberina.*) Here, I'll tell you the answer; but only you, because you asked me once if I never was ashamed . . . (*He smiles and whispers the answer in her ear, nods amicably to her and exits.*)

ANTONIO: What did he say?

BARBERINA: I didn't understand it.

ANTONIO: Always look for, never find, and keep on losing anyway; what could that be?

BARBERINA: Humanity, he said.

SCENE 4

(*Deep in the frontier forest. Susanna and the Count are secretly crossing the frontier in order to return home. One hears only their voices, for it is a pitch-black night.*)

COUNT: Where are you?

SUSANNA: Here.

COUNT: I can't see a thing.

SUSANNA: This is the blackest night of my life . . . (*Emits a brief scream.*)

COUNT: What's wrong?

SUSANNA: I stepped in something soft. (*The moon breaks pale through the clouds, so one can now see the homeward travelers.*)

COUNT: Our moon is on the rise—as it was then. I left my fatherland to avoid being beaten to death, and now I return through the same forest to avoid being locked up again. Necessity knows no law . . . (*He smiles.*) I no longer ask myself what crime I have committed to be forced to sneak across the border . . .

SUSANNA: Now, your Grace, you haven't broken any law at all!

COUNT: Not so: I miscalculated. "In two months this will all be over." (*He grins.*) Figaro was right. (*He looks round.*) Are we across already?

SUSANNA: I know every clearing in these woods, your Grace. Lake on our right, ravine on the left: it's behind us.

COUNT: What do you expect to gain by bringing me along with you?

SUSANNA: (*Puzzled.*) What do you mean?

COUNT: Do you really believe everything will go smoothly when I [just] come popping up again back home?

SUSANNA: (*Puzzled.*) But we've been all through that, your Grace! First we have to go to Figaro secretly and ask him how things stand . . .

COUNT: (*Cutting in.*) Did you really write to tell him we were coming?

SUSANNA: No, he doesn't know yet. I wanted to but I couldn't, I kept tearing up the letters. I have to talk to him [face to face]. (*Silence.*)

COUNT: He's become castle bailiff now, hasn't he?

SUSANNA: You know that, your Grace!

COUNT: And what have I become . . . (*Grins.*)

SUSANNA: Your Grace, I can see a light!

COUNT: (*Not looking.*) I see nothing.

SUSANNA: Come on . . .

COUNT: (*Interrupting.*) No. That tree over there looks like a bed to me. Yes, on the left the bed, the sofa on the right. She slept on the sofa; it was too short for me . . . (*Looks upward.*) Are you happier now? (*Silence.*)

SUSANNA: (*Looking upward.*) It's raining. (*The wind begins to blow, softly at first.*)

COUNT: Go ahead, Susanna, he's called you, no one's calling me. I'm staying.

SUSANNA: Here?

COUNT: It was never really clear to me why I followed you, only now do I understand that I wanted to sleep at home . . . yes, the sofa was too short . . .

SUSANNA: (*Close to tears.*) Oh, your Grace, please don't complicate the situation! What can you do here in the forest?

COUNT: (*Pointing to the tree trunk.*) There's my bed. (*Heavy gust of wind. The moon disappears behind clouds, it's pitch-dark night again, one only hears Susanna's voice ever farther away, disappearing in the storm.*)

SUSANNA: Your Grace! Where are you? Answer me! Your Grace! Your Grace! (*Silence. The moon breaks out of the clouds again, and one sees the Count, alone.*)

He takes off his coat, tries the strength of its belt, while he hums Cherubino's song, "Susanna.")

COUNT: (*Suddenly, to himself*)* My wife used to say we were sitting in the school-room, waiting for the long holiday . . . (*Looks upward.*) Tell me, Teacher: will it be much longer?

A VOICE: Halt. (*Count flinches and listens.*) Who goes there? (*Count stares into the forest and remains silent. The Sergeant of the Guard comes forward: it was his voice.*) Your papers?

COUNT: (*Smiles strangely.*) What?

SERGEANT: Identification: passport or equivalent?

COUNT: (*Grins.*) And what might that be?

SERGEANT: Never mind the stupid jokes! Who are you?

COUNT: I?

SERGEANT: (*Impatient.*) Who [the hell] else?

COUNT: (*Slowly.*) I am Count Almaviva . . .

SERGEANT: Almaviva?!

COUNT: (*Smiles.*) At your service. (*Sergeant stares at him, out of his depth; then pulls himself together and blows his police whistle. Enter the Guards.*)

SERGEANT: (*To Count.*) In the name of the People: you're under arrest!

SCENE 5

(*Back on the former Almaviva estate. Barberina is sitting in front of the gate mending her husband's trousers. She is singing phrases of Cherubino's "Susanna" song to herself. It is a warm autumn morning. After a while Figaro appears in the gate, stops and listens. Barberina doesn't see him and continues singing. Finally she notices him and stops abruptly.*)

FIGARO: What's that you're singing about someone named Susanna?

BARBERINA: Haven't you heard it before? It's the latest song hit, it took the world by storm in a matter of days.

FIGARO: Is that a fact? Pop tunes seem to catch on easier than revolutionary ballads. Has the mail come already?

BARBERINA: Yes. (*Gives him a few letters.*)

FIGARO: (*Looking through them.*) Is this all?

BARBERINA: (*Looking hard at him.*) What were you expecting?

FIGARO: A letter. Something personal. (*Barberina holds out trousers [to look at them].*)

BARBERINA: (*With light irony.*) Who'd ever imagine you having a personal life, the way you dedicate yourself to the castle and the children . . .

FIGARO: (*Cutting her short.*) Do you think the children like me?

BARBERINA: Always the same silly question! Those children would loot and steal and murder for you, you're God Almighty as far as they're concerned

---

*Line interpolated from Act III, Scene 1, which was omitted in 1936 production.

. . .

FIGARO: (*Smiles.*) You think so? (*Looks around.*) When's the next delivery?

BARBERINA: Tomorrow's a holiday.

FIGARO: Hm . . . (*Starts to exit into castle. Sergeant enters quickly from right and salutes.*)

SERGEANT: Good morning, sir!

FIGARO: Morning, sergeant: everything in order?

SERGEANT: Sir, beg to report, an important arrest. A man. He smuggled himself across the border, and we found him not far from the ravine. He says he's Count Almaviva . . .

FIGARO: (*Cutting him off.*) What?!

BARBERINA: The Count? Goodness gracious?

FIGARO: Where is he?

SERGEANT: We locked him in the cellar.

FIGARO: Right, sergeant: come on. (*Exit fast to right.*)

PEDRILLO: (*Enters excited from left.*) Hey, Barberina! Guess who's back! I just heard, down at the tavern: Count Almaviva's back, that monster in aristocrat's clothing! I have a few things to say to that cynical seducer who raped my wife . . .

BARBERINA: (*Cutting him off.*) Pedrillo! Don't get involved in politics again!

PEDRILLO: Rape isn't politics, do you mind? (*Silence.*)

BARBERINA: (*Slowly.*) Pedrillo, I have to tell you something, but you have to promise you won't despise me.

PEDRILLO: I don't despise even a worm, you know that. What is it?

BARBERINA: I'm scared. If you go hauling all that out onto the carpet, what the Count did to me, there'll only be more trouble than ever . . .

PEDRILLO: The law's the law, and rape doesn't go unpunished under our system, we haven't sunk that low yet!

BARBERINA: Pedrillo, I lied to you.

PEDRILLO: (*Stops short.*) What do you mean by that?

BARBERINA: (*Slowly.*) I mean that rape is not exactly the right word . . .

PEDRILLO: It isn't?! Then what is the right word?

BARBERINA: (*Smiles uncertainly.*) Well . . . not rape, anyway. (*Silence.*)

PEDRILLO: (*Staring at her.*) So it was just as much you as him, right?

BARBERINA: Don't be angry with me, please . . .

PEDRILLO: You think I should be glad he didn't rape you?! My world is falling to pieces, my whole theoretical structure of ideals and concepts is in ruins. It's like I said before: what's left *but* the tavern? (*Silence.*)

BARBERINA: What are you going to do?

PEDRILLO: I won't hang myself anyway.

BARBERINA: (*Slowly.*) Are you going to get a divorce?

PEDRILLO: (*Flaring up at her.*) You want to get me in an even bigger mess?! Divorce is out of the question, what about the children? But from now on there's one thing I won't put up with: after this confession of yours, I don't want to hear one more goddamn word about when I go to the tavern or how long I stay there: got that?! (*Leaves her standing and exits left.*)

BARBERINA: (*Alone, gazing after him.*) He doesn't love me any more . . . (*Exit into castle. Figaro enters right with the Sergeant, followed by two children: Carlos and Maurizio.*)

FIGARO: (*To Sergeant.*) That's how's going to be! I take full repsonsibility!

SERGEANT: But sir, please . . .

FIGARO: (*Interrupting him.*) No buts! An order's an order!

SERGEANT: Yessir! (*Salutes and exits left. Figaro starts to enter the castle.*)

CARLOS: [But] Mr. Figaro, sir!

FIGARO: (*Stopping.*) What is it?

CARLOS: The Count Almaviva has to be shot right away, doesn't he?

FIGARO: Who says so?

CARLOS: Me.

FIGARO: (*Gazing at him seriously.*) I see: you do.

CARLOS: Yes. 'cause he's a political criminal.

MAURIZIO: No, tey toodn't toot him, tey ought to keep him in jail forever, toodn't tey?

FIGARO: And just why tood tey to tat?

MAURIZIO: Because jail for life ith *worth* tan det; tat's what our teacher ted.

FIGARO: I see. (*Aside.*) I think I may have to give your teacher a few private lessons to exercise his sense of humor . . . (*To the children.*) Now you listen to me a minute, you two hangmen! First: I'd rather have you breaking windows than getting involved in politics! Second: Count Almaviva is no criminal . . .

CARLOS: (*Interrupting him.*) He's a Count, isn't he?

FIGARO: Have you ever been a Count?

CARLOS: (*Nonplussed.*) No.

FIGARO: Well then! Don't talk about what you don't understand. Listen to me: if you ever meet Count Almaviva, I want you to say hello politely and treat him like a gentleman and be nice, because he's an old man and you are a pair of scallywags and if he did commit a crime it's not up to you two to punish him. And why would you want to shoot a man and lock him up for life anyway? What did he ever do to you? Or you? Aren't you ashamed? You listen to me: maybe when you're old there'll be nothing *but* Counts and they'll pass a law that every orphan is a criminal and shoot them and lock them up. Now go break a few windows: off with you! (*Children leave silently. Susanna enters left.*)

FIGARO: (*Seeing her.*) Susanna! (*He stares at her. Susanna looks at him and remains silent. Disoriented, Figaro passes his hand over his eyes.*) Why didn't you answer my letter?

SUSANNA: (*Can't help smiling.*) Should I have written instead?

FIGARO: What am I saying? I can't get it through my head that you're standing there . . . I've been waiting for a letter for weeks . . .

SUSANNA: Figaro, I heard that you've arrested the Count.

FIGARO: What Count?

SUSANNA: Count Almaviva!

FIGARO: Oh, yes, of course. I'm sorry, I'm still confused . . .

SUSANNA: (*Cutting him off.*) Nothing had better happen to the Count, you hear me? It's my fault he's back at all, and it would be horrible if you did anything to him, he was always a friend to me out there . . .

FIGARO: (*Interrupts her.*) Why are you talking about the Count when we haven't seen each other in so long?

SUSANNA: Because it's more important to me!

FIGARO: (*Alerted.*) More important?!

SUSANNA: Please, promise nothing will happen to him!

FIGARO: You think I'd do anything to hurt the Count?

SUSANNA: I don't know.

FIGARO: You don't know? All right then. There's no hope for the Count, not unless they commute his sentence to life imprisonment . . .

SUSANNA: What?! Figaro, you have to save him!

FIGARO: I can't. What's right is right.

SUSANNA: Right cuts two ways . . .

FIGARO: Since when?

SUSANNA: You ask since when? That was your own theory . . . Oh, now I see how you cheated me with that letter, talking about humanity; it's all talk with you!

FIGARO: No it isn't. You came back, but you still think I'm capable of any cruelty. You deserve to be disappointed.

SUSANNA: You haven't changed.

FIGARO: Haven't I? (*Silence.*)

SUSANNA: I came back because they took my work permit away.

FIGARO: I'm glad.

SUSANNA: I was starving there, that's the only reason I came back to you.

FIGARO: I don't believe you'd do that.

SUSANNA: I would.

FIGARO: No.

SUSANNA: Why should I lie about it.

FIGARO: Why are you lying to yourself? Does it make you feel better? It doesn't hurt me. (*Silence.*)

SUSANNA: Has your conscience been bothering you? (*She grins.*)

FIGARO: When you ask that way, the answer's no.

SUSANNA: Why did you ask me to come back?

FIGARO: Because I need you.

SUSANNA: (*Mockingly.*) What for?

FIGARO: Please don't ask such stupid questions! (*Silence. He approaches her slowly and stops in front of her.*) You asked me once what it would be like when we were old and there was no one there who belonged to us. Our lives would have made no sense . . .

SUSANNA: (*Looking large-eyed at him.*) And you said life doesn't make much sense anyway . . . and I said, if that's how it was I'd rather die . . .

FIGARO: And I said: "I love you." Do you remember?

SUSANNA: (*Softly.*) Yes. But I said that wasn't enough for me . . .

FIGARO: That's right. (*He nods, smiling.*) But that was then. Today I'm not worried any more about the future . . . (*Nearby, the sound of a breaking windowpane. Both listen; another breaks.*)

ANTONIO: (*Enters fast from left.*) Figaro, those brats are breaking windows, I'll tear their ears off.

FIGARO: Get hold of yourself! I told them they could go break windows.

ANTONIO: Told them? (*Another crash.*)

FIGARO: I promised them they could break windows if they stayed out of politics.

ANTONIO: That's the limit. (*Yet another crash.*)

FIGARO: I think you may be right . . . Aren't you going to say hello to my wife?

ANTONIO: We already said hello. (*Count appears in the gateway; his appearance is tidy, but he seems very tired.*)

ANTONIO: God Almighty, his Lordship!

COUNT: (*Smiles.*) Old Antonio . . . are you still alive?

ANTONIO: Not for long, your lordship; not for long!

COUNT: We'll see about that. (*Suddenly looks hard off left.*) What's become of my splendid pine tree?

ANTONIO: Struck by lightning . . .

COUNT: Then I needn't get excited. I thought they might have cut it down . . . (*Smiles and looks around him.*) Yes: the benches still stand beneath the trees and the trees haven't left their places, and the lawns have stayed at home . . . Figaro!

FIGARO: (*Goes to him.*) Your Grace desires?

COUNT: Am I really free now?

FIGARO: Of course, your Grace.

COUNT: And I'll have my [old] room again?

FIGARO: Of course, your Grace.

COUNT: Hm. Then is the revolution over?

FIGARO: On the contrary, your Grace. The revolution is triumphant; so we don't have to lock people in the cellar any more who can't help being our enemies.

SUSANNA: Figaro! (*She runs to him and embraces him. And once more, a windowpane shatters.*)

END

APPENDIX

Act II, Scene 4

(NOTE: *Nearly all the material published as "Excluded Scenes" in the standard German edition of* Figaro Gets a Divorce *is composed of complete scenes which can, with minor revisions, easily be reintegrated with Horváth's original dramatic plan.*

One section of the material is not so easily dealt with. It is clearly an amplification (or perhaps a variant ending) of the scene numbered Act II Scene 4 in the present version, and includes, in my opinion, very important material for understanding the character and motivation of Figaro as it develops in the last third of the play.

To insert this material without inconsistency or loss of dramatic momentum into the scene in question, however, would require extensive cutting and rewriting of the kind which can only be done effectively as part of the rehearsal process. Pending the first production of this translation, I have thought it best to present the additional material in an appendix, so that readers can come to their own conclusions about its relevance and adaptability.)

ANTONIO: I could have told them, but I know when to keep my mouth shut!

FIGARO: (*To Sergeant.*) Sound Assembly! Everybody out!

SERGEANT: Sound Assembly! (*Bugler sounds Assembly and the children, teachers, and staff of the Home come running in.*)

CHILDREN: What's wrong? What's going on?

ANTONIO: (*Maliciously, to children.*) Santa Claus has brought us a new bailiff; there . . . (*Points at Figaro, who has taken a position on the portal steps.*) Hip hip hooray!

ALL: (*Except Barberina and Pedrillo.*) Hip hip hooray!

FIGARO: My dear children! Thank you for your overwhelming reception. I'm deeply touched. Try to see in me not just your new overseer but also your friend. Like you, I was a foundling, like you, a child of the People; but when I was your age, there were no refuges for the less fortunate like this one; I had to make my laborious way entirely on my own. And many a day did I devote more thought and cunning to finding a dry crust of bread to sustain my miserable existence that our former government devoted to the needs and aspirations of our whole suffering nation. That government, praise be to God, has been swept forever out of existence!

ALL: (*Except Barberina and Pedrillo.*) Hip hip hooray!

FIGARO: I salute my noble predecessor, and render thanks to him from an overflowing heart! Truly, it will be no extraordinary feat to continue to build on the firm foundation so heroically laid! Now, exhausted by his superhuman efforts on your behalf, he goes into well-deserved retirement, another self-sacrificing pioneer of our noble new order. My dear children, learn from the example of this extraordinary man! I myself pledge to continue in the course he has set toward your moral and physical improvement, I too will lead you upward on the stern path of self-denial, I too will steel your wills so that no effort will seem to you too demanding, no challenge too severe, no sacrifice too great, of friends or family, worldly goods or heart's blood, love or life itself, in the advancement of the general good of all . . . ! Go forth now; and, in memory of this very special day in our nation's history: school's out! (*Children exit, cheering and yelling.*) My greetings also to you, the honorable custodians of our nation's most precious commodity, the protectors and nourishers of our youth! Let us never forget our duty to grind into them at every opportunity that without the common sacrifice of every individual to the common good, our mighty revolution will lose all meaning. On the one hand, the cultivation by every means of a sense of self-worth in every individual; on the other, the gathering in of the fruits of that sense of self-worth and their exploitation for the good of the community: thus, briefly stated, the pedagogical solution to the central socioeconomic problem of our new order! Oh, gentlemen, how much happier we all would be if we could see that the only way to be worthy of a better life is to give up everything that makes life worth living! Thank you gentlemen; this is the happiest day of my life!

STAFF: Hip hip hooray!

FIGARO: Thank you, Sergeant: that'll be all! (*Sergeant salutes and exits with the Guard. To Pedrillo.*) Well, how was that for a graveside oration, you political cadaver, you? Impressive, hm?

PEDRILLO: You can go to Hell! It's an outrage! A couple of ragged orphans more or less, what does that matter compared to the concrete achievements of a veteran of the vanguard of the battle for the general good? Honest to Christ, it's enough to make *me* emigrate!

ANTONIO: Far as the tavern, anyway.

PEDRILLO: Better a live drunk than a dead revolutionary! (*Exit.*)

FIGARO: Why so quiet, Barberina?

BARBERINA: Nothing.

ANTONIO: Feel a little sick, do you?

BARBERINA: No. It's only . . . (*To Figaro.*) I knew you were a liar. We all are. But how you can lie to the children that way . . .

ANTONIO: (*Cutting in.*) Why not? The child is father to the man, you know . . . (*Grins.*)

BARBERINA: Yes. Men like you. No thank you.

ANTONIO: Now, now, this is your own father you're talking to . . .

BARBERINA: (*To Figaro.*) It's not hard to see you don't have children of your own. I have two, and I when I think about them coming under the influence of a liar like you . . . I'll never let you within sight of them! Susanna did the right thing when she betrayed you!

FIGARO: (*Staring at her.*) You think so?

ANTONIO: (*To Barberina.*) Stop all this personal woman talk!

FIGARO: Let her have her say! (*To Barberina.*) Go ahead, talk.

BARBERINA: (*Cutting in.*) I'd go on talking without your go-ahead! You're corrupt, through and through! Aren't you ever ashamed?

FIGARO: You haven't understood the way the world works yet. Since my wife betrayed me—no, never mind that, even before then, since Haggelburg in fact—it became totally clear to me that no one in the world is better hated and despised than an honorable man with brains, and there's only one way out: you have to decide, honesty or brains. I've made my choice. We live in times where the workings of the world are more important than people. Unfortunately. Because there's only one thing that lies beyond corruption . . .

ANTONIO: (*Grins.*) Oh, a riddle!

FIGARO: Yes, a riddle, a big one: what is it that we're always looking for, never find, and keep on losing just the same . . . (*Antonio shrugs his shoulders. To Barberina.*) Here, I'll tell you the answer, but only you—because you gave me such holy hell . . . (*He smiles and whispers the answer to her, then gives her a friendly nod and exits.*)

ANTONIO: (*Looking after him, surprised.*) What did he say?

BARBERINA: I didn't understand him.

ANTONIO: Always looked for, never found, and lost just the same . . . what's that?

BARBERINA: "Humanity," he said.